MAKING AN EXIT

"There could be no better guide than Sarah Murray – so smart, thoughtful, and wickedly funny – to this remarkable and illuminating exploration of the rituals of dying and burial, both familiar and exotic, as they are practiced around the world." Richard McCann, author of *Mother of Sorrows*

"From Ghana to Bali, Mexico to Sicily, Sarah Murray has travelled the world to find the most wondrous, moving, and surprising departures. This is a fascinating look at our most sacred ritual." Melissa Milgrom, author of *Still Life: Adventures in Taxidermy*

"With a keen eye, ready wit, and very big heart, Murray leads us on a Grand Tour of deathcare practices that are celebrations of both the dead and the creative human spirit. *Making an Exit* will forever change the way you think about death and dying, and that last passage to the Great Hereafter." Mark Harris, author of *Grave Matters: A Journey Through the Modern Funeral Industry to a Natural Way of Burial*

"Her intimate account of the ways death is celebrated and commemorated around the world is exhilarating, insightful, and chock-full of fascinating information." Penny Coleman, author of *Corpses, Coffins, and Crypts: A History of Burial*

Sarah Murray is a journalist, editor, longtime *Financial Times* contributor and author of *Moveable Feasts: The Incredible Journeys of the Things We Eat*. Born in the UK, she lives in New York City.

Cover image: La Catrina, Day of the Dead Festival, Oaxaca, Mexico

MAKING AN EXIT

From the Magnificent to the Macabre: How We Dignify the Dead

Sarah Murray

Coptic Publishing
London
Xoptic

First published in Great Britain in 2011
by Coptic Publishing

Coptic Publishing, Office 408,
10 Great Russell Street, Bloomsbury, London WC1B 3BQ
www.copticpublishing.com

Published in the United States in 2011 by St. Martin's Press

A catalogue record for this book is available from the British Library

ISBN: 978-0-9558771-3-1

Design: Kate Gowrie

Printed and bound in Great Britain
by Lightning Source UK Ltd

✦

For Fa

CONTENTS

Ready to Go

Weary of plying,
Exhausted by trying,
Irked by spying,
And well meaning prying,
Accused of lying,
No money for buying,
Can't see for untying,
No longer denying,
No tears for crying,
A fear of dying
But a
Longing for dying.

Nigel Stuart Murray
(date unknown)

INTRODUCTION

The trouble with death is what comes before it. I struggle to replenish my memory bank with images of my father, not as he was in illness – tired, shrunken and grey – but as he was in health. He was at his happiest out and about in the countryside, in brown corduroys, rubber boots, a green padded jacket and a tweed hat. With eyes twinkling beneath unruly brows, he was always ready for a good walk, a good debate – and usually a good laugh.

We called him Fa. Neither of my parents wanted to be known by "Mum" or "Mummy", "Dad" or "Daddy". But somehow while my mother, Sam, acquired a rough-and-ready boy's name as her substitute (her actual name is Pamela), my father settled on a rather fey alternative – something I had to keep quiet at school, where my classmates competed on the ferocity of their rows with "the old man". To fit in, I played along, but the truth is, Fa and I got along like familiar friends, enjoying debates on politics, economics and art, battling it out on turf that was intellectual, not emotional.

Fa's approach to family relationships was unconventional. He thought the idea of raising children in a kibbutz (a Jewish collective community) an excellent one. And while he and my mother fell in love at first sight and remained devoted throughout their marriage, they never once celebrated their wedding anniversary, claiming neither could remember the exact date (they celebrated a relationship requiring no formal buttressing). For Fa, close bonds with friends and family were essential, but only those forged by genuine affection, not by obligation or tradition. Even Christmas was a casual affair, sometimes spent not at home but in London, with my parents turning up bearing a picnic hamper of smoked salmon, a selection of cheeses and a bottle of wine.

Few events caused my family to flap or panic. One afternoon during Fa's time at the Joseph Weld Hospice, word came that Prince Charles was to visit and wanted to meet a patient. The nurses immediately chose my father, and in excited tones, told Sam, who was lunching at the hospice, that she, too, could meet the heir apparent. Sam, as she told me later without a hint of irony, asked what time he was arriving, looked at her watch and said: "Oh no, I'd better not – I've got to be getting on. And he'll only be late."

My family's no-nonsense approach to life was one my father applied to death. He dismissed the idea that what was left after a person took their last breath had any significance. "Organic matter," he called it. After my grandmother died, he insisted that her body was simply flesh, skin and bones, with no connection to the person who once inhabited them. That person was gone. He even managed to get a refund from the undertakers, who'd mistakenly sent her off in a silk-lined wooden coffin with an engraved plate on it bearing her name, despite his request for what she'd wanted – a simple cardboard box.

On another occasion, he stood in the kitchen, cheerily claiming he'd be happy if, after his death, the hospital would simply dispatch his remains in the most efficient, hygienic way possible. That would be that.

Yet for Fa, that wasn't quite that. He was to make other arrangements altogether. And it's these arrangements, set down on paper a few months before he died, that have got me asking questions – questions about the way we humans mark the passing of our fellows; questions about how we approach our own mortality. This book is an attempt to answer some of them.

While it plunges us into chaos and grief, death also forces us to plough through piles of paperwork and fill in dreary forms. We close bank accounts and cancel insurance policies. We make special trips to hospitals, nursing homes and hospices to collect half-read books, unwanted glasses and sad sets of pyjamas (we come away without their owners). We arrange family parties, make speeches and pass around cocktail sandwiches and sausages on sticks.

Initially, Sam and I were spared much of this activity. After my flight from New York, I arrived at Summerfields, my parents' home (now just my mother's home) the day after my father died. It was Christmas afternoon. England was shut for the holidays. Shops were closed, offices empty. Not a bus or train was running (I managed to borrow a friend's car to get home from London). The country's seasonal shutdown seemed for once appropriate. "Stop all the clocks, cut off the telephone," wrote W.H. Auden. "He Is Dead." A life has stopped in its tracks and so should we.

So my mother and I ambled quietly around the house, assessing what needed to be done. It was a strangely happy time we spent together. Neither of us discussed it, but we both felt a tremendous sense of relief – relief that my father's painful battle with cancer was at last over.

Soon after I arrived, Sam handed me a brown envelope on which in Fa's spindly handwriting was written the words: "To be opened after my death." Inside was a document he'd typed up six months earlier on his computer in "The Hut", the converted garden shed that housed his much-loved office.

Actually, The Hut was much more than his office. It was his home at home. In it, he had his 1970s stereo system ("But the sound is superb," he protested whenever we suggested something more modern) and the Remington typewriter he reluctantly relinquished in favour of a second-hand computer. The shelves in The Hut were full of clues about his life – small model boats, giant industrial bolts, tape measures, set squares, boxes of fishing flies. On the walls were framed photos – Fa as a small boy in shorts in the annual school picture; his late brother Gavin, a military officer, standing in line with his regiment, the Fifth Royal Inniskilling Dragoon Guards.

It was in The Hut that my father loved to spend time writing letters and essays, listening to jazz and compiling photo albums and scrapbooks. And it was in The Hut that, with his death approaching, he composed the letter I was about to read.

The text of Fa's document starts ominously with: "To Whom It Will Concern." Yet in each sentence, the gravitas of his legal terminology is interrupted by light-hearted phrases or exclamation marks that betray his sense of fun and desire to dismantle convention. Re-reading this letter, as I sometimes do, I hear his voice in every line: serious and authoritative, matter of fact, yet ready to enjoy the amusing side of any situation – even his own death.

"Following cremation I would like my ashes to be scattered in the churchyard of North Poorton Church," he tells us. "Subject to any prior approvals necessary, the scattering requires no formalities, or ceremonial baggage attached to the act of scattering!" A local undertaker should arrange for the cremation and delivery of the ashes, he continues, without supplying "any expensive coffin. No 'oak coffin with brass gilt handles' should be necessary; no brass casket to contain the ashes is needed; a cardboard box, or polythene bag will suffice." (Remembering his request for a refund for my grandmother's mistakenly ordered coffin, this bit certainly makes sense.)

He includes practical considerations: "The weather needs to be calm, with no more than light winds." This sentence always makes me smile – because I know he means it. As an agricultural surveyor who advised farmers on business and legal matters, Fa liked things done properly.

His letters, while sometimes philosophical and always affectionate, included instructions for things like "keeping wet out of old windows". In one, he worries about my sister Kate's "tricky problem with her flat roof". In another, he's interested to hear that his brother Alastair's water supply has "a consistent overflow running at the springhead". A note I found from *Country Landowner* magazine thanked him for his "fascinating piece about drainage". Preoccupied with the practical throughout his life, he wants to make sure we don't "make a nonsense", as he would have put it, of the practical side of his death.

But he trusts us, too. "Everything can be left, safely in the hands of Sam (Pamela), and Sarah and Kate, who, if they did not know before quite precisely where my preferences lie, they will do so now," he writes – "in the soil of a beautiful Dorset churchyard, in beautiful Dorset landscape!"

There will be no funeral, no fuss, no speeches, and certainly no sausages on sticks. He discourages us from arranging any "formalities" or "ceremonials" and stresses that any suggestion of a "get-together", wake, or memorial would be "anathema" (he always hated formal functions and had a horror of long speeches).

Accompanying the document (and this is my favourite bit) is a photograph – a colour print of a small stone church in a picturesque village sitting at the heart of softly undulating hills and pea green fields. On the photograph, in ballpoint pen, he's drawn a cross next to the church and written the words: "X marks the spot!"

When I first read through Fa's document, I didn't know whether to laugh or cry. Typed out using the computer he valiantly struggled to master, the words went a long way towards restoring my image of him before his illness – of a man whose best attempts to get serious about something were always foiled because he couldn't resist injecting a liberal dose of humour into the proceedings.

And here was my father, in death as in life, doing things properly, tying up the loose ends. This was something I could certainly relate to. I've always liked everything to be in order. When sharing hotel rooms with friends, I have to warn them I'll probably make the bed or rearrange their stuff without even noticing I'm doing it. Even more embarrassing have been moments when I've found myself absent-mindedly neatening the shelves in bookshops and supermarkets. So my father's urge to tidy up before departing seemed entirely logical.

Coming from a confirmed atheist, his request to have his ashes scattered in a churchyard was a bit of a surprise, to say the least. Yet he'd dispelled any notion of a last-minute conversion to Christianity: "My choice of the churchyard is simply that I have my very oldest friends there already (Jim and Dood Anderson), and also that it is a very beautiful place (see attached photograph)."

In fact, the spot he chose is particularly lovely – a village with a charming church, St Mary Magdalene, at its heart in a rolling green landscape that flattens into a hazy blue-grey as it greets the sea. On our rambles around the countryside together, we'd often stopped there to sniff the air and admire the view.

No, what was really puzzling about Fa's document was the revelation that he'd considered having anything done with his "organic matter" at all and had, moreover, left us detailed instructions on how he was to be disposed of, a description of the location he'd chosen for his remains, and an expression of his desire to end up near close friends. His rationalist way of thinking was one I'd always embraced unquestioningly – death as an ending without meaning; an absence where once there was a presence. So this final acknowledgment of a connection between his living and his dead self seemed to me a reversal of his entire philosophy.

As well as filling us with sadness and a sense of loss, the death of someone we've loved presses the shadow of our own mortality into a sharper image. Fa's death has coincided with my growing realisation that, at some point in the coming decades, I too will come to an end. I've noticed an alarming acceleration in the passage of time, as each year represents an increasingly small proportion of my life. I find myself wondering whether packing in as much as possible will make it seem to stretch out for longer, or if periods of inactivity might persuade it to advance at a more leisurely pace (I end up favouring the first option).

But if my father's death has got me thinking about the notion of human transience, his last request, with its implicit acceptance of the significance of his remains, has prompted me to consider a question that's entirely new to me – what might I ultimately do with my own physical leftovers? What kind of send-off do I want? For if arranging some form of final passage turned out to be important to a man who once pronounced his future dead self to be merely "organic matter", then perhaps these things are important after all.

In thinking about my eventual exit, I face a singularly modern challenge – as an atheist and someone who lives alone (with no particular desire to change this arrangement), I may well be the only one with any incentive to make preparations for my funeral, or at least for the disposal of my body.

Still, I have a great starting point – a blank slate. For among the things I love about being an independent, single woman is that it's all up to me. I wear what I want, eat out when I like, stay in when I need to, paint the walls any colour I fancy. It follows, then, that I can order any sort of coffin, bury my body anywhere I'm legally allowed to, have my ashes scattered wherever I choose, and leave my money to whoever I deem deserving. With no in-laws to influence me, and no religion to constrain me, I'm free to make choices in death as well as in life.

Ah, but there's the rub – where do I start? Having grown up in a secular family, in an increasingly secular Britain, I don't even have any doctrines to reject. Religion scarcely touched my education, save for a brief weekly prayer during general assembly. A decade in New York has brought me no closer to spirituality. Like so many of the city's residents, I worship at its temples of culture and commerce, not creed. Yet atheism provides little guidance on how to deal with the end of life. People might complain about the strictures of their faith or the limitations imposed by traditional communities, but a few rules come in handy when you're dead.

So I've decided to embark on a series of journeys to see how others do it. I'll visit old haunts such as Hong Kong, where I lived for four years, and Mexico, one of my favourite countries. Other places will be less familiar but ones I'm keen to revisit – the Philippines, Ghana and the Czech Republic. Some destinations will be new to me – ones on my travel wish list, such as Iran, Sicily and Bali. Writers often tell us about places we must see before we die.

I want to explore some of the ones we end up in when we're dead. And when you're looking for death, you find yourself in places you might not otherwise have put on your itinerary.

Of course for most people, a review of their "final arrangements", as they're often called, involves a chat with the family or a visit to a lawyer, financial advisor or funeral director. My response is to hit the road. As a journalist and long-time traveller, it's what I've always done when I want to learn about something – I like to get out there, feel the heat, pound the pavements, taste the wine. And, who knows, perhaps contemplating something as scary as my own mortality will make its approach a little less terrifying.

What's more, if I'm lost for ideas, the traditions of others will surely offer me some inspiration. For disposing of the dead is something mankind does incredibly well. We bury our loved ones in the ground. We burn them in fire (in some cases, we bury them first and burn them later). We dismember them and lay the parts to rest in different places. In certain cultures, we leave corpses as carrion, inviting the birds to pick the bones dry. In others, we hang the dead in trees or stow them in caves. In naval circles, we consign them to the ocean.

Meanwhile, we've created all manner of ceremonies to dignify their removal. We incinerate bodies in decorative paper effigies on funeral pyres. We arrange for riderless horses to accompany the cortege to the cemetery. Amid the sound of bells and the swirl of incense, we toss the remains of our fellows into sacred rivers. We sing songs, recite poetry, engage in mock battles and even play games. In some places, we shout with joy at a spirit's departure. Elsewhere, we might wail and moan and tear at our clothes (in my own British culture, we snivel quietly into our hankies).

The way we deal with the dead speaks volumes about the human race. Death rites and gravesites are the focus for astonishingly diverse forms of expression. They echo our thoughts about the afterlife (the Yanomamo people of Venezuela and Brazil, who believe their souls are eaten by cannibals in the netherworld, consume the ashes of their cremated dead after the funeral). They reflect the way we live (in Japanese Shinto funerals, families use chopsticks to transfer the ashes of the dead into their urns).

Funerals and burials reveal all kinds of things about us, from our social status to our thoughts on marriage and where our religious affiliations lie (Muslim graves are aligned so the face of the deceased points towards the holy city of Mecca). They are windows on to the world's most deeply held philosophies, superstitions, hopes and fears.

So what will mine say about me? What method of disposal should I select for my own dead body and what ceremonies might accompany its removal? Most importantly, where do I want to leave my remains? Some societies believe the spirit cannot rest until the corpse is returned home. But what if it's unclear where home is?

For my father the answer was easy – his beloved Dorset countryside. Yet while born in Dorset, I've had homes in many places – Scotland, Hong Kong, Vietnam, South Africa, London, and now New York, home to the United Nations and the city that welcomes the world's citizens. Most I've loved with enough passion to qualify them as a home for my "organic matter". So which should I choose? At this point, I'm not sure. But I'm off to find out.

1

THE LAMENT

A Tear Jar in Iran

A s I step out of the car, I'm struggling to adjust the headscarf I'll be wearing for the next two weeks. Gravel crunches beneath my feet and my breath turns to white vapour in the sharp air of a bright January morning.

It's my first day in Iran and Maryam, my guide, is taking me around some of Tehran's museums and palaces. Sprawling out from the foot of the Alborz Mountains, the city feels a little like eastern Europe before the fall of the Soviet Empire. The colours are muted, the cars are beaten up and faceless concrete blocks have appropriated sites once occupied by elegant mansions. But in a nineteenth-century Qajar dynasty villa, the Glass and Ceramic Museum offers a flavour of the old Tehran. Its delicate brickwork façade blends traces of European Rococo with the courtly geometric details of a Persian palace.

Inside are artefacts from distant civilizations – the Achaemenids, Parthians and Sasanians. Maryam, who has a degree in art history and a passion for Persian culture, knows the collection well. Born in Tehran, she speaks immaculate English with an accent picked up from television and from the many American tourists she's accompanied on trips around her country. Like many younger Iranian women, she interprets the Islamic dress code loosely where she knows she can, covering herself modestly in the required knee-length *manteau*, pants and headscarf. But rather than swathing herself in the dull black or brown worn by most Iranians, she usually dresses in her favourite colour – turquoise – and wears a large pair of wrap-around sunglasses.

When it comes to Persian art, it's the unexpected details Maryam loves. As I gaze at a set of decorated plates, she explains that the almond-shaped eyes of the figures depicted on them are the legacy of a wave of Mongol invaders who barged in from the east on horseback in the thirteenth century, razing towns and villages to the ground, killing even the dogs in the slaughter.

It was one of Iran's most violent periods of history, yet Persian artists continued depicting the eyes of their invaders long after they'd left, creating a new tradition from the detritus of violence and upheaval.

Amid the cabinets of exquisite glasses, bowls and plates, something catches my eye. It's a glass vase with a bulbous base and a narrow sinuous neck that twists upwards towards the rim, where an oval flower-like opening resembles a small ear trumpet. Maryam sees me admiring this strange and beautiful object. "Can you guess what it is?" she asks. I shake my head. "It's a tear jar," she says. "It was used by women while their sweethearts were away at war. They'd collect teardrops of sadness as a gift for them on their return." Ah, yes, that makes sense – looking again at the little flower-like opening, I can see it's shaped to fit over an eye.

Capturing and storing tears is an idea that seems quite remote from the culture in which I grew up, where expressions of sorrow tend to be muted or even suppressed. Yet in many countries, self-control is absent from the process of grieving. We've all seen television coverage of parts of the world in which the bereaved mourn their dead in an unrestrained display of emotion, whether it's crowds of ululating Turkish women in the aftermath of an earthquake, or Iraqi mothers shrouded in black, rocking back and forth in vociferous grief after losing a family member to a suicide bomb.

And it's hard to forget the extraordinary scenes of emotional public grief that followed the death of the Ayatollah Khomeini in 1989. Loud, unselfconscious and highly public, these kinds of laments give visual and vocal shape to mourning.

To get a glimpse of powerful ritual laments, I've come to Iran during Muharram. This holy month commemorates the martyrdom in AD 680 of Imam Husayn, grandson of the Islamic prophet Muhammad. Culminating in the sacred day of Ashura – the day on which, centuries earlier, Husayn was killed in battle – this is Iran's most important religious holiday. It's not a joyous occasion, but a time of intense sadness, when Iranians get together for a period of collective mourning.

Of course, unlike the anguish captured on TV newscasts, the mourning here will be for an individual who died many centuries ago. Moreover, the weeping and acts of penance performed for Husayn and his family are inextricably bound up with deeper bonds uniting Shi'a Muslims across the globe. But while the lamenting ceremonies won't be the same as the grief you might see at a funeral, I want to get a sense of a culture in which mourning is embraced, not hidden away.

The man Iranians weep for every year at Ashura died in the Battle of Karbala (now a city in Iraq) after leading his small band of family and followers in a march across the desert to seize Kufa, a city ruled by Yazid, who was said to be flouting the teachings of Islam. Before reaching the city, a group of soldiers surrounded Imam Husayn and his men, cutting off their water supplies, subjecting their families to terrible thirst.

At the end of several days of bitter fighting, Husayn, his followers and their relatives lay dead on the battlefield. Husayn's death, considered a martyrdom, was a critical moment for the Shi'a movement, heralding the separation of the Sunni and Shi'a branches of Islam.

Iranians know the story of the battle by heart. It's been told to them since they were children. Yet, year after year, they mourn Imam Husayn's martyrdom and remember his death with great outpourings of grief – as if he'd died only yesterday.

Ceremonies and activities, even civic decorations, are all designed to promote weeping. In theatres around Iran, *ta'zieh* or history plays, recreate the battlefield scenes with elaborate costumes, male-only casts, live animals and audiences who are encouraged to cry at the most poignant moments in the performance.

On streets and in religious halls, people watch lamentation ceremonies in which groups of men stand together, slapping their arms hard against their chests in powerful rhythms as they shout out Husayn's name. In public places, posters depict his riderless horse weeping for its lost lord and water gourds spurting with blood. Fountains are filled with dye so that they, too, appear to be running with blood.

Until recently in Iran, men marked this occasion by whipping themselves with barbed chains or blades – popular images in the western media because of the high drama and bloody nature of the ceremonies. This practice was banned in Iran several years ago (although it continues in other countries and secretly in parts of Iran). In a new penance tradition, mourners give blood during Muharram, and instead of blades, men beat their backs with clusters of chains attached to wooden handles. In mournful street processions moving to the slow rhythm of drums, chain clusters rise up in unison before falling back heavily on to the shoulders of their owners. Even young boys join in using child-sized bunches.

I get a taste of what's to come on my second day in Tehran, as Maryam and I stroll through the Grand Bazaar, the ancient market in the city centre. This is a place that's usually alive with activity – in open-fronted stores beneath nineteenth-century brick arches, women in chadors haggle with traders over the price of a pound of mutton and small boys run around with trays of hot tea, dodging boxes of dried fruit and stacks of china plates.

Today, though, the storefronts are shut. The cobbled streets are quiet. Draped across the majestic arches of the bazaar are green and black velvet banners with prayers and eulogies dancing across them in elegant Persian script. Some have photographs pinned to them in memory of deceased former merchants.

Up ahead of us something's going on. A group of old men has

gathered around a bearded man who's singing into a microphone. The song, explains Maryam, is a lament for the death of Husayn and the martyrs of Karbala. The men shuffle their feet, hang their heads and add their quavering voices to the sorrowful chants of the leader. Theirs is the weary melancholy of the older generation. Some rub their hands into their eyes. Others cross their arms and tap their chests gently with the palms of their hands, in the ancient Middle Eastern gesture of mourning.

Meanwhile, outside the bazaar, passions are mounting. Heavily amplified chanting, drumbeats and the shouts of young men wielding chains penetrate the bazaar's deep brick walls. Large loudspeakers send laments echoing down the cobbled alleys. Maryam translates the lyrics of one for me: "I will mourn for you even if you cut off my head."

Until recently, when reality TV swept trembling voices and watery eyes on to British shores, stoicism characterised my countrymen's response to death. You found it in the stiff upper lips of the musicians on board the Titanic, performing on deck until the moment the ship sank into the ocean, or the quiet heroism of Captain Titus Oates, one of Robert Falcon Scott's fated 1910 Antarctic exploration team. In a bid to help save his colleagues, Oates headed out of the tent into a blizzard and certain death. His last words, recorded by Scott, were famously unemotional: "I am just going outside and may be some time."

British reserve often triumphs over human tragedy. One friend recalls an incident that took place the day his father died. On leaving the hospital, he ran into a family friend he'd not seen for some years. After exchanging a few pleasantries, the friend enquired after his father. Exhausted and emotionally numb after weeks of watching his parent suffer the last throes of Alzheimer's, he could think of nothing to say, except, "Actually, he's dead." Surprised and lost for words, the friend had spluttered, "Oh – so not so good then," before they both exploded with laughter at the absurdity of the exchange.

British stoicism once even became a propaganda tool. In the 1942 film *Mrs Miniver*, producer Sidney Franklin wanted to help win sympathy for the Brits to garner US public support for America's entry into the Second World War. In *Mrs Miniver*, a British housewife (played by Greer Garson) is unflappable, displaying fortitude in the face of disaster as, first, their home is bombed and, later, her daughter-in-law Carol dies beside her on the sitting room floor after being hit during an air raid. "Dear, won't you try to get a little rest," she tells her son next morning, stifling tears, as he returns from duty to see his wife's body.

My family, at least its more senior members, comes from this tradition. When Fa's mother died, I was a child and barely remember the day's events, except for the tone of his voice when he answered the phone, telling me something significant had happened. There was certainly no sobbing in the house.

Some years later, when a call came in the middle of a dinner party with news that my uncle Gavin had died in a car crash, Sam recalls that Fa remained stony faced, as did the dinner guests who, after his announcement, offered their condolences and quietly left.

For us Brits, disaster is met not with weeping and wailing but with pragmatism, etiquette and control. When faced with loss, we make a pot of tea. We encourage the bereaved to "get a little rest". At funerals and memorials, we try not to bawl, but instead weep as discreetly as we can. "She bore up well," we say admiringly of those who remain poker-faced when their hearts are broken by loss.

We try to avert emotional displays, too. "There, there, don't cry," is something we're always being told as children, instructions that seem to retain their influence over us well into adulthood. Yet why should we not cry for the loss of a dear friend or close relative? Surely it's the most natural thing in the world?

Nevertheless, I did not weep when Fa died. For me, the worst moments came during his illness. There were the sad car rides with Sam after visits to the Joseph Weld Hospice, when talk of his approaching death seemed somehow easier to conduct from within a moving vehicle. There was the anguish of watching someone endure a pain and discomfort that could only get worse. After a year of this, the end came as a relief, for him and for us. But for that year, frequent, tense sighs were the way I mourned him.

It's early evening and Maryam and I are sitting on the floor of the upper balcony of a Husseinia (a religious hall) looking across at a blaze of fluorescent light. The balcony is high up, near the roof of the building, supported on ranks of iron columns painted in a lurid green. We're waiting for a Tasoua ceremony to begin. *Tasoua* means "ninth", for this is the ninth day of Muharram, the day before Ashura, and it commemorates the eve of the Battle of Karbala. Below us, on the ground floor, a carpet-covered expanse of concrete is where a pageantry of woe will soon be taking place.

This Husseinia is in Yazd, an ancient desert city in the centre of Iran, about four hundred and fifty miles south of Tehran, and known for religious conservatism. Along its narrow alleys, heavy wooden double doors puncturing mud and wattle walls still have paired knockers, each making a different sound to distinguish male from female visitors and let the women inside know whether or not to cover themselves before answering. Out on the streets, women are shrouded in full-length black chadors, turning them into anonymous inky shapes; shadows casting shadows.

These shadows have become real people on the balcony of the Husseinia – cheery, chatty, gossipy women. While the men sit quietly in neat rows on the floor below, up here, everyone's busy handing around drinks and snacks and sorting out the children. It's an indoor picnic.

The only problem is the heat. Because it's mid-winter in Iran, waves of hot air are rising from four huge cylindrical heaters on the ground floor of the hall. I'm in my thick, woollen coat, long shirt, trousers and boots. I'm sweltering, and longing to take off my headscarf. But Iran's strict dress code makes this impossible in public without censure or even arrest.

After almost an hour, with nothing happening and the temperature rising, I'm tempted to leave, but then the announcer starts talking and Maryam tells me the ceremony is about to begin. I hear a noise from the street – singing and rhythmic drumming. It's quiet at first, but it gets louder as a troupe of men enters the hall. As they insert themselves into the spaces between the men sitting on the floor, I realise that the drumming sound is actually being made by slaps, as the performers beat the palms of their hands against their chests. They stretch their arms out and pull them in again; in and out, in and out. Slap, slap, slap.

From up here, it's an astonishingly beautiful display, as a sea of arms rises and falls. Pale hands stand out against black clothing, creating an effect like a shoal of flying fish leaping from a deep lake or a cloud of migrating butterflies fluttering above a stormy landscape. Although the men stand close together, they never once flinch or strike each other, even as they throw their arms wide to the heavens before reining them in to meet their chests.

The visual drama is heightened by the way the performers are standing – not facing the same way but positioned in all directions. They're dancing with their arms. And through it all, there's a slow rhythm, one found in mourning ceremonies and funeral marches of all kinds – a relentless regularity of sound that seems designed to keep the heart beating when really it wants to break.

This is a *noheh*, or lamentation song, and like most of the rituals taking place at this time of year, it tells of the bloody battle at Karbala. In between the lamentations, the leader calls out through a microphone, addressing the members of the holy family directly. "Come to see what has happened to your son!" he cries to Husayn's mother. Then: "Husayn, where is your commander? Husayn, where is your sweet son Ali Akbar?"

The answer, of course, is that Husayn, his commander, Ali Akbar and the others are all dead or mortally wounded and caked in blood, arrows piercing their hearts, limbs severed from their corpses.

Everyone in the hall knows this and has heard the cries many times before. But these direct appeals to the holy family bearing the dreadful news about relatives and kinsmen are delivered as if their deaths had just happened. The cries have a powerful effect, unifying everyone in a moment of shared grief and anger at a common enemy. Well, almost everyone – a small girl in a pink dress stands up in front of me. Grinning cheekily, she stretches her arms out and slaps them on her chest a few times, mimicking the men. She is plainly enjoying herself.

Elias Canetti, the Bulgarian-born writer, once called the Shi'a faith "a religion of lament more concentrated and more extreme than any to be found elsewhere". Yet while the ritual mourning for Imam Husayn might be bound up with Shi'a beliefs, lamenting in Iran has deeper cultural roots. Mourning is at the heart of Persian legends and poems, which invariably end in tragic deaths that are recounted in poignant language designed to elicit tears.

In the epic *Shahnameh*, tenth-century poet Ferdowsi tells the history of Persia from its earliest days to the Arab conquest of the seventh century. In one part of the story, the great hero Rostam, unaware that he has a son by a princess called Tahmineh (a woman he's not seen for many years), finds himself opposite his son Sohrab in battle. Father and son have no idea they're fighting each other.

After a single-combat struggle, Rostam delivers a fatal stab wound to Sohrab before seeing on his arm the bracelet he'd given the princess years earlier. He realises, to his horror, that he's just killed his own offspring.

The mourning for Sohrab takes on monumental proportions. On learning of her son's death, Princess Tahmineh "heaped black earth upon her head, and tore her hair, and wrung her hands, and rolled on the ground in her agony", writes Ferdowsi. "And her mouth was never weary of plaining."

Her father, the King of Samengan, "tore his vestments" in anguish. Meanwhile, the house of Rostam, Ferdowsi tells us, "grew like a grave, and its courts were filled with the voice of sorrow".

Lamenting is enshrined in courtly Persian poetry, in stanzas that are awash with tears. Take the verse of a poem by Hafiz, the revered fourteenth-century poet from Shiraz:

My face is seamed with dust, mine eyes are wet.
Of dust and tears the turquoise firmament
Kneadeth the bricks for joy's abode; and yet . . .
Alas, and weeping yet I make lament!

Or the mournful lines of eleventh-century Sufi poet and mystic Baba Tahir, who produced words such as these:

'Tis Heaven's whim to vex me, and distress,
My wounded eyes hold ever briny tears,
Each moment soars the smoke of my despair to Heaven,
My tears and groans fill all the Universe.

Other cultures have embraced lamenting, too. During weeping rituals in Hellenistic Greece, mourners would tear at their hair and rip their clothing in movements that were violent and agonised, yet choreographed to follow melodies played on a reed pipe. The traditions have proved surprisingly long-lived. Until the mid-twentieth century, ritual laments featured in the death rites of countries as diverse as Ireland, Greece, Russia and China. Unrehearsed yet guided by a format familiar to everyone, mourners sang weeping songs and recited elaborate poems. Words and music gave expression to the inexpressible. As Steven Feld, the anthropologist and musician, puts it, "tears become ideas".

The trick was balancing powerful emotion with ritualised control; standardised formats with improvised content. Stylisation gave room for emotion, but set boundaries for the mourners, preventing unfettered anguish from being let loose. It was a form of grief that was formulaic yet skilful in its improvisations. At times, it was extremely beautiful.

Still, it didn't always meet with state or religious approval. After Athenian statesman Solon introduced laws curbing excessive funeral rites in the sixth century BC, only close relatives or older women could follow the body and weep at the graveside. In nineteenth-century Ireland, the Catholic Church feared that loud wailing for the dead might give the impression they'd never rise again come the Resurrection. Classing laments as "abuses", the church made various attempts to quash them, from refusal to deliver absolution to, in one instance, using whips to force wailing women off the coffin.

In Russia, Peter the Great tried to ban funeral lamenting, while the Russian Orthodox Church was as censorious of the tradition as the Irish Catholic Church. Powerful public displays of emotion were, it seems, unsettling to the authorities.

They persisted nonetheless. And usually, women performed the ceremonies. In some places, the ability to sing or recite ritual laments was part of a feminine portfolio of skills, along with cooking, spinning, mending and cleaning.

In her book *Night of Stone: Death and Memory in Russia*, Catherine Merridale explains how young Russian girls once acquired their proficiency in lamenting. "Children played funerals as readily as they played house, and little girls assisted the old women in the laying out of corpses," she writes. "Girls were also made to learn and practise the improvisation of laments."

In Ireland, too, women took on the task of public grieving. Their keening – improvised poems and songs – could have a dramatic effect. One nineteenth-century account describes "the deep, yet suppressed sobs of the nearer relatives, and the stormy, uncontrollable cry of the widow or bereaved husband when allusion is made to the domestic virtues of the deceased". You might call it therapy through elegy.

Keens turned ordinary men into heroes. Arthur O'Leary, who died in 1773, was one such man – shot by a hired gun on behalf of a landowner to whom O'Leary had refused to sell his chestnut mare for five pounds, a price stipulated by a provision contained in a series of statutes known as the Penal Laws. Deeply moved by his death, his widow composed a famous keen that is now considered one of the great works of Irish literature.

The *Lament for Art O'Leary* uses stock metaphors – the tools of the keener's trade – to establish a framework for the poignancy of the tale, creating something epic from what seems to have been an unglamorous death sparked by a quarrel over money. One stanza describes the terrible moment when Eileen O'Leary finds out about her husband's death – through the return of his riderless horse:

> *My friend you were forever!*
> *I knew nothing of your murder*
> *Till your horse came to the stable*
> *With the reins beneath her trailing,*
> *And your heart's blood on her shoulders*
> *Staining the tooled saddle*
> *Where you used to sit and stand.*

And, after a dramatic section in which Eileen mounts the horse and races to where her husband lies dying:

> *Your heart's blood was still flowing;*
> *I did not stay to wipe it*
> *But filled my hands and drank it.*

Russian laments had a similar quality, expounding the heroic deeds of the deceased and emphasising the suffering of those left behind. "Certain words would always recur," writes Merridale. "Grief was always bitter, for instance, a dead son was always brave and handsome, and widows were always destined for inconsolable solitude and hard work."

Like the *noheh* of Iran, traditional laments reinforce the pathos of death. Their archetypal patterns and familiar sounds seem to tell us that death is part of the rhythm of life – both ordinary and extraordinary. And by using art and artistry to transform death into a thing of beauty, they help turn the dull ache of loss into something more meaningful and, perhaps, ultimately acceptable.

Strangely enough, it was not only relatives who conducted ritual laments at funerals. Professionals could also be called in to swell the ranks. In an ancient tradition, once found in many parts of the world, hired mourners were paid in cash or in kind.

In notes from his 1681 tour of Ireland, Englishman Thomas Dineley describes "poor mercenary howlers, who generally at

Church or Church yard, encompass the next heire with an high note, who more silently laments, if he doth at all". His words suggest that the professional mourners were there to provide enough visible grief to dignify the event – particularly when relatives seemed insufficiently moved to do it themselves.

Hiring professionals was often necessary for another reason – the emotionally exhausted state of the bereaved. "When they're overcome with sadness, their bodies begin to weaken," explains a seventy-year-old retired professional mourner called Li Changgeng in an interview with Chinese writer Liao Yiwu. "But for us, once we get into the mood, we control our emotions and improvise with great ease. We can wail as long as is requested."

The point of bringing in ritual mourners was also their emotional distance from the deceased and the relatives. This was something anthropologist Loring Danforth noticed in 1979, when he was studying funeral customs in Potamia, a village in northern Thessaly.

In his book *The Death Rituals of Greece*, Danforth notes how groups of women – themselves bereaved but not close relatives – were usually present to sing laments at funerals, giving mothers, wives and daughters a chance to do the real, unscripted sobbing. Breaks after each verse allowed those with the most intense anguish to cry out messages to the person they'd just lost.

Yet even this more genuine, emotional expression of grief was only given limited voice. Eventually, the bereaved close family members were expected to join the lament. "At a funeral in Potamia where the widow of the deceased was wildly hugging and kissing her dead husband," Danforth writes, "her sister, in an attempt to restrain and calm her, spoke to her sharply: 'Don't shout like that! Sit down and cry and sing!'" The idea of public grieving, in other words, is to maintain control – not to lose it.

On the day of Ashura, the tenth day of Muharram, the mosques in Yazd are full and everyone is out on the streets. It's a public holiday. Schools and offices are closed. From community kitchens, great quantities of food are served free of charge to the faithful. Yet while some men and women are clearly mourning, Ashura is also a rare chance for social activities. I notice that many of the women shrouded in black are talking into mobile phones. Maryam translates the conversation of the young woman next to us. "She's talking to her boyfriend," she tells me. "She's saying: 'I'm on the corner of the street opposite the mosque – come over now and we can have a chat.'"

That afternoon, Maryam and I head out to a town called Mehriz, where we've been told a big Ashura procession is taking place. This turns out to be a variation on the religious play. Rare in a part of the world where visual representation of holy figures is usually prohibited, these performances have provided a form of social entertainment at this time of year (and have, since my trip, been banned).

Here in Mehriz, the drama is being acted out on top of great big trucks. One by one, great floats lurch through the entrance gate into a large open enclosure. Each new arrival elicits screams of delight from the children, while parents take photos with their mobile phones.

On top to the floats, men in medieval garb (good guys in green, bad guys in red) act out the scenes. One shows merchants haggling in the bazaar on the eve of the Battle of Karbala. In another, soldiers in brilliant costumes engage in sword fights. Husayn's riderless horse (a real one) arrives on one of the trucks.

A few moments later, there's the evil Yazid, sitting on his throne, dressed in crimson robes and a helmet with great plumes of feathers sprouting from it. Cigarette in hand, he knocks back slugs of "wine" from a large goblet (topped up from a large plastic bottle of Coca-Cola).

There's also lots of fake pink blood. This is put to dramatic effect on one float depicting the decapitated dead on the battlefield. Covered in white sheets, the bodies on this truck are live people whose heads are hidden beneath sheets, replaced by severed sheep's necks from which fake blood is dripping with the assistance of a small pump.

These motor-driven tableaux vivant provide flourishes of colour amid the crowds of spectators, who are mostly in black. And the carnival spirit is completely at odds with my preconceptions of Ashura as a dark and sometimes violent ritual.

But, at this time of year, happiness is never very far from sadness. Seeing a westerner in the crowd, a young teacher approaches me. In broken English and with an effort that's deeply touching, she attempts to explain the story to me. "He was a very, very good man," she says, with urgency in her eyes. "But they cut him (she slashes her finger across her throat) and killed him; brother, son, cousin – everybody dead. It is very sad day."

For Shi'a Moslems, it's the saddest day of the year, the most solemn in the mourning month of Muharram. The day of Ashura is the day when Imam Husayn and his supporters were murdered on the battlefield at Karbala. And on this day, the most important moment comes at noon, which marks the very instant Husayn succumbed to the arrows and swords that pierced his body.

In Yazd that morning, Maryam and I had participated in this moment, joining a crowd of people who'd gathered for the ceremony at the city centre in front of the Amir Chakhmagh, an arched, open-fronted structure with two minarets that was once used for the performance of religious plays.

Soon, members of the crowd were clapping hands to their chests and singing. From a nearby balcony, an old woman looked down on the crowd, arms crossed, patting her palms gently on to her chest in the ancient mourning gesture I'd seen used by the old men in the bazaar in Tehran.

Women cloaked in black held their palms towards the heavens while a holy man wove his way through the throng, spraying everyone with rose water from a tank on his back, as if irrigating some heavenly garden where humans sprouted from the earth in place of flowers.

At midday everyone turned to face Mecca. As the crowd fell silent, I turned in the same direction and let my head hang down. I might have been in a foreign country, attending a mourning ceremony for an ancient Islamic prophet, but it was a powerful moment of sorrow. And for a brief instant, I felt as if I was attending the funeral for my father we never held.

Tears were once thought to come directly from the brain. In some ways, of course, tears of emotion do. But physiologically, it's more complicated than that. Our lachrymal system has two mechanisms, one producing and the other draining away tears. A variety of lachrymal glands manage the different types of tears we produce, all of which contain varying concentrations of chemicals, hormones and proteins.

We produce three types of tears – basal tears, which continuously lubricate our eyeballs to prevent them seizing up in their sockets, reflex tears, produced when foreign objects such as particles of dust get in the eye, and psychic or emotional tears, which respond to our psychological state. But if production of the first two types is relatively easy to understand, the reason for the third tear category is harder to explain.

That hasn't stopped people from trying. René Descartes, the seventeenth-century philosopher and scientist, identified the fact that extreme emotions stimulated increased blood flow to the eyes, acting as a catalyst for the production of tears. However, as Tom Lutz explains in his book *Crying*, Descartes mistakenly based his assumption on principles of condensation. As hot blood came into contact with cool vapours in the eye, he surmised, the vapours were turned into tears.

William James, the nineteenth-century American psychologist and philosopher, had a theory that put the egg before the chicken. He argued that sadness was a physiological state. In response to some event, so his hypothesis went, we respond by producing tears – it's the sensation of crying that provokes in us the emotion of sadness.

If the causal link between sentiment and tear production puzzled early scientists and psychologists, the effect of weeping was easier to understand. From ancient times, crying was considered cathartic. In Hellenistic Greece, Aristotle's definition of tragedy used the word *katharsis* to refer to a calming of the audience brought about by exposure to a tragic drama and the portrayal of intense fear and pity. In other words, moving the audience to tears helped them leave the theatre happier than when they arrived.

And if tears can be shown to serve a function, it's no surprise that the great evolutionary theorist Charles Darwin wanted to find out why humans cried. In a chapter of his book *The Expression of the Emotions in Man and Animals*, Darwin examined the workings of tears. After covering in exquisite detail the physiological process of crying, particularly in infants, Darwin concluded that crying was a way of alleviating suffering.

The catharsis hypothesis holds true today. In a study called Is Crying Beneficial?, Jonathan Rottenberg, Lauren Bylsma and Ad Vingerhoets, asked more than three thousand people to recall recent weeping episodes. Sixty to 70 percent of respondents reported beneficial effects, ranging from a release of tension to feelings of relief.

The explanation may be both chemical and physical. Emotional tears contain manganese, which affects temperament, and prolactin, a hormone associated with depression. It's thought that releasing these elements through tears helps balance the body's stress levels, relieving tension. Meanwhile, in another study, Rottenberg, Vingerhoets and Michelle Hendriks found that the cardiovascular rates of people rose while weeping but slowed after the crying episode ended, producing a calming effect.

So if crying is good for you, perhaps we don't do it often enough. I wonder whether this phenomenon might offer a business opportunity for an entrepreneur to found a chain of "crying halls" for collective mourning. They could feature regular performances of doleful music or heartrending stories and charge a modest entrance fee. But, I'm forgetting – we have the movies.

During his physiological examination of tears, Darwin noticed that the English "rarely cry, except under the pressure of the acutest grief", whereas in continental Europe, "men shed tears much more readily and freely". What Darwin had spotted was that the way we weep differs from culture to culture – whether that's muffling our sobs or howling wildly. So is the way we cry something we learn or does it come naturally?

The truth is, cultural conventions and spiritual beliefs play a powerful role in shaping expressions of grief, prompting some to weep in situations others might think unlikely causes for tears.

Alfred Radcliffe-Brown, an English social anthropologist, noticed this when he was in the Andaman Islands in 1906, observing that friends would wail violently together when reunited after a period of separation. He was surprised to find no difference between this type of crying, a show of joy, and the reaction of islanders to the death of close relatives.

On the other hand, some people don't cry when you might expect them to. At funerals in central Thailand, crying is not part of the funeral ceremony, as it's considered inauspicious for teardrops to fall on the body. In Bali, weeping at cremations is frowned on as it's thought to prevent the spirit from reaching heaven. In Russia, women were warned not to weep too much after the death of a child, lest it damage the soul, preventing its ascent to heaven. Yet in other places, unfettered wailing is the most common reaction to loss.

I first noticed the existence of contrasting expressions of grief while watching television on a running machine at the gym. Staring absently at the ranks of screens in front of me, I realised that the two opposite me were both showing footage of people crying. On one, a young girl was talking to reporters amid subdued sighs and a few tears. On the next screen, another was bawling, unable to control her heavy sobs. I wasn't listening to the soundtrack but the subtitles told me these two women's stories. The one weeping quietly was a Thai girl recalling the death of her father in the Asian tsunami. The one sobbing uncontrollably was an American on a reality TV show.

Occasionally, two styles of grief collide. Stewart Wallace, an American friend, recalls this happening at the funeral of his uncle, who died at the age of fifty-five. During the funeral, his grandmother, who came from a village in Ukraine, threw herself on the ground and started grasping at the earth and wailing violently for her youngest child. The rest of the family, who were born in America, stood around staring unhappily at the ground. "It had a ritualised quality to it," Stewart told me. "I don't know if it was something learned or something felt – or both. But it was pretty shocking to all of us."

In his essay *Mourning and Funeral Customs of African Americans*, Hosea Perry describes a clash of mourning cultures that occurred after a mortally wounded teenager was admitted to a Midwestern American hospital. The boy's relatives stood outside wailing so violently that hospital staff called the police, who sent in a riot squad to arrest them. "The hospital doesn't understand how black people grieve," said a community leader after the incident.

So in modern society why are we so squeamish about putting death and mourning on display? Death is a human experience that's inevitable, universal and inescapable. Yet we'd rather it were banished from sight. And while grieving is clearly a necessary reaction to this experience, we appear to want to hide the bereft from public view.

Contemporary society, it seems, no longer has a place for traditional lamentation obsequies. Danforth witnesses the transition. In his book, he notes that the young Greek women of an emerging middle class "regard the singing of laments as a source of embarrassment, indicative of rural backwardness and superstition".

In Victorian England, too, a once flourishing tradition of emotional, public demonstrations of grief eventually faded. The tradition had developed alongside Romanticism, an eighteenth-century artistic, literary and intellectual movement, and the rise of Evangelical Christianity.

In paintings and novels, the deathbed scene, depicting grieving relatives gathered in a domestic bedroom, became a popular theme. Composing lines that might have been written by the Sufi artists of Persia, British poets infused their stanzas with tears, as did Lord Byron in lines such these, from *And Thou Art Dead, as Young and Fair*:

As once I wept, if I could weep
My tears might well be shed,
To think I was not near to keep
One vigil o'er thy bed;

Public displays of sentiment were accepted, and even encouraged. "They were not shy about expressing the depth of their suffering in tears and in words," explains historian Pat Jalland, who cites contemporary accounts describing the behaviour of bereaved individuals.

There was the man who, having lost his only child, became "almost frantic" and started "rolling on his bed and tearing his hair", and George Lyttelton who, on his wife's death in 1857, sobbed uncontrollably for days after, and wanted only to "weep and muse and pine".

As the century drew to a close, however, the influence of Evangelicalism and Romanticism waned. Meanwhile, advances in medical science led to a sharp fall in the death rate. In the process, public and even private emotional outbursts of grief became less acceptable. For Englishmen, says Jalland, the process was accelerated "by the ethos of the public [private] schools with their cult of manliness and masculine reserve". It was this masculine reserve, this stoicism, that shaped my father's generation in their responses to death and bereavement – and perhaps mine too.

In the early hours of August 31, 1997, the British way of death was turned on its head. All of a sudden, that notorious stiff upper lip betrayed a distinct wobble. What caused the wobble was the death of a princess. Within hours of a black Mercedes crashing into a Parisian tunnel, killing Diana, Princess of Wales, and Dodi Al Fayed, her companion, flowers started arriving at the gates of Kensington Palace, where Diana had lived. With bouquets, teddy bears and other gifts piling up outside the palace, the nation became swept up in an extraordinary – and highly uncharacteristic – public outpouring of grief. Even Tony Blair, the British prime minister, allowed his voice to crack just for a moment in his television broadcast on the morning the "people's princess" died.

The night before Diana's funeral, I paid a visit to Kensington Palace. It was a warm summer evening, and the stench of rotting flowers combined with the heady aroma of scented candles and joss sticks to create an ambiance more like a temple in India than a park in Great Britain. Facing a sea of cellophane-covered floral tributes, teddy bears, photos and hand-written signs, people sat on the ground, alone or in groups, around small personal shrines. Heads were bowed. Some wept quietly.

Early the next morning, some friends and I joined the crowds on Kensington High Street to watch the cortège pass by on its way to Westminster Abbey. The atmosphere was unlike any I'd previously encountered in England. The city had fallen silent. The air was leaden. Barely visible, the ghosts of clouds lurked in the immaculate blue of a late summer morning. The only sounds were the tolling of a church bell and a few muffled sobs from members of the crowd.

Finally, draped in the Royal Standard, the lily-laden coffin emerged from the palace gates. It advanced slowly and majestically on a gun carriage pulled by the horses of the King's Troop and accompanied by foot soldiers from the First Battalion Welsh Guards, decked out in their scarlet livery and bearskins. Following behind were the two young princes, their father, the Prince of Wales, their grandfather, the Duke of Edinburgh and Charles Spencer, Diana's brother. It was a state funeral, with all the trappings of a royal pageant.

Through it all, though, the modest box carrying the body of the dead princess appeared to float above everything, detaching itself from the pomp and circumstance swirling around it as it proceeded through Central London. How strange it was, I thought with wonder as it passed in front of me, that inside that box was a person – a person who had walked, talked, laughed, cried, eaten, bathed, made love, slept, and who had, on every morning until the morning of August 31, 1997, woken to a new day.

It was the death of this person – now a body in a box – that had sent British stoicism into a tailspin. Newspaper headlines talked of "A Nation United in Mourning". TV newscasters spoke in hushed tones. I wondered, privately, if the country had gone mad. Plenty of my friends and fellow Brits, it turned out, felt the same. A few commentators claimed the media were overdoing it (as indeed they had during Diana's life).

Nevertheless, the change of mood in the United Kingdom during that time marked a shift in the country's emotional history. And the spontaneous outburst of mourning across much of the nation was about more than the loss of a glamorous princess. It was also, I think, a time in which everyone felt permitted to contemplate their own personal loss; to pull those deep reserves of grief out from their hiding places. In short, the occasion gave everyone in Britain a chance to have something they'd denied themselves for so long: a really good cry.

Ironically, the Ashura ceremony I most want to see – the reciting of the *majalis*, or lamentation – I cannot, since I'm a woman and so barred from the main hall of the mosque, where it generally takes place. But back in my hotel that evening, I catch one on Iranian television. The camera pans across a large hall (it looks a lot more comfortable than the Husseinia Maryam and I sat in) packed full of men sitting in rows. On a stage at the front is a man dressed in a grey suit, a cape and a black cap. Speaking in Persian, he's recounting in detail the suffering at the Battle of Karbala and the martyrdom of Imam Husayn.

At first he speaks in solemn tones, pausing for effect from time to time. But as the story unfolds, something strange happens. The leader appears to have something in his throat. He coughs and starts blowing his nose. Soon, whimpers accompany some of the phrases he utters. Gradually, full-blown sobs are being woven into his recitation.

Meanwhile, the same thing is happening in the audience. People start sighing and murmuring. Pained expressions come across the faces of many of the listeners as they break into quiet moans, many clasping their hands to their brows, hiding their faces with handkerchiefs or shaking their heads. Shoulders shudder and some people have tears streaming down their cheeks (the camera tends to zoom in on these ones). Pretty soon, the hall is heaving with sobbing men.

I'd heard about these lamentation ceremonies but it's still strange to see one, particularly since the participants are all male. In societies with lamentation traditions, men are not usually the weepers. Yet perhaps that's the point. Here is a safe space where men are allowed – even encouraged – to cry.

Curiously enough, there was one thing that would unfailingly reduce my father to tears – the sound of English church bells. I remember him telling me this many years ago. Then, going through his essays and letters, I found a description of the effect they had on him. He had experienced this, he wrote, from an early age and interpreted it as a child's "involuntary, and deeply emotional" response to a sound. "I soon learned to control the visible signs of emotion," he wrote. Even so, he went on, throughout his life church bells continued to work their "emotional magic" on him, "the reasons for which I have never yet found an explanation".

Music and mourning have always had a close relationship. Music can move us to tears even without the presence of the dead, so it's hardly surprising that it can also help give voice to grief.

When Steven Feld was studying the culture of sound in Papua New Guinea, he noticed that the mourning songs of the Kaluli people – whose weeping-singing voices are, according to Feld, intimately connected with rainforest birds, which are considered spirits – had common features. The songs were delivered in breathy voices with "choking sounds and slight vibrato". They were always descending in their melodic contours, and several songs could overlap, creating complex polyphonic layers of sound.

I once saw some of these musical traits at work in the performance of a Caribbean wake drumming song by Dominican singer-songwriter Irka Mateo. Accompanying herself with a small drum and a wood maraca, Mateo's rendition started brightly with melodies rising sharply before falling again. Once more, rhythm played its part. But in addition, as the verses were repeated, her voice grew hollow and her head sank lower over the drum. By the end of the song, a distinct breathiness had entered her singing and the performance ended in what was almost a sob, mixing music and mourning.

Towards the end of Fa's life, it was music that turned my restrained sighs into tears. One evening shortly after returning from England – my last visit before his death, as it turned out – I was at home in New York, paying bills and filing papers. I put on a CD I'd ordered that had just arrived in the mail, a recording of Bulgarian choral singers. Halfway through the third track, *Kalimankou Denkou* – a slow wash of dissonant harmonies over which the powerful vibrato of the lead singer soars only to descend again and again – I found myself hunched over the table, tears running down my cheeks.

I let myself cry for a while. The tears seemed to be part of the music; soft and warm, like a consoling caress. My tears ended as the song drew to its quiet close, and I sighed again as I'd done so often that year, but this time with breath drawn from the deepest recesses of my lungs. It was a new sigh – clear, unrestricted by tension, and one that seemed to bring with it a sense of calm I'd not felt in months. I was not in a Husseinia. This was no Irish keen or Greek funerary lament. Nor was it rehearsed or planned. But at that moment, I realised that – with the assistance of the doleful voices of the Bulgarian singers – I was performing my own mourning ceremony.

Crying might be good for you. It certainly helped me through a dark moment during my father's illness. Still, I'm not sure I want to encourage public wailing at my funeral. Despite almost a decade in America, I can't shake off my British discomfort at the thought of making a scene, even in death. And personally, I prefer the guidance of the old Hebrew proverb: "Say not in grief 'he is no more' but live in thankfulness that he was," or the words of Henry Scott Holland, canon of St Paul's Cathedral, who in a 1910 essay suggested the bereaved should "wear no forced air of solemnity or sorrow" but "laugh as we always laughed at the little jokes we enjoyed together".

I'm not the only one who feels like this. Romantic poets, tragic heroes and dying heroines have often entreated those left behind not to weep too much at their deaths. In one of the most moving death scenes in opera, Henry Purcell's Dido, of *Dido and Aeneas*, tells the audience that when she is "laid in earth" they should remember her, but forget her troubles: "May my wrongs create no trouble in thy breast," she cries as her life ebbs away. Others have specifically forbidden any weeping by their graves. In his 1812 poem *Euthanasia*, Lord Byron asks that no "band of friends or heirs" or "officious mourners" attend his funeral because, he writes:

> *I would not mar one hour of mirth*
> *Nor startle friendship with a tear.*

Perhaps a similar sentiment lay behind my father's last request. Maybe Fa's wish that there should be no funeral or memorial service for him was motivated by this same idea – a desire to save us all from an event bound to provoke tears.

2

BEAUTIFUL FIRE

A Burst of Flames in Bali

I f there were an award for the world's most elaborate funerary tradition, the Balinese would surely win it – and their victory would surprise no one. For on this small Indonesian island, even banal daily activities are executed with the utmost grace and style (and usually a ceremony or two). In Bali, dance dramas in dazzling costumes are staged at the drop of a hat and even rice gets treated to elaborate rituals. To prevent tower blocks from marring the lush green skyline, the law stipulates that buildings can no rise higher than the palm trees. Oh yes, and the garbage trucks are painted with pictures of lotus flowers. *Of course* Bali's funerals are fabulous.

Even for non-royal individuals, cremations are astonishing affairs, accompanied by spectacular decorations taking weeks – sometimes months – to construct. Often involving the immolation of dozens of individuals in a single day, these events are more carnival than funeral. Immense floats made of paper and bamboo deliver the bodies to the pyre, drummers cavort around the procession and street traders sell snacks and drinks to the crowd.

"It is in their cremation ceremonies that the Balinese have their greatest fun," wrote Mexican artist Miguel Covarrubias in his 1937 book, *Island of Bali*. "Hundreds of people in a wild stampede carry the beautiful towers, sixty feet high, solidly built of wood and bamboo and decorated with tinsel and expensive silks, in which the bodies are transported to the cremation grounds." Everything is set on fire, he explains, with "hundreds and even thousands of dollars burned in one afternoon in a mad splurge of extravagance by a people who value the necessities of life in fractions of pennies".

Most dazzling of all are royal cremations, throwing power, politics and status into events that, even for ordinary citizens, are packed with drama and spectacle. On July 15, 2008, a royal Balinese individual is to be cremated – Tjokorda Gde Agung Suyasa, first son of the tenth child of the last king of Ubud, a small hillside town at the centre of Bali. I hear about it a couple of months before it's due to happen. Because it's to be a Pelebon, a royal cremation, it will be on a grand scale. In fact, I'm told it will be the biggest of its kind in three decades. Thousands will probably attend.

Knowing this comes as something of a relief. For on one website, I learn that the island's funerals are visitor attractions. "If you go to the local tourist centre in your town in Bali, you should be able to find out if there are any cremation ceremonies taking place," writes one travel blogger. For about fifteen dollars, the writer explains, local guides will pick you up from your hotel and take you to the ceremony.

Fortunately, the Ubud royal cremation will be such a huge event I won't have to contemplate the grotesque prospect of paying to see a funeral. And since it will be so public, I'll have no worries about the prospect of intruding on private grief. Still, if I want to explore the world's death rites and burial traditions, being part of the tourist industry is something I'll just have to get used to – the dead and their gravesites are firmly on the tourist trail.

After all, cemeteries such as Père-Lachaise in Paris, London's Highgate Cemetery, and Arlington National Cemetery in Washington often welcome more tourists than families visiting relatives. And, of course, some of the world's most visited tourist sites are mausoleums or memorials – think of India's Taj Mahal, China's Ming Tombs or Egypt's pyramids. The Egyptian dead have always been huge visitor attractions. The unwrapping of mummies brought back to England by Victorian archaeologists drew large audiences and in museums, the sections displaying mummies of the pharaohs are always packed. Embalmed dictators pull in the crowds, too, most famously Lenin in Moscow, Mao in Beijing and Ho Chi Minh, the Vietnamese leader (who in fact wanted to be cremated). Death, in short, is a crowd pleaser.

In Bali, death is perhaps at its most spectacular. And aside from wanting to attend what will clearly be a once-in-a-lifetime event, I'm curious to see what a "happy funeral" looks like. Bali's royal cremation will surely have drama and ritual to match the mourning ceremonies laid on every year in Iran for Imam Husayn. Death is certainly not hidden away in Bali, far from it. But rather than favouring rituals intended to provoke weeping, as the Iranians do, the opposite applies here – no one is supposed to cry.

The blatantly celebratory mood of Balinese cremations might seem inappropriate at events many of us would consider distressing. But the Balinese believe any sadness or strong emotions displayed at a cremation will hamper the journey of the soul into the next life, so visible signs of grief are frowned upon. Instead, elaborately choreographed ceremonies are designed to elicit the laughter and joy needed to liberate the souls from their earthly bonds. I like this idea – death as a happy ending and a glorious beginning.

Too bad the latter isn't part of my belief system. After my death, I foresee no beginning, glorious or otherwise. Nothing in my upbringing prepared me for it. Apart from a brief spiritual awakening at age nine (which consisted of me purchasing a plaster angel at a jumble sale and imagining myself looking angelic as I knelt before it in the small chapel I would ask Fa to build in our garden), I had a thoroughly non-religious childhood, and not just at home.

At school, "divinity classes", as they were known, focused not on the Bible but around social issues such as poverty and drug addiction (I still have a surprisingly accurate drawing I did as a twelve-year-old of what my caption explains is a "joint or reefer").

"But what if we end up at the gates of heaven only to find we've made a horrible mistake?" a friend asked me many years ago. "It simply won't happen," I told her, and I'd say the same today. Still, my certainty on this front poses a more difficult question – if nothing follows death, how can I approach my own expiration date without fear? Should I belatedly embrace a religion? Should I invent some new philosophy in which I can envisage an afterlife? Perhaps the Balinese way of death will offer some inspiration.

Tjokorda Gde Agung Suyasa was born in 1941. He died aged sixty-seven leaving behind two wives, six children, twelve grandchildren and one great-grandchild. Greatly respected in the community, he was head of the Ubud royal family and was a national advisor on cultural and religious matters.

His body won't go alone to the funeral pyre. He'll be cremated with Tjokorda Gede Raka, another member of the Ubud royal family and once a senior official in the Bali police force. Gede Raka died a week before his cousin. A third royal Ubud personage, Desak Raka, will join them. Born in 1917, she was cremated soon after her death in December 2007. On July 15, she'll be represented by a symbolic effigy – an idealised representation of her body – and given a full cremation ceremony, too.

On the day of the Pelebon, the remains of sixty-eight Ubud citizens will also go up in flames (although for some, as for Desak Raka, the effigy will be the only thing on the pyre). These sixty-eight citizens have until now been lying in the ground. Several years earlier, their families buried them without coffins in simple graves and waited for an auspicious date on which to cremate their remains. Agung Suyasa's death has provided that date, for being cremated at the same time as royalty is extremely propitious.

When the time comes for the cremation, the families will go to the cemetery to exhume the bones. They'll pick off the dirt, cleanse them, wrap them carefully in cloth and take them home, treating the bones with the reverence with which they'd carried the actual corpse. Once at home, they'll re-enact the death, standing around and sighing all over again, as if their relative's breath were weakening for the first time, hanging their heads as he or she fades from the world. Then, as they would with a recently deceased person, they'll ceremoniously wash the fleshless bones and, using tiny combs, softly brush at non-existent hair.

For nobles it's slightly different – the body of Agung Suyasa was never buried; instead he was embalmed and has been lying in state. But first, as all Balinese do, the family visited a medium to ask him for his last wishes (he wanted to be cremated with his cousin). Then relatives carried out the cleansing of body, washing it gently and rubbing it with sandalwood paste. At that point, anyone overcome by grief would have left the room, adhering to the principle that runs through all Bali's funeral rites. For by the time the cremation comes around, the most visible emotion is joy and excitement.

Yet the truth is, maintaining a separation between the happiness that Balinese tradition demands and the grief that surrounds loss is not always easy. Anthropologist Linda Connor noticed this at a ritual body washing she attended in Bali in 1990. With about sixty friends, relatives, and neighbours standing around in a courtyard to watch the corpse being washed, the scene was one of extreme distress, with many people weeping or choking back tears. "After five to ten minutes of the initial washing and rubbing down with fragrant sandalwood paste, some of the mourners around the corpse appeared to become overwhelmed by the situation," Connor writes. "They fell swaying to the back of the ranks in what appeared to be a faint."

Halfway through the ceremony, attention shifted from the body itself (Connor says it looked "ghastly" with its blistered face and bloated form) to the effigy on the corpse's chest. The effigy signifies the rebirth of the soul, so it must be made of materials that symbolise renewal and revitalisation. Mirrors form the eyes, so they are clear and sparkling, iron nails stand in for strong teeth, and fragrant flower buds become the nostrils.

The creation of this effigy had a striking effect. "Although the women who fainted had not come back, those who stayed were no longer sobbing openly, and the expressions on their faces were more composed," writes Connor. The second-eldest daughter took the leading role in putting together the effigy. "And she became visibly more serene as the ceremony neared completion."

In Bali, disconnecting the dead from the living is a long, elaborate process, often stretching across years, from the initial (and temporary) burial, to the exhumation of the bones, the cleansing ritual, the creation of the effigies, and the cremation itself, a ceremony designed to break the material bond between the soul and its body.

It's something you see at work in many traditions, from the year-long process of Jewish mourning to the rites of Orthodox Christians, who hold prayers on the third, ninth and fortieth days after the funeral, then on the third, sixth and ninth months, and thereafter annually. Like lamentations and funeral marches, these practices have a distinct rhythm, one whose pace slows over time. With schedules set for mourning, rote and routine ease us from intense grief to fond remembrance.

In Bali, the five elements from which Balinese believe humans are made – earth, fire, water, ether and air – come together in death to return the body to the universe, and to regenerate the soul. It's called *Panca Maha Bhuta* – the energy of nature. Each new rite brings the soul of the deceased just that bit closer to this new life. It's like matriculation and graduation only without the exams. And for those left behind, familiar customs guide the bereaved through their mourning.

Like a play with many acts, death unfolds gradually until in the end, as a brilliant fiery conflagration sends the soul up towards the heavens through swirling smoke and showers of sparks, grief is transformed into joy.

I wake at 5am on my first morning in Bali. I'm in time-zone hell, having made an unholy jet-bound leap across the globe from New York. There's no chance of getting back to sleep, so I throw on some clothes and head out of the hotel to have a look around Ubud.

In the soft morning light, it soon becomes clear that the charms of this place more than match the reveries of the travel brochures. The town clusters around a small palace, the Puri Saren Agung, which will be the central nervous system for the cremation. Behind the main thoroughfare are enchanting leafy streets and beyond lie emerald rice paddies. Brilliant green and glistening under the pale morning sun, the stalks of rice push their slender, spiked leaves through small lakes of glassy water in a collective expression of energy and renewal.

As I dive down narrow alleys, villagers in floral sarongs and embroidered shirts are starting their day on bicycles and by foot. Religious statues, too, are stylishly dressed, wrapped in black-and-white gingham fabric with gold sashes. They flank carved stone entrance gates to homes that look like small temples.

Behind enclosure walls of each house, clusters of tiny, eccentric-looking towers support oversized roofs of thick thatch topped with metal crowns. These are shrines representing the cosmic Mount Meru. Bali is often called the "island of a thousand temples" – a claim I can now see isn't so far-fetched.

Miraculously, my jetlag seems to have faded. With the scent of frangipani in my nostrils and tropical birdsong filling my ears, I'm smitten by the place – and perilously close to composing some of the purple prose you find in those travel brochures. And that's even before I've encountered the giant cow.

Growing up in a rural part of England dominated by dairy farming, cows were an important part of my childhood. Cows, I was always told, see things at three times their actual size, turning humans into towering monsters. Well, here in Ubud, I finally understand how they feel. Approaching the royal palace, I find myself face to face with the biggest cow I've ever seen. It's absolutely huge – it must be at least fifteen feet high.

I walk over to inspect it. Standing erect in a defiant posture, its hoofs planted firmly on to an ornate plinth, the cow is made of paper, wood and bamboo, and is painted black, with muscles and other anatomical details picked out in red and gold. It has bulging eyes and flared nostrils. Its horns are gilded, its gold mane sparkles with tiny mirrors and pieces of coloured glass, and strings of gold beads hang around its neck. When I reach its hind legs, I catch sight of a large red appendage. Okay – so it's not a cow. It's a bull.

But, whether it's a bull or a cow (it turns out that in Balinese tradition, bulls are used for men, cows for women), this magnificent creature will – with the assistance of a giant ceremonial pyre – be what takes the spirit of Agung Suyasa on his journey to the next life.

But why has a bull, however ornately decorated, been chosen as the form for a ceremonial cremation sarcophagus? The answer lies in Bali's curious religious history. Surrounded by Indonesia, which has the world's largest population of Muslims, Bali is a religious anomaly – its dominant faith is Hinduism.

Quite how or why Bali, which lies thousands of miles away from the Indian subcontinent, became "Indianised", as scholars put it, remains a mystery.

Some direct contact existed between India and Bali from the first century AD. Then, in the ninth century, Indian traders came to the Indonesian archipelago. The real impetus behind the spread of Hinduism came when the kings and nobles from the neighbouring Hindu Majapahit kingdom of East Java (the main island of the Indonesian archipelago) fled to Bali, escaping the fourteenth-century Islamic conquest of the region.

As Islamic rulers took over the rest of the archipelago, the Majapahit kingdom declined. Yet somehow Bali's Hindu culture remained intact.

Anyone familiar with Indian Hinduism would find the Balinese version quite different. This is partly because elements of Bali's early animist beliefs still make their presence felt in the island's culture, as do some Buddhist ideas. Yet the two branches of the religion have much in common. Both follow the Hindu caste system (although in Bali, the social divisions are far less complicated than they are in India).

Another important shared belief is that the cow is the most sacred of animals. Meanwhile, the Balinese also adopted the Indian Hindu custom of cremating the dead on a funeral pyre. What could be better, then, than to combine the two traditions by cremating the dead *inside* a cow?

In the west, the practicalities of modern cremation are unromantic. There are no bull or cow effigies dripping with decorative necklaces. Instead, jewellery is removed from the corpse, as are pacemakers, which can explode during incineration. Using a motorised trolley, the coffin is loaded, or "charged", in the industry jargon, into the cremation chamber (known as a "retort"). There, a series of computer-controlled burners bring the temperature up to 1,800 degrees Fahrenheit. To get things going, a column of flame is directed at the chest cavity, the part of the body containing the most fat, and so the part that burns most quickly, making it the human equivalent of kindling.

With body fat acting as an efficient fuel, the bones soon dehydrate as the organic constituents become charred. When the char oxidises away, the bones calcinate, shrink and fracture. As the internal moisture turns to steam, the bone can also flake off.

After roughly two hours, the intense heat will have consumed the "organic matter" (a description for which, it turns out, my father and the funeral industry share a fondness), leaving just the bone fragments. For heavier bodies made up of larger amounts of fatty tissue, a longer burn is required (another hour per hundred pounds) at lower temperatures, since fatty bodies generate more heat than leaner ones, causing the cremation chamber to generate smoke, reducing its efficiency.

What's left at the end is put into a cremulator – a rotating drum like a small spin drier with heavy steel balls rolling around in it – which crushes the remains into fine particles leaving no recognisable bone pieces.

It's an industrial process, conducted beneath fluorescent lighting in stainless steel chambers with equipment managed by computer chips. The most involvement the family members get is, in crematoria that offer this facility, a view through small glass windows through which they can watch their relative disappear into the cremation chamber. Sometimes faint echoes of traditional rituals make their way into the process. In adherence to the Hindu funeral rite – in which the oldest son or brother lights the pyre – Indian families often request to be allowed to press the button that ignites the burner.

Considerable advances have been made in cremator technology in recent years. The brochures and websites of companies that manufacture them show pictures of sinister-looking steel boxes with names like the "Millennium II", the "Newton", or the "Joule" (named for a unit of energy). Cremator makers cheerfully boast about dramatic reductions in fuel usage, space-saving designs, environmental integrity and significant increases in the "throughput" of their machines.

And, of course, greater "throughput" means lower prices. In the United States, a cremation can cost as little as a fifth of the price of a traditional funeral with a burial. Customers who choose cremation no longer need to purchase caskets costing thousands of dollars. Even if they want an open casket funeral, rental options feature coffins that come in two parts – a decorative one that can be reused and a simple lined combustible box that slides out of the back of the main casket and is cremated along with the body.

The growing popularity of lower-priced cremations has created something of a challenge for the funeral industry – how to stem the erosion of its profit margins. As a result, the industry has recently been coming up with some inventive cremation-related products and services.

Many hearses, for instance, now have a special fitting in which to secure urns (the industry calls it an "urn enclave"). With "adjustable bier pins" accommodating different sizes and shapes, urn enclaves flip up from the floor of the hearse and are neatly stowed again when the vehicle needs to carry a coffin.

And if using a hearse to transport a pot of ashes seems like taking a sledgehammer to crack a nut, the Pennsylvania-based Tombstone Hearse Company will carry your urn in a scaled down Victorian-style hearse drawn by a motorcycle.

Nor do the innovations stop at transportation. Even the act of scattering can be motorised these days. A company in Meridian, Idaho, called Release Urns has devised what inventor Scotty Crandlemire, in a promotional video, explains is a "new revenue producing tool". It's a box funeral directors can lease to their clients. It comes in a variety of finishes with a small round hole in one side (it looks rather like a birdhouse). On reaching the edge of the lake, mountaintop, or whatever spot designated for the scattering, friends or relatives simply press a button and, with the aid of a motorised device inside the box, the ashes come spurting out of the hole, making the dispersal, says Crandlemire, "an awe-inspiring, reverent event each and every time".

The royal palace in Ubud is where most of the preparations for the Pelebon are taking place so, on my first morning in Bali, I head over there to see what's going on. It's early and in the main courtyard of the palace, something's clearly about to happen. Dozens of men dressed in the traditional combination of a sarong, a shirt and *udeng* (a small patterned turban) are waiting expectantly. Suddenly, on the dot of 8am, they all stand up and start work on a collection of ambitious-looking structures, sawing up bamboo stems, fastening them together or splitting them into long strips and weaving them into various shapes.

The objects they're constructing are two *badés*, giant pagoda-shaped towers made of wood and bamboo that will transport Agung Suyasa and Gede Raka to the cremation grounds on July 15. Tapered towards the top, these towers represent the Balinese concepts of earth, body and soul, with the uppermost section representing the heavens and a wide turtle-shaped base symbolising the earth, the foundation on which the world rests.

The more tapering roofs in your tower (the number is always odd) the higher your social status. For these two royal corpses, the *badés* will soar heavenwards, each with nine floors, rising to more than ninety feet. On the journey to the cremation pyre, the bodies travel in an open platform between the towers and the turtle.

Weighing more than ten tonnes, each structure will take scores of men to carry on the journey from the home (in this case, the palace) to the cremation ground. They'll also have to heave over two more structures – high bamboo bridges that, rather like aircraft boarding staircases, will be used to bring the bodies down from their towers to be placed in their bull sarcophagi (Balinese funerals require a lot of heavy lifting, it seems).

Progress on the *badés* is moving fast. Workers are busy affixing a large demon head with bulging eyes and pointed fangs to the front of one (having plenty of demons on your *badé* helps frighten off evil spirits). And both towers are already lavished with gold leaf, colourful paper and mirror decorations. Eventually they'll each have huge symbolic wings. For now, these are lying on the ground, but when finished they'll be lashed to the sides of the towers so that, like the appendages of gargantuan phoenixes, they can carry the royal souls upwards to paradise – to their glorious beginning.

As funeral hearses go, these are pretty impressive. And as I gaze up at this collection of enormous and dazzling structures – all crawling with workers busy hammering pieces of bamboo together, securing them with rattan strips and fastening decorations to the surface – I can't help thinking of the phrases Fa used in his final instructions: "swift and practical", with "no formalities, or ceremonial baggage".

Well, it's hard to imagine how you could get more "ceremonial baggage" into a cremation than what's sitting outside this Balinese palace. If I didn't know better, I'd say someone was putting on an opera or a play, not a funeral. Gamelan players constantly hone their skills as if rehearsing for a concert. Processions of women bearing offerings on their heads look like a chorus arriving. And foreign guests and dignitaries showing up at the palace in national costume could just as easily be actors about to go on stage.

Every day, more decorations appear, more monsters and demons are unveiled. Often, it's as if adornments have grown without human intervention – black, gold and purple fabric will overnight have wrapped itself around a pillar. Mythical creatures emerge from behind bamboo scaffolding with no sign of how they were made. Newly cut banana-leaf fronds appear on balustrades in the afternoons, and each morning small offerings are pinned on to every column inside the palace. It's like a game of Spot the Difference. Something's always been added while you looked away.

It's all enchanting and exotic. Yet to my amazement, I'm beginning to feel part of this whole event. I know my way around the complex of pavilions that make up the royal palace. Monitoring the progress of the preparations has become a sort of duty. Strange ceremonial structures are becoming familiar friends.

Of all the ceremonial beasts, my favourite is the dragon, or *Naga Banda*. With a twenty-three-foot-long sinuous tube of a body covered in brocaded silk, his huge jaws reveal fierce splayed teeth. His eyes bulge wildly. This magnificent creature – rarely seen, even at royal cremations – will also go up in flames on July 15.

One afternoon, the dragon is to be ceremonially installed in the palace after being "retrieved" from the nearby village of Peliatan (he was actually constructed in the palace so they've had to take him there secretly in order to bring him back again). Waiting for his arrival amid hundreds of onlookers, the atmosphere is one of excited expectancy. A royal prince and princess arrive, dressed in purple, pink, white and gold and conveyed on two golden palanquins shaded by parasols and lifted high above the crowd. Then the gamelan players strike up a tune. Hearing cheers from down the road, I quickly find a spot at the top of some steps, from where I can peer out over the palace walls. Below is a sea of people all looking in one direction.

Finally, here comes the dragon, and he looks truly splendid. His golden head, gilded adornments and purple, pink and blue silk body are resplendent in the fading sunlight. Slowly and majestically, he inches down the street towards the palace gates. And, coming up behind the dragon is – oh, how fabulous – another giant bull. It turns out that the bull I encountered next to the palace is merely the more modest version, destined for Gede Raka.

This new arrival is for Agung Suyasa himself, and at about twenty feet high, it's a much bigger beast. The bearers reverse it into position so that the two funereal bovines stand side by side.

As the dragon approaches the courtyard, the gamelan players' tempo rises to a frantic pace and, to roars from the crowd, the *Naga Banda* enters triumphant. His jaw seems to have opened wider. His eyes seem to be bulging even more wildly (mine are, too). Floating above a carpet of people, he makes his way through the narrow gates and tiny passageways of the palace and, after much heaving and shouting on the part of the bearers, he's finally positioned on the stage that will be his temporary resting place.

The stage – surprise, surprise – is even more ornately decorated than it was the day before, with all manner of offerings in banana-leaf baskets piled on to it. Cages of live birds hang stage right and stage left and, on two pedestals below, a couple of real cow heads on giant platters look like something out of a banquet scene painted by Rubens.

It's about now that I realise I've wandered into a fairy tale. Everywhere I turn, there are demons, dragons and princesses (and the princesses are real). The air is filled with an eclectic mixture of tuber roses, incense and cigarette smoke. The music of gamelan players echoes around me and the lights twinkle like it's Christmas. A few days ago, I was wondering how to fill my time in Bali until the cremation ceremony. Now, I don't want to leave. Who knew a funeral party could serve up such generous portions of joy?

Yet it's at times like this that I fear death the most, or at least regret the fact of it. For when I'm dead, there'll be no more new discoveries, no more exotic, enchanted experiences. Nothing will make my heart race because my heart will have stopped. Death, as poet Philip Larkin puts it, is the "anaesthetic from which none come round". Of course, when I'm actually dead, I won't miss anything because I'll be gone. But while alive, I miss these moments on behalf of my dead self. And perhaps that's what makes them all the more delicious.

I was not there to see my father's body enter the Weymouth crematorium. I was thousands of miles away, travelling along a potholed road in northern India. Sam didn't want me to cancel my trip. She decided to go to Fa's cremation with just her brother Anthony to keep her company. "I prefer to have my grief privately," she told me. And after all, she reminded me, Fa had specified that the arrangements for his cremation should be "swift and practical" with no unnecessary "formalities" or "ceremonials".

Fa's instructions also stressed that the cremation should be, "above all considerations – Secular!" It certainly was. A small piece of paper I eventually found embedded in the ashes provides a prosaic record of the event. It read:

Weymouth & Portland Borough Council
Murray, Nigel Stuart
Crem no: 58809
Time & Date: 1.00 pm on Thursday 4 Jan 2007
Service: Committal
Fun Dir: [he would have enjoyed this abbreviation] *A J Wakeley*
Disposal: Remove By Representative of Applicant to A J Wakeley
Funeral Service
Authority to Cremate: [signed] *Helen Hornell*

There it is again. That uneasy marriage of something so momentous, a last rite of passage, a human body (my own father's, no less) cast into fire, with something so mundane – a bureaucratic record, complete with serial number, date and the official marks of the local administration.

On January 4, 2007, as my mother and uncle were driving to a crematorium in West Dorset, I was hurtling along a Gujarati highway staring out at streams of huge trucks, each groaning under the weight of its cargo, horns blaring. I looked at my watch. Sam and Anthony would by then have left Summerfields. They'd be winding along the sinuous coastal road that runs past the villages of Burton Bradstock, West Bexington and Abbotsbury (famous for its sub-tropical gardens).

From this road you can, on a clear day, see Portland and the magnificent Jurassic Coast that stretches for eighteen miles along the south coast of Dorset. The journey, passing some of the county's most spectacular views, would take about forty minutes.

Meanwhile, in Gujarat, we still had hours ahead of us. Dusk was falling and I was fixated on the road, not sure whether I was more afraid of being crushed between two lumbering juggernauts or of ramming into one of the barefoot pedestrians who every so often, without warning, strolled into the oncoming traffic. We passed billboards for the Why Wait Restaurant and for a company claiming to offer the "World's Second Largest Appliances".

On one stretch of road, a "Corpse Hotline" sign helpfully displayed a phone number above a simplified picture of a dead animal. We overtook camels and donkeys (happily none of them yet corpses). Between roadside chai shops and half-finished buildings, brilliantly lit gas stations loomed up, islands of the rich world transplanted into the poor.

At 1pm Greenwich Mean Time on January 4, 2007, as Fa's remains passed into the capable hands of the "Representative of Applicant to A J Wakeley Funeral Service", dusk was falling over northern India. The sun was enjoying its final burst of energy, its incandescence magnified by clouds of dust, which captured and redistributed millions of tiny particles of light across the horizon, creating a glorious fiery haze. I looked down at my watch again. Right now, if I'd calculated the time difference correctly, my father's coffin would be sliding into the furnace at the Weymouth & Portland Borough Council crematorium.

While the Balinese started cremating their dead after they adopted Hinduism, elsewhere this method of corpse disposal dates back as far as the Stone Age. The Romans embraced the practice (emperors such as Augustus, Nero and Caligula were cremated) and the ancient scriptures of Hindus and Buddhists describe cremation. From Homer's Iliad, we learn that the Hellenistic Greeks favoured burning their dead, believing that this liberated them from their bodies, allowing them to enjoy eternal life.

Early cremation varied in its efficiency. Given enough wood

and peat, it's thought early pyres could achieve temperatures of up to 1,800 degrees Fahrenheit, putting them on par with modern crematoria. The Anglo-Saxons managed this, as analysis of their remains reveals. However, bones could be left charred and often in one piece (a bonus for archaeologists, of course).

And as in Bali, early cremations could provide moments of intense drama, as we learn from the great English epic poem *Beowulf*, celebrating an eighth-century Scandinavian hero and culminating in his cremation. "The wood-reek went up," writes the poet, "Swart over the smoky glow, sound of the flame / Bewound with the weeping (the wind-blending stilled), / Until it at last the bone-house had broken / Hot at the heart."

Early European Christianity disapproved of such drama. The young religion deemed cremation a primitive, pagan practice and from the fifth century it fell out of favour, at least in the west. Above all, cremation was at odds with belief in the resurrection of the flesh, a central doctrine of Christianity. When Christ eventually returned, the church believed the dead would need their bodies in order to rise up again. Eighth-century French ruler Charlemagne subscribed to this logic. He banned cremation, making it a crime punishable by death (one wonders if the criminals were then cremated to compound their castigation).

Interest in cremation revived in the late nineteenth century, as the industrial revolution gave rise to new technologies and as populations swelled, putting cemeteries under huge pressure and sparking worries about the spread of disease. By burying the dead, society was "laying by poison", wrote Sir Henry Thompson, cremation's early champion, since future generations would "find our remains polluting their water sources". Thompson, who was also Queen Victoria's surgeon, founded the Cremation Society of England in 1874 and drew up a declaration calling for cremation as a more sanitary alternative to burial.

Debates over cremation were, dare I say it, heated. First, there were religious objections. The Bishop of Lincoln, an influential Anglican leader, declared that the practice would undermine belief in the resurrection of the body and so spark a wave of immoral behaviour. Others said the process would simply be too expensive.

Technology would ultimately triumph over such arguments, and technology was advancing fast. In 1873 at the Vienna World's Fair, an Italian anatomy professor called Ludovico Brunetti displayed the cremation chamber he'd devised. Six years later in 1879, the Cremation Society of England successfully cremated a horse in the crematorium it had built.

Rumours that this was a prelude to a human cremation provoked public outcry and threats of parliamentary and legal proceedings against the society. Others put the law to the test, too. In 1884, when his his five-month-old son died, William Price, an eccentric Welsh doctor and a druid, cremated the body. He was prosecuted but successfully defended himself on the grounds that no law explicitly banned cremation.

The following year, Britain's first official cremation took place when the body of Jeanette Pickersgill, a well-known scientific and literary figure, was cremated six days after her death. The *Times* reported that the cremation, which lasted an hour, "is said to have been eminently successful from every point of view".

With the technology proven, the argument for the sanitary benefits of cremation gained momentum. When, in 1886, William Eassie gave a lecture at the Sanitary Institute of Great Britain (he stood beside a vase containing some of the ashes of the cremated horse) he declared that "the thinking community are perfectly satisfied that the crowded dead injure the living, and that if this source of danger be not removed, or, at least, abated, it will become more and more intensified until an ungovernable climax be reached".

Meanwhile, Americans were starting to take an interest in cremation. Among the pioneers was Francis Julius LeMoyne, a medical doctor and philanthropist. In 1876, he built America's first crematorium in Washington, Pennsylvania, on his own land. On December 6 that year, modern America's first cremation took place when the body of Joseph Henry Louis, Baron de Palm, was incinerated in LeMoyne's crematorium. *The New York Times* later gave a blow-by-blow account of the incineration, which could be viewed through a hole in the door of the retort:

Five minutes after the body was put in the furnace was dark inside. In seven minutes a thick white smoke could be seen. In 15 minutes the retort was lighted up, and the body could be seen distinctly. By 9:45 the head had separated from the body and rolled to one side; the flesh had all disappeared, and all the bones but the skull were red-hot. At 11 o'clock, after two and a half hours of burning, the skeleton was almost entire, and white hot in every part. It was a skeleton of fire. Soon afterward it began to show signs of crumbling, and by 12:30 the cremation was pronounced complete. Some of the larger bones still retained their shape but they needed only a breath of air to reduce them to ashes.

As in Britain, the American public was slow to take up cremation (possibly put off by those descriptions in *The New York Times*). However, by 1913, when the Cremation Association of America was formed, fifty-two crematoria were conducting more than ten thousand cremations a year across the country. Today, about 35 percent of Americans are cremated and that's expected to rise to almost 60 percent by 2025. In Britain, the numbers are even higher, with more than 70 percent of the population choosing to be cremated.

I've thought a lot about cremation. I agree with my father that it seems a swift and efficient method of disposing of "organic matter". However, it's not the most eco-friendly method of corpse disposal, as the furnaces generate smoke and carbon dioxide, as well as mercury emissions from dental filings. As a result, a few crematoria are investigating the possibility of reusing the heat produced by their operations. In Sweden, one plans to save energy by using its crematorium furnaces to heat its buildings – and eventually some of the homes in the town surrounding it. The idea is causing a few raised eyebrows but, if my body heat could help warm up some homes, that'd be fine by me.

One morning, at Ubud's royal palace, I run into one of the caretakers. For a small "donation", he lets me into the private areas behind the main courtyard and leads me to the door of the chamber where the two royal corpses are lying in state. I'm not allowed into that section, so I wander around the other parts of the palace.

At first glance, the buildings look more like temples than royal residences, except that on raised platforms outside each pavilion – the place where at temples you'd normally leave your shoes – is a motley collection of modern sectionals, antique chairs, glass-topped coffee tables, electric lamps and TV sets. There are faded family photographs and kitsch plastic clocks, as well as a plaster bust of Beethoven and a large tank whose occupant – a somnolent turtle – looks like it was born around the same the time as the German composer. All in all, it's an eccentric setup.

At night, however, the palace becomes magical. That evening, locals crowd into the public courtyard to watch legends being re-told, as demons and angels face off in dramatic dance performances. With fingers aquiver, toes curled and masks whose eyes bulge like those of the dragon, the dancers are the epitome of vibrant, nervous energy.

Each performer plays several roles. A youthful devil reappears as a comic figure, first as an old man, stumbling and tripping, then strutting around like a chicken, twitching, pecking and scratching. At times, he opens his cape like a bird of paradise displaying his splendid coloured feathers like a sexual weapon.

Meanwhile, Hindu high priests have arrived at one of the palace's private enclosures. Two of them have black hair tied in a knot on top of their heads while the most senior, wearing an ivory-coloured linen jacket, has grey-blond hair cut in a short bob. They mount a high stage opposite the dragon, where they sit chanting prayers amid piles of offerings and religious accoutrements. They're here to help transfer the souls of the deceased (for now wandering freely) into the body of the dragon. At the precise moment of the transfer, the expression on the face of the dragon will alter. It's pretty heady stuff.

I step outside the enclosure momentarily and when I return, the ground is covered with seated women. Heads bowed, the women open their palms expectantly to receive droplets of holy water being scattered by a priest (I'm reminded of the morning in Yazd, when holy water was sprayed over the crowd that had gathered to mark Imam Husayn's martyrdom).

As they disperse, family members assemble below the dragon's stage. Holding a long rope representing the deceased, they walk around a table piled with offerings and tiny model boats (symbolising the sea into which the royal ashes will eventually be scattered). The relatives smile and laugh to show their happiness as the spirits of the departed royals approach their rebirth.

It's a joyous fond farewell for the dead and an assurance for those left behind of the continuation of the cosmic and social order. Yet watching everything unfold, I find it astonishing that all this pageantry is not for the president or prime minister of a powerful country. It's for members of a royal family who hail from a tiny town on an island about a quarter of the size of Wales. Everything – intricate rituals, giant towers, fantastical effigies, musical performances and, let's face it, extremely large sums of money – is being laid on for a couple of people who've reached their expiration date. Their time might be up, but what a way to go.

The Weymouth & Portland Borough Council crematorium sits on a quiet road called Quibo Lane on the outskirts of Weymouth, a coastal town on the mouth of the River Wey. The crematorium has a garden of remembrance, burial plots for cremated remains and a remembrance room at the side of the main building. It lies eight miles south of Dorchester and the Joseph Weld Hospice, where Fa spent his last weeks surrounded by tubes, wires and wonderfully kind nurses.

Since I hadn't been at his cremation, on a visit to Dorset some months later, I asked Sam if we could visit the crematorium. She said she wouldn't mind driving me there but she'd probably stay in the car. This, she hastened to add, wasn't so much because she didn't want to go in but because, as she reminded me, she likes sitting in cars. It might sound like an excuse, but strangely enough, she does like sitting in cars. As a family, we'd often go to West Bay, our local harbour town, for a walk on the beach, usually in winter when the waves were smashing up on to the pebble shore and we children were carefully packed into sou'westers, Wellington boots and woolly hats. My mother always preferred to stay in the car and read the papers.

So, leaving Sam with the crossword, I headed across the lawn towards the crematorium office. There, I met Ian Price, a man with a warm smile, an affable manner and "Bereavement Service Manager" written on his calling card. He told me a cremation service was taking place in half an hour but in the meantime, he'd happily show me the place, and he led me into the chapel.

It's a simple municipal interior. Built in the 1930s, it has cream walls, plain wooden benches and a blue-grey carpet. Decoration is minimal – just a couple of brass chandeliers and, hanging above the altar, a Baroque-style painting of some religious figures amid swirling clouds.

Of course, that's more than an altar. Behind it are two wooden doors through which the coffin slides on its way into the furnace. After whatever type of service a family requests (Fa, of course, had none), the blue curtains framing the altar close. There's no sliding or burning until everyone has left.

It could hardly be further removed from the theatricality of Balinese funerals. There, everything takes place in public, usually on a stage. Even at non-royal cremations, dozens gather around the pyre, shouting with joy as they watch the body burn and the flames releasing its soul into the heavens. Yet here, friends and family are sheltered from viewing the fire. In the cremations of Europe and the United States, the ultimate ceremony of death is often a solitary one.

Still, perhaps we're starting to get a little more creative. Ian Price told me he was starting to see families personalising cremation ceremonies, with photographs of the deceased projected on to screens, as well as coffins painted or collaged with images from their lives. More wicker caskets were turning up, too, some of them quite elegant, with ribbons or flowers woven through them.

Slowly, it seems, some of the fanfare that traditionally surrounded death is being revived, along with the artistry we once put into honouring our departed. As with elegiac laments, doleful mourning music and exquisitely decorated Mogul tombs, beauty helps bring us though our most broken moments.

I felt rather sad that we hadn't arranged for a wicker coffin to take Fa to his cremation. He'd clearly considered the idea, as I knew from a folder I'd found in his filing cabinet labelled: "How to End it!" The folder contained a collection of brochures from companies supplying caskets made of wicker, willow and seagrass. Maybe a willow coffin woven through with flowers would have been a good way to send him off. Or perhaps we should have put him in a huge wood and bamboo bull covered in gold leaf and mirrors, with bulging eyes, flared nostrils, decorative necklaces and a fabulous golden mane.

In the Indian city of Varanasi, cremation ceremonies have little of the pageantry accompanying the Balinese versions. But for Hindus, who make up more than 80 percent of India's population, reaching this sacred site is the most significant of life's moments. Varanasi (once known as Benares) is where every Hindu would like to die. The River Ganges, India's holiest waterway, is the destination for a constant stream of corpses.

Some belong to people who managed to reach the city while alive. Others pay to be shipped there for cremation. More often, the cremation has already taken place and the family brings the ashes to scatter into the Ganges. But however they reach it, Hindus believe the holy river has the power to release them from the eternal cycle of birth, death and rebirth, allowing them to achieve *moksha*, or enlightenment.

After visiting Varanasi, Mark Twain wrote: "Benares is older than history, older than tradition, older even than legend and looks twice as old as all of them put together." Looking at the Manikarnika Ghat, or Burning Ghat, the biggest of Varanasi's cremation sites, you can see what he means. Looming over the proceedings are three blackened domes surmounting the temple that houses the "eternal flame" used to light each new pyre. Day and night on the sloping riverbank, small fires burn as if in the aftermath of some medieval battle. Dark smoke thickens the air. Cows amble about. Wild dogs howl as fresh corpses arrive on bamboo stretchers wrapped in white winding-sheets.

Underfoot is cremation's detritus – shards of wood, the remains of biers, faded marigolds and shreds of the brightly coloured silk shrouds draped over the body before it's laid on to the pyre. Sandalwood fumes fill the air, competing for attention with the pungent odour of cow dung.

Most ominous is the gloomy hospice overlooking the ghat. This is home to those who've come to die in Varanasi. Inside are some of India's poorest people. They've often travelled to the city ahead of their death since they'll have no family or funds to bring their bodies here after they've died. Some are even forced to beg for money to buy wood for their pyre. Those who can't afford a sufficient supply will have their partially burned bodies launched out into the Ganges.

In the narrow streets behind the ghat, huge piles of that precious wood are crammed into every available corner. Logs and branches gathered from villages around Varanasi arrive here by river barge and are stacked up against the outer walls of small temples and stuffed down side alleys. Wood is everywhere, but it's never around for long: it takes six or seven hundred pounds to burn a corpse so the piles are constantly diminishing and being replenished. Huge green metal weighing scales are on hand to verify that customers have bought the correct amount.

Nearby are other funerary traders – tiny shops packed with sandalwood (to mask the smell of burning corpses) and packets of incense. In open-air hair salons, barbers equipped with little more than a razor, a bar of soap and a tin bowl of water shave the heads of fathers, sons or brothers in a mark of respect for the dead.

Doms – caretakers who handle the corpses at cremation grounds – attend the fires, shuffling around like the downtrodden characters from a Dickensian workhouse scene, adding more logs to the pyres when necessary. Inserting bamboo poles under the knees of their charges, they pull the legs in towards the fire's blazing heart to ensure the whole body is immolated. With the same poles, they poke at the skulls, which pop and hiss as they crack. The workaday atmosphere and the irreverence with which the dead bodies are treated seem brutal. But their actions are all rooted in Hindu beliefs – cracking the skull allows the spirit to escape from the corpse.

The doms are efficient workers. Hundreds of bodies are cremated daily on the Burning Ghats. Yet there are no industrial retorts here, no temperature-controlled burners. What's more, the bodies are doused in the Ganges before the cremation, an act that while spiritually meaningful seems to make no sense when what you're trying to do is immolate a human corpse (which already consists largely of water).

From the maze of tiny alleys behind the waterfront, bodies arrive on bamboo stretchers with the regularity found in factory production lines. Fires burn around the clock. It may be an intensely spiritual moment for the individuals being cremated, but the doms' work on an industrial scale, achieving a "throughput" that would impress modern crematory managers.

As they heave around logs and poke at the fires, the doms look more like blacksmiths than undertakers. It's easy to forget that corpse disposal is the job of work being completed here. That's until you see the unmistakable sign of death in Varanasi – a couple of bare feet sticking out through the red-hot logs.

It's the morning of the Pelebon, and it's clearly going to be a huge event. Local newspapers are predicting that tens of thousands of people will converge on Ubud, so I rise early to get a head start on the crowds. The road leading from my hotel to the palace is lined with smaller cows (these ones are roughly life-sized) and bright red winged lions. These are the sarcophagi for the remains of some of the sixty-eight citizens that will go up in flames today, and although more modest in size, they're every bit as decorative as the regal versions. Even if you're not a royal, in Bali you get to go out in style.

Outside the palace, large teams of men in purple T-shirts are ready for their day's work – conveying the bulls, dragon, stair-cases and towers from the palace to the cremation ground. Their task won't be easy. Hundreds of men will carry these fantastically heavy ceremonial objects, working in teams in a slow relay.

By mid-morning, hundreds of people are lining the street. I feel a little sad. I know this is the last of the magic. And as visitors pour into town, it's getting hard to move through the crowd. I'm worried that before too long, it will be impossible to get near enough to see the cremation itself – the event I've come all this way for.

So two hours ahead of time, I walk down to the cremation ground and secure a place on top of a wall looking directly across to the cremation platform, a raised stage with a high temple-style canvas roof above. Soon the ground below is full of people and I'm wondering how on earth they're going to get those towers and bulls in through the throng.

It's a long, uncomfortable wait, and there's a false start when people start cheering at what turns out to be the arrival of an ambulance. Happily, soon after, the first bull rounds the corner into the cremation ground to uproarious cheers from the crowd. Beneath it, the purple T-shirt crews are putting everything into their work, and enjoying every moment. Guided by a team leader with a megaphone, they manoeuvre both bulls up on to the cremation platform using nothing but bamboo rollers and wooden levers. It's touch and go, so each successful move of the bulls, even by a few inches, draws elated cries.

Eventually the two beasts take up their final position beneath the tented roof, with the dragon in between them. The *badés* have also arrived, as well as the bamboo bridges. Looking at this huge platform, with the two vast bulls on top of it, the giant towers behind and the dragon in the middle – knowing that any minute, it's all going to go up in flames – I'm thinking that this is surely a rather dangerous endeavour. A couple of fire engines are parked behind me, but they're modest in size and not tremendously reassuring.

Now the bodies, inside decorative temporary coffins, are brought down from the cremation towers. Villagers and relatives arrive with offerings on their heads, which they place at the bulls' feet. Meanwhile, men wielding knives slice open the bulls' backs so that the ceremonial beasts can take delivery of their charges.

The sight of the bodies as they're lifted from the coffins is strangely moving. The corpses are heavy and fleshy. And in their simple white shrouds, they seem touchingly modest compared to what's surrounding them. Suddenly amid all this beautiful artifice, here are two real bodies – human beings, like you and me.

On the ground, the priests show up for a last prayer. With the corpses inside, the bulls' backs are repositioned and each is lavished with silk drapes and other offerings, while men pack dried grass around at hoof level. Darkness is drawing in and the crowd has fallen silent. The only sound is the ching of a bell as the head priest administers to the two corpses.

Then, adhering to the ancient Hindu tradition, Tjokorda Raka Kerthyasa, younger half brother of Agung Suyasa, sets light to the dried grass at the bulls' feet. For a few seconds, flames flicker feebly. But soon the fire starts to move with tremendous speed. First, it rips up the bulls' golden beads, giving them spectacular flaming necklaces. Moments later, a thick stream of smoke is pouring out of the mouth of the biggest bull. Now the dragon is aflame. It burns quickly, with a sad tinkle of bells as its tail falls off.

I realise my fears of an uncontrolled inferno were unfounded. Several men move in towards the platform wielding hoses with which they direct powerful jets of water towards its base to prevent the fire from spreading (so that's what the fire engines were for). Above them, the bulls are fantastic black silhouettes amid a raging conflagration. Shrieks go up from the crowd as the biggest wobbles. Flames are coming out of its eyes and mouth. More cries go up as its head falls to the ground with a crash. The smaller bull's head is ablaze too. One of its ears falls off. The dragon has been reduced to a two-dimensional snake-shaped piece of wooden board.

Astonishingly, it takes just half an hour for everything to burn – thirty minutes in which to destroy the fantastical creatures, the huge pagoda-towers, the bulls' bamboo frames, the gold paper, silk fabrics and glass beads.

Gradually the crowd disperses and I climb down from the wall to stand in front of the crematory bonfire. There, I can see the bodies. With their sarcophagi incinerated, the simple iron frames on which they're suspended are now visible. Though blackened by smoke and deformed by fire, the corpses are still intact. Their tenacity in the face of such a patently destructive force seems to speak of the astonishing force that is a human life. "Organic matter", I realise, is not that easy to dispose of.

After about an hour it becomes clear that the only things left burning are the two cadavers. I can see their heads and can't help wondering if this is what my father would have looked like, had I been able to look inside his cremation chamber. Perhaps, one day, I'll look like that, too. I try not to think about this too much.

Then something unexpected happens. Two members of the purple T-shirt crew arrive with huge burners to direct a fat jet of yellow-white flame at each of the corpses. Every so often, like the doms of Varanasi, they prod the bodies roughly with bamboo poles to make sure they're at the centre of the fire. The huge industrial burners and the brusque, irreverent manner with which the men stab their sticks into the remains of royal princes come as a shock after the courtly pageantry of everything that's gone before.

But it's all part of the process; part of the cycle of life. Fire has destroyed the corporeal containers of the royal souls. Tomorrow, another of the five elements – water – will play its part, when the remains are scattered into the sea. With the souls now well on their way to achieving *moksha*, the bodies are simply empty vessels with no further use – objects that, as Covarrubias put it, are "to be got rid of, about which there is no hysteria". This, at least, is something on which my father and the Balinese would have agreed.

3

STARTLING STILLNESS

Death on Display in Sicily

In a northern suburb of Palermo, Sicily, amid 1960s apartment blocks, car mechanics' workshops and a lingerie store called Mutandina Sexy Duck is a small, plain building in the style of a Greek temple. Attached to a church, it has an unassuming door with a sign above reading "Ingresso Catacomb". Entry costs one and a half euros, paid at a wooden desk manned by a monk in a brown habit with a rope belt. The ticket allows you entry to a crypt. It's just below street level, so the conversations of passers-by on the pavement above are clearly audible. Down in the crypt, however, no one is talking. Down here is something altogether different – more than eight thousand mummified figures, fully dressed and in a disquieting state of decay.

This is the Capuchin Catacombs of Palermo. Most of its occupants hang in rows in shallow niches on twenty-foot-high walls rising to vaulted ceilings. Others lie in ranks on horizontal shelves below them. Collectively, they make up one of the world's most macabre collections of corpses.

While the first arrival – the body of Brother Silvestro da Gubbio – was in 1599, most of the dead here took up residence in the eighteenth and nineteenth centuries. The last one to be left in the crypt was two-year-old Rosalia Lombardo, who died in 1920, so the fascination here is not with antiquity. No, what's really strange is seeing at close quarters corpses that are fully dressed – gentlemen in frock coats, ladies in lace-lined skirts, uniformed military officers and monks in the same sorts of robes worn by the man who sold me my entrance ticket.

It's not my first close encounter with mummies. That took place in 1986 in a dingy cave in the Tarim Basin of the Taklamakan, a forbidding tract of desert in China's far northwest province of Xinjiang (Taklamakan means "place of no return"). I was on a sightseeing tour with a group of fellow backpackers and at one point our guide herded us into a shallow cave with no explanation as to what was inside. As my eyes adjusted to the darkness, I found myself looking at a wizened body lying on a stone bier.

Our guide pronounced the mummy to be from the Tang dynasty, China's rulers from the seventh to the tenth centuries, but something wasn't quite right about this assessment – the leathered features didn't look Chinese at all. With high cheekbones and long noses, the face seemed distinctly European.

Since then, scores of what are now known to be Caucasian cadavers have been unearthed from the shifting sands of the Taklamakan. For the Chinese, the discovery in the late 1970s of these "foreign" mummies proved awkward, revealing previously unknown connections between west and east and providing a potential rallying point for the region's Muslims, some of whom want to be free from Beijing's control.

What interested me, however, was the chance to look an ancient corpse in the face. It was of a woman, and her body – dressed in shreds of dusty, decayed clothing – was brown, shrivelled and impossibly thin ("Turn her sideways, mark her absent," a friend's father would have said). Tiny hands emerged from the sleeves of her disintegrating robe, while her legs were skinny sticks that seemed insufficient to have ever supported even her emaciated frame. Time had painted her skin a deep rust colour, as if she'd been charred by some terrible fire.

Still, remnants of the features she'd possessed in life survived. In the dim light, I could make out eyelashes, teeth, fingernails, hair, leathery skin and even the lines on the palms of her hands. She was more than an engraving on a tombstone or a name in a history book – she had a physical presence, one whose shape and form (albeit dried out and shrunken) resembled the one she'd occupied while alive.

Yet time had left her looking far from peaceful. Her open mouth and empty eye sockets gave her a look of extreme suffering. She seemed to be howling. It's the kind of facial expression scholars suggest may have inspired *The Scream*, Edvard Munch's famous painting of 1893 (he made several versions), since several years before he finished the work, an ancient Incan mummy from the Andes appeared at the Exposition Universelle in Paris, a show Munch could well have attended.

I wanted to stay longer, to scrutinise her features and speculate about the kind of life she'd led. But the guide hustled us out of the cave and into the bright sunshine again, ready for the next stop on our desert tour – a lunch of watermelon and kebabs that, as it turned out, gave me food poisoning so severe that, twenty-four hours later, my shrunken body, dehydrated skin and gaunt face looked alarmingly similar to the corpse I'd seen in that cave.

After three days of sickness and crippling stomach pains, I found myself in a bus rattling across the vast empty spaces of the Taklamakan. But the image of the mummy stayed with me. By then, I'd been in China for more than a month. Few people knew of my exact whereabouts and I remember wondering what would happen if our bus were to disappear in one of the sandstorms that had obliterated so many ancient towns along the Silk Road – how long would it take for anyone to find out what had happened to me? How many months or years would I lie beneath the shifting sands of the Taklamakan before being discovered? Long enough, perhaps, to take on the leathery features of the mummy in that cave. Four thousand years later, would tourists be gawping at my hardened skin and surprisingly well-preserved eyelashes?

I don't remember what I thought back then about the prospect of mummification, but I do recall a reckless exhilaration in being utterly (if temporarily) removed from my own world. The idea of disappearing in a remote Chinese desert stirred not the slightest twinge of fear in me. It's funny how, twenty years on, I've fewer of my unused years to be wasted than when I was sitting on that bus; I've less of my life to lose – yet I'm now more fearful of losing it.

Unlike ancient mummies, the corpses in the Capuchin Catacombs of Palermo were mummified without evisceration (removal of the internal organs). The monks used a number of preservation methods. One involved dipping the bodies in arsenic or lime, a method often used when disease was prevalent. The other was desiccation, whereby the bodies dried out in special cells called "strainers" for eight months, aided by the area's unique climate and porous limestone subsoil. Then, they were washed in vinegar, dressed and suspended in wall niches using wires and nails or laid out on horizontal shelves.

Today, they're in an appalling state of disintegration. Some retain facial skin, although mostly it hangs off the skull like a leather mask. But it's the clothes that make the corpses such a disturbing spectacle. Delicate lace collars and cravats emerge from wide-lapelled coats of silk and velvet endowed with decorative details such as covered buttons and brocade. These once-fine garments now droop sadly, many rotted away into dirty wisps of shredded fabric, adding to the sense of decay and making this parade of deceased humans truly shocking.

Some are in glass-fronted coffins but, for the most part, these macabre wall decorations are untrammelled, exposed to the cool, musky air of the crypt, with no cabinets, cages or alarm systems to separate them from visitors. Those lying on the shelves look as if they're languishing in some overcrowded, under-funded medieval hospital. Fingers, toes and bits of rotting cloth hang untidily over the edges of these divans for the dead.

I'm not the first to find this place disconcerting. The ranks of corpses alarmed some early visitors to the Capuchin Catacombs.

"Horror of horrors – what a spectacle!" exclaimed British writer Catherine Gore in 1845. "Brown and skinny arms, extending from sleeves of lace – court-dresses of silk and satin, falling in easy drapery around embroidered silken stockings and shoes hanging loosely upon withered limbs; while caps or coiffures of fanciful device appear to mock the fearful faces whose smiles once constituted the sunshine of some human heart!"

However, one individual seemed strangely unperturbed by the corpses. In 1952, the British writer Evelyn Waugh visited the crypt in the company of his friend Harold Acton. Waugh, who was suffering from rheumatism, responded to the place in a typically eccentric manner. After an hour scrutinising the grisly relics, Waugh emerged from the crypt, recalls Acton, took one last sniff, pronounced the odour "delicious", and tossed away his walking stick declaring his lameness cured.

Embalming and mummification seem to me the most mystifying of all the treatments with which we indulge our dead. The practice of preserving human corpses, of course, dates back millennia to the ancient Egyptians and beyond. Yet as a Brit from an island that has managed to purge from its funeral rites any evidence of an actual body, one of the traditions I find most exotic is that of today's American open coffin funeral. The idea of embalming a corpse, dressing it, applying make-up to it and displaying it in a polished wood coffin – lavished with shirred white satin and often surrounded by videos, images and memorabilia – seems to me, to put it bluntly, weird.

The practice even seems to contradict the recent consensus of psychologists and social historians on the contemporary approach to death – something they believe has been shut away from view. "The more we are making advancements in science, the more we seem to fear and deny the reality of death," argued Elisabeth Kübler-Ross in her influential 1969 book *On Death and Dying*.

Dying "has passed from the home to the hospital", wrote Philippe Ariès in the classic 1981 book *The Hour of Our Death* (or

L'Homme Devant la Mort, in the original French). And if the process of dying is dominated by medicine, we're told, the process of dealing with the dead, too, has become unfamiliar. The bereaved are no longer distinguished by black attire. Funeral arrangements are left in the hands of professionals rather than members of the community. "Modern, affluent societies tend to sweep death under the carpet," say the authors of *Psychiatry and Social Science Review*, while in countries such as England, says Ariès, death has "been evacuated efficiently and completely".

All true. Yet in its preference for the open coffin funeral, the American way of death seems to demonstrate quite the opposite. To my mind, such a theatrical display of mortality in all its glory puts this particular death rite high up there on my list of the world's most exotic funeral ceremonies. The viewing parlour or chapel may benefit from modern conveniences such as air-conditioning, dimmable lighting, plug-in fragrances, canned music and, of course, embalming fluid. But there, in the middle of the room is a corpse – an actual dead body – fully dressed and made up to look as if it's simply sleeping. To me, this seems every bit as outlandish as the Sicilian idea of leaving mummies hanging in a crypt in Victorian finery.

Embalming is not unique to America. In Ireland it's common, while in Britain, the practice arrived from the United States at the turn of the twentieth century. Yet in Britain, it was slow to catch on and until recently, writes Mary Bradbury in *Representations of Death*, "British embalming practices were somewhat crude in comparison to the skills and efforts put into the presentation of the dead in the United States". And while most of my American friends have seen an open coffin, I've so far found only one Brit who has.

I'm not alone in finding the open casket tradition perplexing. Ariès is also bemused by it. In the final section of *The Hour of Our Death*, he's forced to concede that, in his analysis of contemporary attitudes to death, the US case is somewhat different. While he finds the embalmed corpse a rarity in Europe, in America, in what he calls a "resistance of romantic traditions to the pressures of contemporary taboos", the body has become the centrepiece of death.

Jessica Mitford, the British-born writer and political activist, had a lot to say about embalming, calling it "an extraordinary procedure", In 1963, in *The American Way of Death*, an uproariously witty exposé that became a national bestseller, Mitford argued that with their expensive coffins and embalming services, the "funeral men" were constructing "their own grotesque cloud-cuckoo-land where the trappings of Gracious Living are transformed, as in a nightmare, into the trappings of Gracious Dying".

Mitford, whose book prompted a Federal Trade Commission investigation into the funeral industry, wasn't the first to complain about the exploitative practices of the "dismal traders". A century earlier in Britain, Victorians had expressed concern at what they saw as immoderate display at funerals. The events were certainly lavish. Elaborately carved coffins conveyed by glass-sided hearses decorated in silver and gold were decked out in ostrich feathers, drawn by six horses and accompanied by dozens of footmen, pages, coachmen and pallbearers carrying wands and batons. In the 1850s, organisations such as the National Funeral and Mourning Reform Association were established to curb this kind of excess.

In 1948, Evelyn Waugh brought his savage satire to bear on both Hollywood and the American funeral industry in *The Loved One*, a novel set in Los Angeles. The story features a love triangle between Mr Joyboy, the debonair embalmer at Whispering Glades, a Hollywood funeral home (based on California's Forest Lawn), Dennis Barlow, an English poet working in a down-at-heel pet cemetery, and Aimée Thanatogenos, a junior cosmetician at Whispering Glades (and nothing escapes Waugh's wit – Thanatos is the Greek personification of death).

One of the book's most brilliant conceits is the role the dead play in the dramas of the living. When Joyboy's admiration for Aimée is most fervent, he expresses it through corpses, sending the young cosmetician "Loved Ones" that arrive with beatific smiles on their faces, regardless of the requests of the "Waiting Ones" for other facial expressions. However, when Aimée transfers her affections to Barlow, Joyboy's cadavers arrive in her cosmetics room bearing grimaces.

Less amusing but more inflammatory was Bill Davidson's May 1951 article in *Collier's* magazine, "The High Cost of Dying", which accused funeral directors of price fixing and criticised the power of the industry's trade associations. Then in June 1961, the *Saturday Evening Post* ran an article titled "Can You Afford to Die?" by Roul Tunley, sparking letters from more than six thousand readers recalling unfortunate experiences and asking for advice.

While the funeral business has long been at the receiving end of jokes or cynicism, Mitford's book threw it into turmoil. *The American Way of Death* painted a picture of an unscrupulous group of merchants peddling over-priced goods and services and taking advantage of vulnerable consumers for whom the purchase had to be conducted in haste at a time of extreme emotional distress.

Mitford challenges everything from the language invented by the industry (flowers become "floral tributes", coffins are "caskets" and hearses are "professional cars") to sales techniques that, to ratchet up the price of their goods, play on customers' guilt, grief, disorientation and need to make an on-the-spot decision. Citing a casket sales manual, she remarks that the diagram of the selection room "resembles one of those mazes set up for experiments designed to muddle rats".

Mitford reserves some of her most acerbic remarks for the part of the profession devoted to embalming and what's known as restorative art. "Alas, poor Yorick!" she writes. "How very surprised he would be to see how his counterpart of today is whisked off to a funeral parlour and is in short order sprayed, sliced, pierced, pickled, trussed, trimmed, creamed, waxed, painted, rouged and neatly dressed – transformed from a common corpse into a Beautiful Memory Picture."

Describing embalming in graphic detail, Mitford marvels at "the docility of Americans who each year pay hundreds of millions of dollars for its perpetuation". She's surprised to find many people believe embalming the corpse before burial is a legal requirement and a necessary sanitary precaution. Both arguments Mitford convincingly dismantles. Even now, many Americans believe embalming is enforceable by law, even though this has never been the case and, under Federal Trade Commission rules adopted in 1984, it's deemed deceptive practice for a funeral provider to imply that it is.

For the funeral industry, Mitford was "a new menace", as she puts it in the introduction to her revised 1998 version of the book, *The American Way of Death Revisited*. On the publication of her book, funeral magazines, she writes, "fulminated against 'the Mitford bomb,' 'the Mitford war dance,' 'the Mitford missile,' 'the Mitford blast,' and 'the Mitford fury.'"

Yet despite the book's success, the funeral industry seems to have barely skipped a beat, at least when it comes to embalming. Almost 70 percent of respondents to a 2008 survey conducted by *American Funeral Director* magazine said that the funeral they'd most recently attended included a public viewing and about 60 percent of the newly dead are embalmed.

In the end, it may be other factors that prompt a decline in the popularity of embalming, such as cost, a rise in cremation and awareness of the environmental damage caused by burying bodies full of chemicals.

In a 2006 article outlining some of these trends, John Caranci, a funeral director at Wiefels & Son, discusses the changes he has witnessed in the industry. "There was a time when we embalmed just about everything that walked in the back door," Caranci tells the Palm Springs newspaper *The Desert Sun*, before correcting himself: "Well, not walked in the back door."

The forerunner of the modern embalmed corpse is, of course, the mummy. Preserving corpses has been practiced by everyone from the Chinchorro coastal peoples of Chile's Atacama Desert (their mummies, dating back seven thousand years, are thought to be the world's oldest) and the Egyptians (relative newcomers, making mummies two millennia after the Chinchorro) to the pre-colonial mummies of the Inca rulers of Peru.

For the ancient Egyptians, who believed that to continue living after death, you needed a well-preserved body, mummification was at the heart of funerary culture. The process seems unpleasant, to put it mildly. Embalmers would first wash the body with sweet-smelling palm wine and water from the Nile. That doesn't sound too bad. But then they made a cut in the left-hand side of the body through which they removed all the internal organs – except the heart, thought to be essential in the afterlife. In the most disagreeable part of the process, a long hook was used to pull the brains out through the nose.

The organs were washed, packed into natron, a natural dehydrating salt and returned to the body (in early forms of mummification, they were placed in stone jars and buried with the mummy). The body, too, would be plastered with natron to dry it out and, after forty days, washed with Nile water again (embalming centres were located on the banks of the Nile, says writer and academic Christine Quigley, partly because of the setting sun's connection to the underworld but also because of the smell). Oils were applied to keep the skin elastic. To rebuild the body's form, embalmers would stuff it with materials such as linen, sawdust and leaves in much the same way a taxidermist pads out animal carcasses.

Then the wrapping would begin, starting with the head and neck, followed by the finger and toes, then arms and legs, which were tied together. Embalmers used liquid resin to seal the bandages, secreting between the layers amulets inscribed with spells to protect the corpse as it journeyed through the underworld (Tutankhamen had more than one hundred and forty amulets distributed throughout his wrappings). A final piece of fabric encased the entire mummy before it was lowered into its sarcophagus.

It's hard to believe that today anyone would want to subject their body to this sort of process. However, in Utah, a non-profit organisation called Summum (Latin for "the highest good" or "the sum total") will turn your corpse into an Egyptian-style mummy using a process patented by its founder, Claude "Corky" Rex Nowell. A former manager at a Salt Lake City supply company, Nowell established the organisation in 1975 after receiving visits from "advanced living beings" and changed his name to Summum Bonum Amon Ra "for governmental purposes and to reflect his spiritual path" (these days, he goes by the name of Corky Ra).

In Summum's process, blood and organs are removed and the bodies are cleaned and soaked for up to six months in a special preservation fluid after which the organs are replaced, covered with lanolin and wrapped in gauze. A polyurethane membrane is painted on, as well as a layer of fibreglass, and a death mask placed on the face. Contained in a "mummiform", the body is laid to rest in Summum's Mausoleum Sanctuary. Summum stresses that this process is common to many cultures and "based on Nature's own workings". Still, the organisation seems to acknowledge the fact that this form of burial is not for everyone – Summum's slogan is: "Sealed Except to the Open Mind."

Back at the Whispering Glades funeral home, Joyboy gives the final touches to an embalmed corpse. He takes a blank visiting card and a pair of surgical scissors. "In one continuous movement, he cut an ellipse," writes Waugh, "then snicked half an inch at either end along the greater axis." He tests the jaw to check it's firmly set, draws the lips back and places the visiting card against the teeth. Then comes the moment for which the embalmer was most admired – "the deft flick of the thumbs with which he turned the upper corners of the card, the caress of the rubber finger-tips with which he drew the dry and colourless lips into place. And, behold! where before had been a grim line of endurance, there was now a smile. It was masterly".

The ability to fashion facial expressions is just one of the embalmer's skills. Morticians pride themselves on being able to restore even the most disfigured and damaged corpses. "The boys up there surely know their job," explains a Whispering Glades hostess. "Why, if he'd sat on an atom bomb, they'd make him presentable."

Some embalming experts have achieved remarkable reconstructions, as did the embalmers of David Morales Colon who, according to press reports, had not wanted his family to hold a traditional funeral for him – for his viewing in April 2010, he was propped up on a Honda motorbike dressed in a biker's shirt, cap and sunglasses.

The superstar status – in the world of undertakers, at least – of the most skilled embalmers is well represented in an episode of the HBO drama series *Six Feet Under* in which the Fishers, the family at the centre of the plot, are forced to watch as Kroehner Service International, a mortuary conglomerate, poaches their company's best asset – restorative artist Federico Diaz. The loss of Diaz is a blow to the business.

So how does embalming work? Others braver than myself have explored the process at length – the authors of embalming hand-books, for a start. For more entertaining and informative descriptions, turn to Mitford's explanation, as well as that in Mary Roach's *Stiff*, and the chapter on the embalming of Jenny Johnson in Mark Harris's *Grave Matters*. Meanwhile, here are a few details:

The body is laid out in a preparation room, where it's cleaned, groomed and shaved (those who were bearded in life may retain their whiskers). "Purge" – liquid that originates in the stomach or lungs and that, due to build-up of pressure inside the decaying body, can come out through the nose or mouth – is removed with an aspirator.

A trocar (a hollow needle attached to a tube) is inserted into the abdomen to empty the contents of the chest cavity and entrails. Up to six gallons of dyed, perfumed embalming fluid is pumped around the body through the arterial system, in the process forcing the blood back through the veins into the heart, where it's removed either by vein drainage or with the trocar. Another means of vein draining is mechanical, although embalmers prefer the first method, which relies on the pressure of the arterial fluid.

Embalming fluid consists mainly of formaldehyde, a pungent-smelling chemical that vaporises easily and can cause the eyes to sting, and which preserves the corpse for a few days, just long enough for the funeral. Borax is also present to keep the blood liquid so it drains easily, as well as glycerin, which rehydrates the tissues, restoring to the shrivelled body a look of health and vitality.

The face is set. Cheeks are restored to plumpness with the aid of cotton wool. The mouth is sutured together using a curved needle and strong thread or a needle injector, a mechanical device that sends metal pins through human bone. Once its tissues are firm and dry, the body is ready for the "restorative work", when creams and fillers are injected into hollowed and sunken parts of the face and hands. "If the tissues do not fill out," advises the 1987 textbook *Embalming: History, Theory and Practice*, "seal the lips with glue, then rebuild the corners of the mouth with a surface restorer wax".

To the uninitiated, embalming might well seem an odd practice – part theatrical, part surgical, and using many of the same techniques and tools deployed by those professions.

Hypodermic syringes, forceps, clamps and suture needles link the embalmer to the surgeon. But no one is getting cured of anything in the undertaker's preparation room. After all, how many self-respecting surgeons would have among their instruments a shear designed for removing a patient's ribs? And few doctors would offer this kind of advice to their students: "If there is a problem of 'buck' teeth, it may be necessary to glue the lips prior to injection of the arterial solution to achieve good mouth closure" (From *Embalming: History, Theory and Practice*).

After restoration is complete, cosmeticians such as Aimée Thanatogenos wash and brush the hair and apply make-up to the visible parts of the body (funeral homes sometimes call this "cosmetizing"). Charts provide guidance on how to counteract skin discolorations caused by conditions such as Addison's disease (orange), carbon monoxide poisoning (cherry red), jaundice (bright yellow) or bruising (purple). The technique, generally speaking, is to apply make-up in the opposite primary colour.

For funeral cosmeticians, the challenge is not unlike that faced by Hollywood make-up artists – creating the illusion that people are something they're not. Occasionally, the two professions overlap. Bobbie Weiner, who made up the actors playing floating corpses in the movie *Titanic*, is famous for make-up collections such as the popular Bloody Mary Makeup and Goth Cosmetics lines. Meanwhile, among her products is her Final Touch range of powders, foundations, concealers, bronzers, blushers and sponges for funeral directors. So as well as making living people look dead, Weiner's clients can also make dead people look alive.

I have a copy of Jessica Mitford's book with me the day I show up at the National Funeral Directors Association expo in Orlando, Florida (You Have Found Your Ticket to Paradise reads the banner above the entrance to the Orange County Convention Centre expo hall). As I approach the glass doors, the slim paperback feels like a bomb inside my handbag, ready to go off at any moment. If caught with *The American Way of Death* on my person, will it be confiscated and my entry barred?

Happily, I walk unimpeded into the vast hall, where I find a sprawling encampment of exhibition stands displaying a range of unfamiliar products. Who knew, for example, that a need existed for the Zontec PA600, which eliminates odours and controls crypt flies (*crypt flies!*), or that a "non-tapered interior" was desirable in a niche space? Even the promotions are puzzling. To attract visitors to its stand, one company is running a competition whose prize is a $2,500 certificate for a "Fresh Getaway" – but to where?

Another first for me is the "widow's chair", a one-armed high wooden stool on which bereaved can sit while greeting guests. The stool, explains a company rep, puts her at the same level as the arriving guests but also ensures she's supported on one side. Not far away, I see some more chairs – a row of mechanical massage seats, the ones you sometimes see in department stores. I sincerely hope they're for tired exhibitors, not stressed-out corpses.

All in all, it's a strange experience – here's a multi-billion dollar industry about which the average consumer knows almost nothing and to whom its brand names are obscurities. I feel I've entered a hidden world.

I spend a few moments talking to a man whose firm makes vaults – encasements to protect the coffin and its contents once below ground. His, he explains, are made from a material into which a special gas has been injected, making it light but strong. To prove it, his stand displays a series of photographs showing disinterred coffins that, after many years below ground, remain in perfect condition. According to Mitford, funeral directors once told clients these kinds of products could keep the body from decaying, too, a claim it's now illegal to make.

Another vault company is offering custom-decorated versions, with lids on to whose polished-steel surface you can have family photographs etched. Sometimes, explains a woman in a black dress and stilettos barking through a microphone, customers don't even bury these lids but keep them as a memory of their loved ones (I'm thinking it might be easier just to have a framed photo). In case the lids aren't sufficiently eye-catching, the company has employed a woman in a red sequined evening gown to play songs on a large harp (she's currently in the middle of a rendition of *Somewhere Over the Rainbow*).

In this brave new world, I'm constantly asking company reps about their products. At one booth, a white mannequin hangs suspended by straps from what looks like a small crane on wheels. The whole setup brings to mind a scene from the movie *Coma*, but the machine turns out to be a mortuary lift. It's a piece of equipment much in demand, particularly as corpses get larger and heavier, explains a woman at the stand. As I leave, she hands me one of her corporate giveaways – a stick of lip salve with "Em-Balm" written on it.

While my day is filled with new discoveries, nothing seems as peculiar as what I find in the brochure of an embalming supplies company. Inside are products I had no idea existed. To start with, I learn, pre-injection chemicals can do everything from breaking up "blood clots caused by the congealing of the blood cells in the plasma" to inhibiting the "swelling of the capillaries" and improving "drainage qualities". Arterial fluids have even more impressive properties, from their "firming action" and ability to "alleviate effects of edema" (build-up of fluid between tissue cells), to their prowess in preventing "wrinkling due to astringency" and producing "a more lifelike texture". Tissue-building chemicals are available for rebuilding facial features and filling in wounds.

In the "Sundries" section of the catalogue are headrests and arm and hand positioners (which help the deceased achieve a comfort-able-looking pose). Casket liners and cranium pads can be cut to size, and what looks like a clear plastic jumpsuit without holes for hands and feet, is available "for use in extreme cases where entire body leakage protection is needed".

Meanwhile, rubber eye caps covered in tiny little spurs are available by the dozen (pink or colourless) to keep the eyelids firmly closed as well as plastic "mouth formers" – the high-tech equivalent of Joyboy's deftly snicked calling card.

Often, I find myself longing to hear Fa's laugh again. Laughing was a family tradition. And while everyone wanted to be the one to initiate the joke, it was usually Fa who set off the giggles. Somehow, he made the lamest jokes sound hilarious. In one of his most well-worn, he'd lampoon the words of a TV ad for Head & Shoulders, the anti-dandruff shampoo. "Yeah, Head & Shoulders is great," he'd say. "I used to have dandruff on my head. Now I've got it on my shoulders too!" We'd groan and roll our eyes. We'd heard his jokes many times before. But really we loved them, consuming each one eagerly like a candy treat.

Fa liked to make fun of death. In a letter advising me about my finances, he suggested prepare a will in case I were to "sud-denly 'get dead.'" He'd often solicit a laugh by slapping his fist on his chest and addressing his heart, telling it to "keep going, you fool!" And among his favourite quotations was one from Somerset Maugham: "Death, like constipation, is one of the commonplaces of human existence. Why shy away from it?"

Once, after it had become clear his illness was terminal, he and I were discussing whether or not to sell my grandmother's cottage, which had been rented since she died. Should we put it on the mar-ket now, or wait, we wondered? I felt no urgency as the real estate market seemed strong. "Let's see how the cookie crumbles," I sug-gested, to which with a dark smile Fa replied: "And this cookie is crumbling."

As the cookie crumbled, the laughter faded. Watching Fa during his last year, the thing that shocked me most was learning the grim but obvious truth that death is not only painful and undignified. It also triggers depression. For me, the day Fa died was the moment at which I could start to rebuild my image of him as the funny, clever optimist I'd known. No amount of embalming fluid, tissue-filling chemicals or make-up could have helped me to accelerate that process.

While some feel the need to see the body, not everyone who attends an open coffin funeral finds it helpful. In a 1990 survey of attitudes to death and deathcare, 32 percent of respondents said they found viewing of the body to have been a negative experience. In informal polls of my American friends, many have told me they found seeing the body disturbing. One recalled how, when living in an Irish Catholic-dominated town near Boston, she was surprised to find that funeral etiquette required congratulating the family on what a marvellous job the embalmer had made of their dead relative. Not to do so was considered impolite.

Yet it seems embalmed corpses don't always resemble the individuals while alive (people often use the term "empty shell" in their descriptions). In her book, *Caring for the Dead*, Lisa Carlson, executive director of the Funeral and Memorial Societies of America, a non-profit that protects consumers' rights, interviews numerous people who'd attended open coffin funerals. Some, she says, reported that the body "looked like nothing more than a statue or mannequin, a caricature of the departed friend or relative".

Waugh's character Dennis Barlow has a similar experience. After his uncle, Sir Francis Hinsley, hangs himself because his writing contract at the Megalopolitan Studios is terminated, Barlow visits his embalmed corpse in the Whispering Glades Slumber Room and is shocked by what he sees: "The complete stillness was more startling than any violent action." Barlow finds his uncle's face "entirely horrible; as ageless as a tortoise and as inhuman; a painted and smirking obscene travesty by comparison with which the devil-mask Dennis had found in the noose was a festive adornment, a thing an uncle might don at a Christmas party".

Most funeral directors would disagree. They argue that the

"memory picture" created by the embalmed corpse helps grieving relatives navigate their sorrow and achieve "closure". In an article on the website of Dodge, one of the world's biggest embalming equipment suppliers, psychologist Donald Steele writes that, "by seeing the deceased, and even by touching the deceased, we have a visual and tactile image of what the fact of death means. We know that being dead is different than being alive, and we know that the person whom we loved is truly dead, not simply gone away".

Elisabeth Kübler-Ross begs to differ. "The elaborate expensive display of an open casket with all the make-up in the slumber room enforces the belief that the person is only asleep," she writes in *Questions and Answers on Death and Dying*. This, she adds, will "only help to prolong the stage of denial". Mitford of course was also sceptical. She claimed the funeral industry's insistence on the importance of the "memory picture" was simply part of an "assortment of myths based on half-digested psychiatric theories".

I would have once wholeheartedly agreed with these critics – that is, until I read a moving essay by Thomas Lynch, the undertaker poet. While embalming still seems to me a strange, intrusive procedure, Lynch's essay provides a powerful insight into why those who embalm the dead can perform a critical service, particularly in the case of a death that was far from peaceful.

Lynch describes the tragic case of a small girl abducted, raped then murdered by a madman with a baseball bat. Most funeral directors would have suggested a closed coffin. However, one of Lynch's colleagues, Wesley Rice, spent all night working on the corpse. "Eighteen hours later the girl's mother, who had pleaded to see her, saw her," writes Lynch. "She was dead, to be sure, and damaged; but her face was hers again, not the madman's version. The hair was hers, not his. The body was hers, not his. Wesley Rice had not raised her from the dead nor hidden the hard facts, but he had retrieved her death from the one who had killed her."

If embalming corpses is a very American way of death, its origins are very American too – they lie in the Civil War. With slaughter, on a scale never before seen in the young nation, came dead bodies; bodies in their thousands, often mangled and disfigured, with arms and legs missing. Between 1861 and 1865, it's estimated that more than six hundred thousand people died. The question was how, physically and psychologically, to deal with so many corpses.

"Americans had to identify – find, invent, create – the means and mechanism to manage more than half a million dead," writes Drew Gilpin Faust in *This Republic of Suffering*. "The work of death was Civil War America's most fundamental and most demanding undertaking."

Part of that undertaking was getting the dead home for burial. New preservation techniques would facilitate this process. Earlier physicians, surgeons and anatomists had experimented with ways of preserving bodies using arterial embalming. Frederik Ruysch, a Danish anatomist and botanist born in 1638, conducted pioneering work in the technique. With injections of mercury and red wax, he was able to show the anatomical course of blood vessels. However, he used it mainly in the preservation of animals, bones and human organs, which he used to produce strange decorative tableaux (one showed a skeleton playing a violin made of arteries).

Thomas Holmes, a New York doctor born in 1817, was among the first to apply the technique to human corpses and to commercialise it. His method of arterial embalming – using a solution of chemicals injected into the body – soon took off, particularly after he displayed the body of Colonel Ellsworth, Abraham Lincoln's friend and one of the first Union officers killed in the war. After he died in 1861, he was embalmed by Holmes and publicly displayed in New York, Washington and Albany, where the quality of the preservation generated much favourable media attention.

Embalming made Holmes a rich man. He claimed to have embalmed about four thousand soldiers from the war, charging families a hundred dollars for each officer and twenty-five for enlisted men. Others followed his example and a fledgling industry was born, with a licensing system and its own trade body, the Undertakers Mutual Protective Association of Philadelphia, established before the war had ended. Of course, tens of thousands were buried where they fell. But during the American Civil War, about forty thousand bodies were embalmed and shipped home.

After the assassination of Abraham Lincoln in 1865, the president's corpse helped put embalming on the undertaker's map. A shocked nation queued up in the hundreds of thousands to view the embalmed body, which travelled from Washington to Springfield, Illinois, by train, allowing viewings wherever it stopped, giving people a chance to inspect the impressive preservative powers of the new technique.

Embalming owed its success to something deeper, though. Demand for the services of embalmers was also linked to nineteenth-century religious concerns over the fate of the soul. The Victorians had revived the medieval concept of *Ars Moriendi* (the art of dying), which was enshrined in a body of Christian literature giving guidance on how to secure a "Good Death". While attitudes, actions and prayers contributed to the soul's salvation, of profound importance to achieving a Good Death was the presence of family at the deathbed.

Relatives could, of course, comfort the dying person. But more importantly, they were essential observers of life's last moments – moments during which the dying were supposed to seek forgiveness for their sins, pardon those who'd wronged them and put their soul in God's hands. Facial expressions were thought to mirror the soul so, explains Drew Gilpin Faust, "family members needed to witness a death in order to assess the state of the dying person's soul, for these critical last moments of life would epitomise his or her spiritual condition". In other words, how you died made a difference to what you could expect in the afterlife – and your family had to be there to see it.

War threw this tradition into chaos. The carnage was such that thousands of bodies had to be tossed into shallow graves or mass burial pits. Letters from fellow soldiers provided first-hand descriptions of comrades in their last moments. But that wasn't enough. If families couldn't see for themselves that their father, son or husband had made peace with God before he died, they wanted to see his face before he was buried. Embalming provided a solution (for those that could afford it), giving the dead a calm, peaceful countenance.

Born in the midst of conflict, embalming served a number of needs. It preserved the body during the journey home. It gave families certainty that those they'd lost had been correctly identified. Most critically, by making them look as if they were merely asleep, it created the "beautiful memory picture", as today's funeral directors would call it, needed to fulfil the *Ars Moriendi* requirements. By providing visual evidence that the individual had experienced a Good Death, the fledgling embalming industry delivered more than well-preserved corpses – it gave families the confidence that the souls of their loved ones were on their way to heaven.

Before leaving Palermo, I return to the Capuchin Catacombs for one more tour of the dank corridors and their unsettling array of bodies. As the monk hands me my ticket, he gives me a knowing look as if to say, "See – you think you're horrified by this place but you're actually fascinated."

He's right. And what's perhaps most arresting is the range of emotions on display here. While the "Beautiful Memory Picture" of the modern embalmed decedent creates an image of rest and peace, there's no evidence of it in this Sicilian crypt. Here, gravity combined with years of decay has endowed the occupants with such a ghoulish range of expressions that even Waugh's debonair Joyboy would have a hard time fixing them into something more acceptable.

With skulls sinking on to shoulder blades, many of the figures have acquired a melancholy shrug. Others simply smile, but with an expression that's turned into an unsettling grimace. Worse still, many of them appear to have picked up the same type of food poisoning I came down with in China. With arms crossed over their bellies, they appear to be suffering from painful stomach disruptions. In fact, the twisted, tormented torsos look as if they're struggling to break free of their niches to make a dash for the bathroom.

One woman wearing a blue-and-white striped dress and what

were clearly once smart kid gloves has a particularly striking pose. With her head tilted back, chin sticking out and empty eyes rolling towards the heavens, she seems to be in some sort of physical agony – or is it spiritual passion? Anyone who's seen the *Ecstasy of St Teresa* will know the pose. Like Bernini's shockingly sensual sculpture in St Peter's, Rome, her head is thrown back, her mouth open (whether in pain or pleasure is uncertain). But unlike the beautiful sculpted marble face of St Teresa, this woman's features have imploded, leaving her with a mash of crumpled yellow leather.

For nineteenth-century British writer Catherine Gore, the contrast between the attire of the unmarried women and their decayed facial features was most disturbing. While they were "arrayed in their white robes, with their spotless coronals [small metal crowns symbolising virginity] upon their brows", she remarks, beneath these headdresses, "the sunken yellow temples and distorted lips impart to the accessories of an angel the countenance of a fiend!"

There's anger and frustration here, too, for some of the corpses have fallen forward and appear to be shouting at an invisible enemy. With a shrivelled mask of a face, a torn hole for a nose and a toothless open mouth, P. Rozario Dal Parco (who died in 1793, according to the handwritten cardboard note pinned to her chest) seems to be wailing silently at some unknown horror. One priest whose lower jaw has been lost and whose head has slipped on to his chest appears to be chomping into his own robe with what's left of his mouth.

Dark humour also echoes through these dingy corridors. A few, with hips hitched up to one side, look as if they're dancing, while others appear to be cackling with laughter, jaws wide open, arms gripping their sides to control their shaking bodies.

Fr. Modesto da Marsa, who died in 1855, seems in a particularly playful mood. As the dead priest peers down at the corpse below him, his foot, which has slipped down from the edge of his niche, pokes at the shoulder of the fellow below. With skin covering only one side of his face, one eye closed and the other a hollow socket, a bishop appears to be winking at us.

The section for children is most upsetting. The small figures hang together like a collection of horror-movie dolls. As American traveller Nathanial Parker Willis put it in 1844, "a more horribly ludicrous collection of little withered faces, shrunk into expression so entirely inconsistent with the gayety of their dresses, could scarcely be conceived".

What were their families thinking? True, this was once seen as a prestigious burial place. But would you really want your dead relatives pinned to a wall and left looking miserable in a cold, dark corridor? Anyone seeking evidence of a Good Death according to *Ars Moriendi* traditions would be hard pressed to find it here.

Today's skilled embalmers certainly wouldn't leave their charges looking like these Sicilian mummies. Even so, I'm thinking that somewhere in my will I must leave a prominent note that says in big, bold letters: "DO NOT EMBALM ME!" If I need to be preserved for any reason, the refrigerator at the morgue will do just fine. But the prospect of having formaldehyde pumped through my arteries and veins does nothing to alleviate my fear of mortality, quite the opposite in fact.

As I leave this extraordinary Sicilian necropolis, I can't help wondering whether the individuals hanging along these walls would have chosen this as their final resting place. For me, this strange display of crumbling "organic matter" might be chilling, but it's also fascinating. I'm amazed by the desperate human need to project beyond the grave not only our spiritual selves but our corporeal ones, too. We want to live on in body as well as in soul.

It's a desire that persists. After all, until recently, claiming their products could prevent a body from decaying was a powerful marketing tool for casket makers. And, at cryogenics labs, people are still signing up to have their bodies deep-frozen in the hope that medical advances will one day permit their reuse.

Perhaps the Capuchin monks made similar claims. At any rate, their clients clearly had no clue as to how ultimately ineffective the monks' preservation techniques would prove. With hindsight, is this really the eternal image of themselves they would have wanted to present to the world?

4

INSIDE THE BOX

A Fantasy Coffin in Ghana

As soon as we shake hands, I know I'm going to like Eric Kpakpo Adotey. He's got sparkly eyes and the sweetest smile. He's sturdily built, and has about him a look of youthful vitality, something I feel is a good thing to find in a person – particularly when that person is going to be your coffin maker. Eric and I meet at his workshop in Teshi, a suburb of Accra, the sprawling capital of Ghana. Here, strung along a coastal road like beads on a necklace, are ramshackle shops, and shacks housing the offices and workshops of traders, car mechanics, fishermen – and coffin makers.

In terms of natural beauty, this section of coastline is not one of West Africa's finest features. Along a weather-beaten highway, cars and trucks spew diesel fumes into the sticky tropical air while waves from the Atlantic Ocean pound angrily up against the shore. Dusty banana trees are the only signs of green amid an urban land-scape of half-completed buildings whose rusted steel rods sprout from unfinished walls. Commercial enterprises – the Lord Our Banner Paints and God's Way Hairdo among them – share the roadside with stalls whose neat pyramids of oranges are shaded by tattered beach umbrellas. Everything seems to be leaning slightly, with wooden posts propping up plastic awnings and unstable-looking sheds turning for support to equally unsteady neighbours.

And there's plenty of time to take it all in. Traffic in Accra achieves an unusual level of awfulness. It makes for a stressful visit, even when you're not on a mission to commission your own coffin. Still, two things about Ghana have, after previous visits, left me wanting to return. First, I always come away convinced that Ghanaians are the nicest people in the world. Second, they have the craziest coffins.

Ghana's tradition of fantasy coffins is a recent one. It started by accident in the 1950s, so the story goes, when a chief from the Ga tribe who made his fortune in cocoa farming commissioned Ata Owoo, a well-known carpenter, to build him a giant cocoa pod as a ceremonial palanquin. The chief died before his palanquin was finished, so it was transformed into a casket and used for his burial.

Inspired by the chief's unusual coffin, a Ghanaian furniture maker called Seth Kane Kwei decided to create a personalised casket for his grandmother that would fulfil her lifelong dream – to ride in an airplane, something she never managed to do when she was alive (references to her "final flight" are usually introduced at this point in the story, but I'll spare you the puns).

Today, Ghanaians who can afford it are buried in anything from a giant Coca-Cola bottle to a sack of flour or a massive fish. Monstrous chickens and scaled-down elephants are popular models, as are luxury cars. A mechanic who repaired outboard motors went off in a Yamaha 40. Majestic eagle caskets are generally reserved for chiefs and giant vegetables for farmers. Boldly carved and painted in bright colours, they're more than coffins – they are works of art.

Over the years, human bodies have been buried in all kinds of things – baskets, jars, earthenware pots, animal skins, dugout tree trunks, canoes, Viking ships, cerecloths (special wax-treated wrapping cloths tied at the head and feet) and even whole suits of armour. For Muslims and Jews, the traditional burial container is a simple linen shroud. For the Egyptians, the preference was for a lavishly decorated mummy sarcophagus.

The ancient Greeks used stone sarcophagi to inter their dead, and while you might think stone was chosen for durability and protection, this was not the case. The word sarcophagus in fact comes from a combination of the Greek words sarx, or "flesh", and phagein, "to eat", and referred to the limestone used for burial containers, which it was thought accelerated the rotting of corpses (they weren't so far off, as limestone is an alkaline, solutions of which can be used to decompose corpses).

Coffins were not always used for burial. In seventeenth-century England, many parishes had a coffin that was loaned out to parishioners to contain the shrouded body during the funeral service. Moreover, for many centuries, the graves of ordinary people were merely temporary homes, for eventually their bones would be dug up and placed into crypts, charnel houses and ossuaries.

Nor do we always bury people in the earth. Local conditions may demand surface interments, as in New Orleans, where a high water table and marshy ground made it difficult to bury the dead in the earth, leading to the tradition of above-ground tombs.

And do we always have to be buried lying down? Some would say no. George Hancock, a nineteenth-century Virginian plantation owner, is thought to have been buried sitting upright so he could continue to watch his slaves at work in the valley below. In Buenos Aires, Juan Facundo Quiroga, a nineteenth-century Argentine strongman, is said to have been interred standing up because he wanted to meet God "face-to-face". Ben Johnson, the English poet and playwright who died in 1637, was buried vertically in Westminster Abbey for a more prosaic reason – by the time he died, it was the only slot left in the part of the abbey he'd requested. Today, managers of cramped cemeteries in Britain and the United States are considering stand-up burials to save space.

The modern coffin has been through several evolutions. Early American caskets, like their British counterparts, tended to be plain, often made of pine, although hardwoods such as chestnut or walnut were the choice of more affluent customers. Anthropoid shaped (wide at the shoulders and narrow at the feet), they were known as "toe pinchers".

Changes came with nineteenth-century industrialisation, when toe pinchers gave way to models with straight sides that could be machine made. In the United States, the first patent for a coffin was awarded to Almond J. Fisk in 1848 for three cast iron models, while other companies such as Cane, Breed, & Co of Cincinnati, secured licenses to produce the Fisk caskets. As factory-produced metal coffins became popular, the role of the undertaker – for whom carpentry had once been an important part of the job description – changed. Funeral directors became middlemen for the sale of caskets and burial accoutrements. In recent years, they've become more like event planners and grief counsellors.

Today, caskets can be churned out in impressive volumes. From Batesville, Indiana, the world's biggest coffin maker produces a thousand a day. Batesville Casket Co compares what it does to car manufacturing. It buys the paint from the same suppliers and has even found that trends in car colours are later reflected in casket choices. However, the form of the casket – an anthropoid shape or an elongated rectangle – remains much the same, the proportions of the human body having barely changed over the centuries.

That is, until recently. Rising obesity has prompted the arrival of new super-size coffins. In Indiana, one company has made a business from "serving the oversize needs of the funeral industry". With names like "Harvest", "Heartland", and "Homestead", the Goliath Casket company offers a variety of sizes – ranging in width from twenty-nine to a massive fifty-two inches (the standard is twenty-four inches). But while the coffins might be larger than average – Goliath's can handle loads of up to seven hundred pounds – they still conform to the familiar rectangular proportions.

Having said that, in some countries, other shapes are preferred. In parts of rural Southeast Asia, bodies are still buried in the foetal position, calling for a shorter, wider box. The Chinese favour the long rectangular format but one constructed of smoothed, polished and varnished sections of tree trunks, resulting in caskets with four rounded sections on each side (retaining the original curve of the trunk) enclosing the central shaft. And, let's not forget Ghana where, when it comes to coffin shapes, anything goes.

A longstanding family joke – one my father liked to repeat whenever he got the chance – was born one morning after Fa had just come out of hospital, when Sam, with a slip of the tongue, asked him whether he would like "tea or coffin" with his breakfast. "Coffin; definitely coffin," was Fa's swift response. Towards the end of his life, he became set on the idea of being cremated, which he considered the most practical and efficient means of disposing of his "organic matter". However, at various points in his life, Fa had looked at other options.

There was the time he'd toyed with the idea of an ocean burial. Fa "went to sea", as he put it, when he joined the merchant navy as a teenager. At eighteen, he wrote a detailed technical explanation of nautical navigation, including beautifully executed diagrams and an impressive section on the "Apparent Motion of Heavenly Bodies" (astronomy was another great interest). He remained passionate about ships and the sea. During retirement, he'd collect pictures of his favourite vessels and, out in The Hut, spend hours putting them into scrapbooks and adding explanatory notes. So it's hardly surprising he'd considered a sea burial.

However, Sam – ever the practical one – knew how difficult it would be to arrange such a thing and told him in no uncertain terms she wasn't prepared to take responsibility for organising it (I believe her exact words were, "Over my dead body").

Then there were the brochures for wicker coffins I'd found in his "How to End It!" file. He also seems to have investigated the possibility of a green burial. In the same folder was a list of notes written to himself on a piece of yellow foolscap, dated 1997 (nine years before he died), reminding himself to "find out details of plots, costs included and the presentation of arranging the interment and transport and burial of the body in its willow coffin" and to "write to W.D.D.C. [West Dorset District Council] and ask if any woodland burial graves are in that district". Most of the items on the list had ticks marked against them so he'd clearly been serious.

When the law in Britain changed to allow burial outside sanctified ground, I remember he and my godmother discussing the idea of being buried at the bottom of our garden. Of course, unless done in secret, this might have seriously affected the resale value of the house. Who wants to buy a place with the corpse of the previous owner fertilising the flowerbeds?

In the west, the graveyard was the traditional destination for the dead. I've seen what this might look like for me. On a recent trip to Hong Kong, I found myself wandering around the old colonial cemetery. Amid the gravestones of nineteenth-century British soldiers, sailors and administrators, there was one that stopped me in my tracks. On a sturdy marble tombstone in bold capital letters was engraved simply: "SARAH". Nothing was written about this Sarah's life, and the name of the man to whom she had been "The Beloved Wife" was no longer legible. The headstone recorded her death, as November 20, 1864 (she was just twenty-eight). But what struck me most was the single word, chiselled above the date in alarmingly large letters: "DIED".

In spite of the rather unsettling experience of coming across my own name on a gravestone, a burial place amid trees and lush greenery is certainly an appealing idea. And while talk of burial as a "return to nature" seems odd, since I don't remember coming from soil, becoming part of the earth on which I've trodden for so long might be a good way go.

There are other ways to "return to nature". Some cultures rely on birds rather than worms to remove the bodies of their dead. Traditionally, the corpses of Zoroastrians in Iran were wrapped in white muslin and left in circular towers on top of mountains – Towers of Silence – where vultures picked off the flesh in a matter of hours. In Mumbai, another Tower of Silence serves many of India's Parsis, descendents of Zoroastrians. Here, though, the practice is coming into question since a shortage of the birds (India's vultures are facing extinction) is posing a tricky problem for the city's Parsi community as bodies pile up.

For Zoroastrians and Parsis, leaving the dead to birds reflected their respect for the earth, which they believe should not be polluted with human corpses. Tibetans, on the other hand, see their sky burials – in which corpses are cut into pieces and left as carrion for mountain birds – as acts of generosity to the natural world, with the dead bringing sustenance to living creatures. A similar idea shaped an ancient practice in the Solomon Islands, where corpses were left out on rocks as gifts for the sharks.

I'm not sure I'm ready to honour nature with my body through any of these methods. But while backyard burial poses real estate conundrums, and as an atheist I'm hardly first in line for a plot in the cemetery, there's another option – the one my father had at one time considered – the green burial, or natural burial.

Modern burial has become anything but natural. By some estimates, enough embalming fluid to fill eight Olympic-size swimming pools is lowered into the ground every year, where it slowly leaches into soil and groundwater. Not to mention the pressed steel caskets, brass handles, adjustable beds, fabric lining and foam padding that accompany the embalmed bodies into the earth, turning the modern cemetery into a new form of landfill.

Green funerals and woodland burials mean going into the ground in a biodegradable coffin, without being pumped full of embalming chemicals. They first took off in Britain, where chunks of rolling countryside are being opened up to those looking for a more natural type of interment. In the United States, too, green burials and "conservation burials" are catching on, with a number of eco-graveyards appearing around the country.

Pioneers in this respect are Kimberley and Billy Campbell, who've been restoring a park in South Carolina to its former beauty as a mature hardwood forest where orchids and other rare wild flowers can grow – and people can be buried. At Ramsey Creek, the dead are buried without preservative chemicals, steel caskets or leak-proof coffins. Grave markers are simple inscriptions on rocks or stones. Coffins must be biodegradable (and not made of endangered tropical woods) so that, as they naturally break down, their owners are released into the earth as part of a glorious rambling wilderness. Some modern technology is at work here, however, in the Campbell's intriguing way of helping visiting families locate their relatives – by keeping records of each grave's GPS co-ordinates.

It's not often that you look at a picture of a casket and say, "I want one of those!" But this was my reaction to the Ghanaian fantasy coffins. I was captivated by their brilliant colours and crazy designs. And it seemed to me that knowing you'd be leaving the world in a giant orange fish or a huge wooden banana could make it slightly less traumatic. So I've decided to head to Ghana to put in an order for one of these eccentric funerary artworks. In the event that I pick burial for my remains, I want to go down in something stylish (even if I'm cremated, I'll need something to get me to the furnace on time).

I'm aware that in ordering my own coffin in advance, I might be seen as slightly odd, if not downright eccentric. "Pre-need" is, of course, an important chunk of the funeral industry – one in three Americans over fifty has embarked on some sort of pre-planning for a funeral or burial, according to the AARP (which represents the interests of the over fifties), and just under a quarter have pre-paid a portion of their "final expenses" for themselves or someone else. Companies with names like Forethought Financial Group and Funeral Financial serve these customers ("Is your pre-need program really changing your firm's destiny?" was one of the burning questions asked recently by *American Funeral Director* magazine).

But while many people purchase such policies and secure burial plots ahead of time, pre-need consumers of coffins and other funeral-related products remain part of a niche market; the smallest notch on the revenue charts of the "death care industry", as it would like to be known.

Even so, some companies are catering to people who want to make more imaginative choices. Colourful Coffins, a British firm, helps clients create customised designs. It's based its entire business model on offering its "Pre-Design Service" only to those who will eventually occupy their coffin. "It cannot be purchased by any third party, or on behalf of someone else," says the company.

Those who like the buy-now-die-later option can purchase coffins that serve as pieces of furniture in the interim. Baltimore-born artist Charles Constantine's pine-built "Memento" is a coffee table and coffin combined. It stores books and personal possessions until it's needed as a burial casket. Canada-based Casket Furniture's products ("Furniture for a Lifetime ... and Beyond") include the traditional-looking Adam's Coffin Coffee Table, a polished wood coffin with six short legs, as well as the velvet-upholstered Salvador Casket Sofa in a chic contemporary design, and which, says the company, "will always provide you with the ultimate place of rest, whether it's taking a load off, or doing the final send-off".

But if in commissioning my own coffin, I'm part of a fledgling pre-need casket market, I'm by no means doing anything new. Over the centuries, great rulers have generally liked to get this kind of thing sorted out before heading to the next world, ordering the construction of ambitious tombs or mausoleums while still alive – leaving us, by the way, with some of the world's greatest architectural landmarks. Take the pyramids of Egypt. As pre-need sarcophagi go, how much more impressive can you get?

While the pharaohs deployed armies of slaves to work on their tombs, the wealthy and the influential commissioned artists and architects. Luckily for Pope Julius II, he got Michelangelo. In 1505, eight years before his death, Julius commissioned the Renaissance artist to create a huge tomb of Carrara marble that was to be three stories high with up to forty-seven sculpted figures adorning it. "The quantity of stone was enormous, so that, when it was all spread out upon the square, it stirred amazement in the minds of most folk," wrote Ascanio Condivi, Michelangelo's biographer.

The project suffered constant setbacks, partly because Michelangelo broke off the work to carry out a few other papal chores – the Sistine Chapel ceiling, for one. In the end, Julius got neither the tomb nor the location he'd wanted. When Julius died in 1513, Michelangelo signed a contract for another seven years, but to work on a greatly reduced version of the tomb, and even this scheme was scaled down. Eventually, forty-five years after

Michelangelo's original commission, in what Condivi calls "the tragedy of the tomb", a modest version was installed in the Church of San Pietro in Vincoli in Rome, far from St Peter's, where Julius had wanted to rest in papal splendour.

The "tragedy of the tomb" shows just how tricky it can be to secure the right kind of burial for yourself, even if you're a powerful Catholic prelate. Still, some practical matters can be taken care of – what to wear, for example.

The American funeral industry has made a business of this, offering a range of what you might call "casket couture". The garments are slightly different from ones sold to the living. First, they open at the back to facilitate dressing the corpse. High collars and scarves cover the skin around the neck, which is probably not looking its best. Sleeves are cut on the long side to allow arms to be crossed over the chest. A lower shoulder-line means the garment won't ride up awkwardly over the neck when in "repose" position.

Funerary tailors also offer "fabric, textures, and colours that work well with casket interiors" in "traditionally stylish" one-piece frocks, negligees for the "soft and peaceful" look and "flowing" gowns (quite why it needs to flow is unclear). What's more, you don't have to invest in a whole outfit. As well as "full couch" attire, there's the "three-quarters couch" option, for those who only intend the top half of the body to be viewed in the coffin.

Most of these garments are sold to customers who are buying them for dead relatives. But in some countries, people make advance preparations for the clothes they'll wear in the grave. In her photograph series *Clothes for Death*, London-based photographer Margareta Kern documents the tradition practiced by women in Croatia and Bosnia-Herzegovina of making and arranging the garments in which they want to be buried.

In a moving set of images, Kern highlights the poignant contrast between the modest interiors and tired old work clothes in which the women are photographed and the beautiful lace and embroidered garments and sheets (for placing on top of the coffin) they've laid out around them for the photo session.

Kern is struck by the way the women store their burial clothes

– in travel bags and suitcases. "One of the women, Jovana, who is 97 years old, pulled out a dusty old suitcase from underneath the bed and inside of it was a floral dress, long woollen socks (which she probably knitted), petticoat and many family photographs," writes Kern in her blog. "It was as though she was preparing for a journey and needed to be ready at any moment."

These days, people tend to react to this kind of planning with a shudder and move on to a new topic of discussion, as I've discovered when talking to friends about drawing up a will. Yet along with necessities such as eating and sleeping, the fact that we are destined to die is one of the most important aspects of our existence. We readily make provision for eating and sleeping, and, it's true, those activities are more appealing than the prospect of our annihilation. But dying is no less real, so surely we should prepare for this, too?

Still, it can be a little discomforting. On one occasion, I inadvertently became involved in the burial preparations of an elderly couple. When living in Vietnam, my great friend Sandro Lovatelli and I would drive out of Hanoi at weekends to explore the villages and temples around the city. We had with us Sandro's trusty driver Mr Tan – well, perhaps I should say trusty in character (he was blind in one eye and had only 70 percent vision in the other).

One afternoon we found ourselves in the home of a Vietnamese family. They hung on Mr Tan's every word, nodding enthusiastically as he told them all about us, while Sandro and I smiled back politely, unable to understand a thing. As we got up to go, Mr Tan indicated that the family wanted me to take photographs of them. In the days before cheap digital cameras, the arrival of foreigners provided a rare chance for a family picture.

I took a few snaps of the children and the father, and wrote down the address so I could send them the prints. Then an old couple came forward – the grandparents, who'd been sitting quietly in a corner. They, too, wanted a photograph and were trying to describe what they were after. It was clearly not a family snap.

As I adjusted the camera, the two stood together on the front terrace of their tiny house, striking up a pose of great seriousness, no hint of a smile on either face. With their simple wooden home behind them, I couldn't help thinking of Grant Wood's iconic 1930 painting *American Gothic*. I squinted through my viewfinder and adjusted the camera lens. Suddenly it became clear what it was the old couple had requested – a picture to use on their tombstone. I took the photograph and, a few weeks later, sent it to them. But I remember feeling uneasy as I pressed the camera shutter. It was as if somehow I'd participated in their deaths.

The first part of my plan to commission a coffin – booking a ticket to Ghana – is straightforward enough. There's even a direct flight from New York to Accra. The coffin shops are easy to find, being dotted along the coastal road at the point where it runs through Teshi. And I'm pretty certain one of the Ga coffin craftsmen will be happy to make and sell me one of his wilder creations. But I've no idea how I'm going to get it home. I picture myself negotiating with logistics agents in dusty shipping offices and filling out customs forms: "Item for shipment: One coffin."

Oddly enough, I visited those West African shipping offices many years ago, when I was hired to collect publicity material for a shipping company. The trip took me down dirt roads following container trucks to pineapple plantations and rubber factories across Ghana, Senegal and Cote d'Ivoire. On a short flight in a two-seater Cessna over Abidjan harbour, I leaned out over the wing to take photos of giant cargo vessels docked below as the great gantry cranes lining the quays heaved up from their holds the cargo of steel shipping containers.

So it's strangely appropriate that I'm once again heading to West Africa in pursuit of containers. And this time, I'll need to use the services of those shippers to get my coffin home. I consider tracking down the agents I met last time. But my contacts in the Ghanaian freight-forwarding industry are well out of date.

Then, poking around on the internet, I come across an online fair-trade retailer called eShopAfrica. It's based in Ghana and sells African craft products. When the company's founder, Cordelia

Salter-Nour, a Brit who has worked all over Africa in the technology departments of aid organisations, moved to Ghana more than a decade ago, she decided to use the internet to generate work for African artisans by connecting them with global customers. Today, from its tiny office in Accra, eShopAfrica sells and ships everything from shawls, beads and wall hangings to barber signs and tribal drums. Coffins are a recent addition to the product range.

I call up Cordelia, who's in Rome working at the United Nations World Food Programme. "When I moved to Ghana," she tells me, "the first thing I did was order a coffin." She has two scaled-down coffins – in the shape of a computer mouse and, for her very much alive son, a football. She treats them as decorative objects to brighten up the house. "Personally, I love them," she says. "I think they're wasted on the dead."

When I tell her I want to travel to Ghana to order one, Cordelia suggests I contact her colleague Kawther el Obeid, a Sudanese woman who's lived in Ghana for twenty years and runs the business from her home in Accra. Kawther, says Cordelia, can introduce me to a young coffin maker and help me with my order.

So here I am, several months later, sitting on a paint-spattered bench next to Eric, my charming coffin maker, discussing my order. Kawther has joined me for the visit to introduce me to Eric and discuss materials with him (US customs regulations mean I can only import something made of the right kind wood and decorated with lead-free paint).

It's a sticky day at the tail end of the rainy season and the drive to Eric's workshop has left me feeling hot and bothered. But, strange as this seems, meeting my coffin maker has lifted my spirits. His voice has a delightful timbre – a gentle pitter-patter that that turns into a chortle whenever humour enters the conversation. He doesn't look remotely like someone from the funeral business. He's wearing jeans and flip-flops and a sky blue T-shirt on which the number 838 is embroidered with little wave crests picked out in white below it. There are no men in black suits and dark ties here.

Eric is from the Ga tribe. He lives in Nungua, the suburb next to Teshi. He got into coffins (so to speak) after dropping out of school because his parents could no longer afford the fees. He apprenticed himself to a well-known master coffin maker, also from the Ga tribe. Since Eric had no money to set up shop alone, he stayed on for several years after completing his apprenticeship. Today, he's got his own business with two apprentices and a workshop with an open-air showroom above it sheltered by a flat roof.

Eric leads me up the wooden steps to his showroom past a sign reading "God First Furniture Works" (this, it turns out, isn't a euphemism for Eric's trade but the name of the business with whom he shares the building – a furniture maker). It's good to be above ground, with the sea breeze carrying off some of the sticky sweat that's making my shirt cling to my sides and causing my feet to slip around in my sandals. With a roof shading me from the angry sun, I'm feeling more relaxed. In any case, it's hard to focus attention on bodily discomfort when you're staring into the bulging eyes of a huge green, yellow and pink crayfish that's made of wood and designed to house someone's remains.

Up here on Eric's showroom platform, there's also a scaled-down model of a "Ghana Int. Airline" plane with detachable wings, a scaled-up model of a Nokia cell phone, a couple of giant bottles of Star (Ghana's favourite beer), an oversized sack of GMG flour (with Pride of the West written across it), a huge white chicken and a gigantic red tropical fish. They've all been decorated in brilliant colours – and they will all one day contain a dead person.

Can these really be coffins? I wonder. With their cartoon-like designs and cheery coats of paint, they seem a million miles from the dour "Ambassador", "Colonial" or "Chancellor" models whose dull grey pressed steel and walnut-veneer finishes fill the pages of funeral directors' catalogues back home.

Eric's "catalogue" is rather different – it consists of dozens of photographs of some of the coffins he's made over the years. Soon, images of all kinds of carved objects are spread out on my lap – a giant key, a large gun, a snake (for a fetish priest), an enormous drum and, for a pastor, a six-foot-high bible. Eric's most unusual commission was a giant womb for a doctor. Then there are animals – lions, fish and other creatures. I'm reminded of the huge decorated bulls in which the Balinese royals were cremated, but Eric's work is designed to go below the ground, not up in flames.

Some of the coffins in the photographs contain corpses, one with a cigarette stuck in his mouth (he loved smoking, explains Eric). Others, such as a humongous root vegetable, are being paraded through the streets on their way to the cemetery.

I ask Eric where he gets his inspiration. "First, I listen to the people," he says. "After I hear them talking, I start to know them. Then I get my ideas. And usually, they know what they want."

Often, that's something relating to their lives – a favourite car, perhaps (Eric's current project is a Mercedes C360) – or a symbol of their profession. I'm not sure if the beer bottles are for brewers or drinkers, but the fish are for fishermen, the keys for locksmiths, kiosks for storekeepers, planes for pilots and, of course, uteruses for doctors. Occasionally the visual references have tragic origins. One young man, Peter Borkety Kuwono, was buried in a wooden replica of the oil tanker that killed him when he crashed into it.

Building these coffins requires years of training. The craftsmen work from memory or from photographs of the objects, drawing the shapes on to planks of wood. They cut the pieces, glue them together and, before painting them, sand them down to produce a silky-smooth finish. The coffin craftsmen make sure they get every detail right, from the logo on the label of a beer bottle to the registration plate of a Mercedes or the scales on the surface of a fish.

The variety of things they can produce is remarkable, but the coffins all have one thing in common – a sort of mad, comic, pop art look that seems at odds with something as sombre as death. Eric tells me that the tradition has changed the way people in Ghana feel about death and funerals. "Before, when we saw a coffin, we were scared or we felt unhappy," he says. "Now people are not afraid, because these coffins are something they know – it's part of them, part of their life."

Eric's comment brings to mind something I'm seeing in a lot of the death rites and funerary objects I've encountered so far – the human search for some kind of immortality. These coffins provide more than flamboyant means of making an exit. They're also a way of continuing in death what you did while living, whether that's spending eternity catching fish or taking your Mercedes for a spin on heaven's highways.

Before I left for Ghana, I'd spent quite a while thinking what part of my life I wanted reflected in my coffin. As a writer who spends so much time in front of a laptop, a computer mouse seemed the most obvious – but there was something too depressing about the idea of leaving this world in a piece of IT equipment. A newspaper or a book might be appropriate, given my trade, but they'd be the wrong shape. A pen seemed a little anachronistic and unexciting, given Eric's evident powers of creativity. No, I needed something that reflected my life in another way.

If coffin manufacturers in some parts of the world show a distinct lack of imagination compared to the Ga craftsmen, this is starting to change. These days, the traditional box is not the only option. Nor does it have to be bought from a funeral director. As consumers have baulked at shelling out several thousand dollars for a casket, online retailers have started to offer basic coffins for lower prices. You can even pick one up at, appropriately enough, big-box stores such as Costco, the discount retailer, where prices start at just over nine hundred dollars, and Walmart, which sells caskets at similar prices with payment over a year at no interest.

As environmentally conscious customers start to worry about the amount of junk humankind is shovelling into the earth along with its mortal remains, a new kind of coffin is also gaining popularity – the eco-coffin. Some have an old-fashioned, rustic look and are constructed of seagrass, bamboo and wicker, rather like the ones in the brochures my father collected.

Others are high-tech containers, such as the Ecopod, a sleek casket that looks more like a cocoon than a coffin. Produced by a British company and made from recycled newspaper, it has a smooth surface of recycled silk and mulberry leaves. Also in Britain, Hainsworth, which manufactures fabric for, among other things, the uniforms of the Royal Guard, has devised a biodegradable woollen coffin that is supported on a recycled fibreboard frame.

One Dutch "green" coffin producer has taken a radically new approach to the manufacture of its products – it leaves customers to assemble them. The EveryBody Coffin arrives as six flat pre-cut pieces of wood, with simple handles integrated into the pieces. Sections snap together without the aid of tools, screws or glue and the untreated wood, says the company, allows "personal decoration involvement".

Then there's what you might call the adaptive-reuse coffin. When Ed Kienholz, an installation artist, died in 1994, his wife and artistic collaborator, Nancy, arranged his body in the front seat of a 1940 Packard Coupe, with a bottle of 1931 Chianti beside him, a dollar bill and a deck of cards in his pocket and the ashes of Smack, his dog, in the trunk. "He was set for the afterlife," wrote Robert Hughes, the art critic. "To the whine of bagpipes, the Packard, steered by his widow Nancy Reddin Kienholz, rolled like a funeral barge into the big hole. All in all, it was the most Egyptian funeral ever held in Idaho."

Meanwhile, the fantasy coffin is no longer a phenomenon that's confined to West African shores. At Michigan-based Eternal Image, sports fans can have coffins decked out in the colours and logos of the Mets, the Red Sox and other major league baseball teams (The Star Trek line is among the latest additions to the collection).

From Jenks, Oklahoma, Hot Rod Caskets designs and produces models for firefighters such as the Smoke Eater, which has attachments for pike poles. For members of the military, the Uncle Sam model comes in desert sand and olive green with hex bar handles and a camouflage lining. The company also caters to Harley-Davidson fans with coffins that have plenty of tread plate trim. "Some might claim that our caskets are overbuilt," says owner Corey Parks on the company's website, "and my answer is always, 'That's the whole point.'"

In Nottingham, Vic Fearn & Company, coffin makers since the 1860s, has taken a leaf out of Ghana's book. In recent years, the company has been making personalised coffins to the specifications of families, or their eventual users. Its craftsmen have created, among other things, a river barge, a vintage Rolls-Royce, a yacht, a giant guitar and a huge egg for a woman who wanted to be buried in the foetal position.

For building contractor John Gratton-Fisher, the firm built a dumpster into which his "organic remains" will eventually be deposited. And for Pat Cox, a nurse and music teacher with a passion for the ballet, a giant dance shoe covered in pink silk will be what lowers her into the ground, with the aid of reinforced satin laces. "It doesn't daunt me, the thoughts of lying in there afterwards," Pat told a reporter. "But it would in a box. I think an ordinary standard coffin is just so morbid, so scary." My coffin maker Eric would no doubt agree.

Shortly before leaving for Ghana, I decided on a shape for my coffin. It's something with great meaning for me. For a start, I live close to it, and if I stick my head far enough out of my apartment window, I can just see the top of it. More than a decade ago, it served as a kind of lucky charm for me when I was wondering how on earth I was going to move to New York (my lifelong dream). I kept a miniature version of it with me wherever I went and I'd put it next to my bed, whether at home in London or in a hotel on assignment overseas. It now sits proudly on a chest of drawers in my New York apartment. "It's the nearest thing we have to heaven in New York," Deborah Kerr tells Cary Grant in the 1957 movie *An Affair to Remember*. It's my favourite piece of modern architecture. It's the Empire State Building.

And now I'm sitting next to Eric, showing him a tourist souvenir model of the building I picked up before heading to Ghana. Eric has never seen the building before, nor has he heard of it, so I've given him a postcard, which I also brought with me to show him what it looks like as it soars skyward through the forest of skyscrapers that is my Manhattan home.

On the flight over, I'd been slightly worried that the Empire State Building might be too difficult for a coffin maker to replicate. After all, its surface is extremely detailed, with hundreds of windows, vertical Art Deco lines and a delicate spire. But as I sit here admiring a giant crab to my left and a jumbo jet in front of me, I realise my commission will be easy. "Yes, I can do this," Eric says confidently. I believe him. Eric suggests making the lid as a hinged double door on the front of the building. It seems a good idea. I ask whether, to save money on shipping, the spire could be detachable and could travel inside the main structure. No problem, says Eric.

Then he gets out the tape measure. It's the moment I've been dreading. I stand up and try to look as if getting measured up for a coffin is something I do every day. But I can feel my heart racing, and the smile on my face is quickly turning to a rictus (one I feel must resemble the ghoulish grimaces of those mummies in Sicily). In an attempt to distract myself, I gaze out at the waves crashing on to the beach opposite, but it doesn't help – being measured for one's own coffin is, let's face it, extremely unsettling. Eric does the job cheerfully and efficiently, like a tailor measuring someone for a suit. But unlike a new suit, it's not something I'll necessarily look all that good in.

A few months later, back in New York, I receive by e-mail the first of a set of photographs taken by Kawther at eShopAfrica. She's helping me arrange the shipment of my coffin and sweetly promised to send me pictures of the various stages of construction. First to arrive is a shot of a simple wooden tower. A few weeks later, Art Deco details have been added to the façade and the spire is complete. Next comes a photo of the whole structure, painted with an undercoat. One of the pictures – my favourite – shows Eric inside it, peering out through the doors at the front.

By January the coffin is ready, bar the painting. At this point, Kawther e-mails me to say Eric wants to know what colours I'd like it decorated in. We'd discussed this in Accra. Eric agreed with me that replicating the grey-pewter colour of the original souvenir model would make the thing dull and rather depressing when enlarged to coffin size. We'd decided to make it more colourful.

Now, here's my dilemma – the adventurer in me says I should

let Eric come up with some wild, crazy colours of his choosing. That would make it more authentically Ghanaian, after all. But my adventurer's spirit is in constant battle with my inner control freak. I know which will win – and in the end, the control freak decides that, because this coffin is going to sit in my apartment for a while, it should really go with the décor. I look around for something to photograph and send to Eric so that he can match the colours. I know almost immediately what that should be – Kit's painting.

Kit Barker was a British painter and a great family friend. In the 1950s and 1960s, he produced bold abstracts based on landscapes. He lived in New York for a few years, joining the bohemian set in the Bowery in the 1950s with his wife, Ilse, a German-born poet who wrote under the name of Kathrine Talbot. Kit died many years ago, but when I was a child, he was one of my favourite adults. He always said I was his favourite person – something I loved, chiefly because he called me a "person" rather than a little girl, which made me feel very grown up.

His *Stone Falling into Water* – a large abstract in cobalt blues, turquoises and blacks with flashes of white and dashes of brick red – hung on loan for many years in the sitting room at the house where I grew up, Pear Tree Farm. It was my father's favourite art-work. I was always fascinated by it, too. I'd spend hours gazing into its deep shadows and ambiguous forms, imagining all kinds of far-off places.

When Kit died in 1988, Ilse asked for the painting back again, since her only assets were by then her late husband's works, some of which she hoped to sell. Yet for years, *Stone Falling into Water* sat in her garage. I dreamed of buying it and bringing it back into our family's possession. But I was living in London at the time, and my small flat had no space for a painting on such an ambitious scale. Then I moved to New York. After renovating my apartment, I decided it needed a piece of art – and I immediately thought of Kit's painting. One wall seemed to be asking for it to be hung there. I rang up Ilse and arranged to see it again.

On my next trip to England, I had lunch at Ilse's house. She told me stories of New York and the heady days when she and Kit had partied with famous abstract expressionist painters. By the time I left, I'd written her a cheque and the painting was in the back of my car. A couple of months later, it was hanging on the wall of my New York apartment, looking as if it had been commissioned for that very space. Even the colours matched the spines of the books on my shelves and the Chinese ceramics dotted about the place.

Now, as I contemplate the painting of my coffin, there's no question about it – Kit's colours must decorate it. I e-mail a photograph of the painting to Kawther and wonder which hues Eric will pick out for the windows, doors, Art Deco lines and spire of my own Empire State Building.

About a month later, Kawther tells me the coffin is finished. She's attached a final photograph of it standing in Eric's workshop, ready for shipment. Opening up the attachment, I can't believe what I see – instead of simply picking red, blue and black for the different architectural features of the building, Eric has actually recreated the painting itself across its surface. It's astonishing – he hasn't copied it exactly, but he's captured perfectly the spirit of the work, the deep blues, the shadows and the splashes of red, the mysterious far-off places. My coffin is a work of art.

What's more, so many people are bound up in it. Some of them are alive – me, for one, and Kawther, who helped me arrange all this, and of course Eric. But the dead are in there too – Gregory Johnson, the architect who designed the Empire State Building, for instance, and the hundreds of workers who bolted the beams together. Then there's my father, who loved Kit's painting so much, and most of all, Kit himself, the first grown-up to treat me as an adult and perhaps the first to guide me into the afterlife. His art has found new expression at the hand of a coffin painter from the distant shores of West Africa – people certainly live on in the most unexpected ways.

My coffin has arrived in New York. On the airway bill under the section for "Nature and quantity of goods," is typed: "State Empire Coffin. DIMS: 83x55x184cms x 1." (I'm wondering what the customs officials made of it.) With the packing case removed, the spire restored to its rightful place on top of the main shaft and the smell of fresh paint lingering about it, my Ghanaian Empire State Building is now standing in my apartment. It looks nothing short of fantastic. On the opposite wall is Kit's painting. The two versions are looking at each other, perhaps a little suspiciously at first but, yes, I think there's mutual approval.

But now the unpacking is over, that moment has come – the moment when I have to try it for size. In fact, the prospect of stepping into my coffin reminds me of story I once read about a South Korean craze whereby, as part of "well-being" courses, participants write then read their wills, dress up in shrouds and get into coffins. The lids are nailed down and there they lie for about fifteen minutes, supposedly contemplating how better to value their lives. My favourite quote in the article is from Chung Jae-hyun, a board director at the Korea Association of Thanatology, a group of academics who study death-related issues: "Real death is totally different than this," he sniffed. (Really, Mr Chung, you think so?)

The prospect of being buried alive has long been a source of terror. In its most extreme form, it's known as taphophobia (from the Greek taphos or "grave") and several famous people have suffered from it. Frédéric Chopin's dying wish, for his heart to be removed before his burial, stemmed from this fear (the heart of the Polish composer now sits in a jar of alcohol in Warsaw's Church of the Holy Cross). On his deathbed in 1799, George Washington insisted that he should not be buried for three days after his death, just to make sure he'd really gone.

Edgar Allan Poe captured these fears in *The Premature Burial*, a horror story in which an unnamed narrator describes his terror of being buried alive. Poe's narrator, whose fear regularly sends him into an unconscious state, provides a horrifying description of waking up in a confined space. He tries to scream "but no voice issued from the cavernous lungs, which oppressed as if by the weight of some incumbent mountain, gasped and palpitated, with the heart, at every elaborate and struggling inspiration". On moving, his arms strike "a solid wooden substance, which extended above my person at an elevation of not more than six inches from my face. I could no longer doubt that I reposed within a coffin at last".

Poe's narrator, as we discover, turns out simply to have been unconscious in a boat. But such stories no doubt contributed to the Victorian practice burying people in a grave with a bell hanging on their tombstone linked to the coffin below by means of a rope or chain. This could be pulled so that, in the event of an overly hasty burial, the occupant would be saved by the bell.

In 1852, George Bateson, a British inventor, patented a device under the name Bateson's Belfry that incorporated a miniature campanile on top of the casket equipped with an iron bell (the inventor's own terror was such that eventually he committed suicide by dousing his body in linseed oil and setting himself alight in what was a premature cremation). These days, of course, one could take a contemporary approach by requesting to be buried with a mobile phone – with its battery well charged, of course.

With such thoughts in mind, I've decided to get into my coffin only in the presence of someone else. My friend Lisa Waltuch has kindly offered to indulge me before we head out for dinner together. I'm glad she's standing there as I close the doors, shutting myself in. Once inside, it's a tight fit. Eric certainly got his measurements just right – the top of the main section, just below the spire, is almost brushing my head. Strangely enough, being inside is not as bad as I'd expected (although I'm quite pleased to get out).

As the weeks go by, I get quite used to my coffin. It's part of the furniture now. Full of curiosity, friends have been trooping around to have a look. I even get to pass on news of its arrival to Tony Malkin of the Empire State Building Company. By chance, soon after taking delivery of my coffin, I'm commissioned to write a feature about the building's ambitious energy efficiency programme, part of a plan to make it a green building. At the end of a phone interview with Tony, I can't resist telling him why my own version of the building is sitting in my apartment. After finishing the call, I e-mail him a picture. A few minutes later, I get the reply. "I hope you correctly licensed the use of our image!" he deadpans. "If not, we will hunt you down to your grave!"

5

PACKING FOR ETERNITY

Gifts for the Afterlife in Hong Kong

In a small shop in Hong Kong, I'm looking at a large plasma television set in a matte silver finish. On its screen is an image of a Chinese water lily pond on which delicate pink blooms hover above layers of waxy green leaves. The TV comes in three sizes, each with a natty little remote. But I'm finding it hard to operate and when I do manage to hit the channel-down button, the lily pond shot remains stubbornly on the screen.

This is partly because the remote has no batteries in it. Oh, and it's made of cardboard. What's more, it'll be tough getting a different picture (or any sound, for that matter) as the TV is also made of cardboard. The lily pond view is a colour photocopy, enlarged to fit the screen and stuck on with glue. Its surface has bubbled slightly in one corner. This won't bother the set's eventual owners, however. They're dead.

This is the Tin Chau Hong Worshipping Material store and the TVs, remotes and everything else here are destined for the deceased relatives of Chinese families. Set light to them and, as pieces of silver cardboard turn to flakes of black ash, they'll be whisked off into the afterlife for the enjoyment of the ancestor spirits. One of the biggest annual remembrance celebrations of the year is approaching. At Qing Ming (which falls on the first day of the fifth solar term, usually in early April), thousands of people go out to cemeteries on the hillsides around Hong Kong, tend to their family graves and burn paper gifts for their ancestors in the netherworld.

The ancestors are a demanding bunch, it seems. To judge by what's on the shelves here, you'll need pretty much everything in the afterlife that you had (or would have liked to have had) in life. Most important – let's not forget, this is Hong Kong – are paper gold ingots, as well as chequebooks, cardboard Amex cards and paper money, complete with serial numbers and Chinese bank chops. Known as Hell Bank notes, each bears the signature and image of Yu Wang, the bearded and fearsome-looking Jade Emperor, and is countersigned by Yen Loo, the King of Hell.

Keeping up appearances is important in the netherworld, too, for the store is well stocked with shoes and clothing, as well as with accessories such as a shaving set, a hair dryer and a set of dentures. There are gold wristwatches (Rolex, of course), and items of jewellery.

The ladies' shoes are particularly chic – yellow and pink ones with high heels, thin straps and gold foil buckles. Smart paper suits, shirts and ties and mandarin jackets are all folded neatly into boxes wrapped in cellophane. You can pick up a paper T-shirt or perhaps a zip-up jacket, for a more stylish ghostly moment. A cardboard iron (complete with string wiring and paper plug) will keep those paper clothes neatly pressed.

You've no reason to be bored in the afterlife either. As well as the plasma TVs, diversions include a cardboard mah-jong set, a Game Boy and an electric guitar. A couple of paper footballs and a cardboard-and-string tennis racquet hang above the store entrance. For the super-rich, whole houses are available for incineration, complete with effigies of servants. They take weeks to make and come fully furnished (although I don't suppose they're covered by fire insurance).

Meanwhile, the dinners for the dead will leave no one hungry. A display table in the centre of the store is piled high with dim sum sets in small round baskets (steamed dumplings are crafted from tissue paper), fancy sponges and cupcakes (made from rubber foam) and boxes of swallow's tongues, a rare Chinese delicacy, if rather tasteless in the cardboard version. For those who prefer junk food, there are six-packs of Coca-Cola (the name has been changed to "Caixin-Cele"), tubs of pot noodles and a boxed set with a paper burger, fries, ketchup and a soda. It's an unhealthy diet on which to nourish your ancestors, but then since they're already dead, why worry?

Burning paper objects for the ancestors is a Chinese tradition dating back centuries and reflects the traditional reverence for printed paper, which was associated with literacy and the trappings of a civilised society.

However, manufacturers have always managed to keep up with times. A photograph taken by Sidney D. Gamble in Beijing in 1924 shows a life-size paper version of a Ford Model A, with movable wheels, working doors, a steering wheel and a chauffeur dressed in a Chinese-style coat and a big western hat.

When I lived in Hong Kong in the 1980s, I was always intrigued as Qing Ming approached, and shops would fill up with paper clothing, cardboard electronics and other flammable goods. I love Hong Kong for this insane blend of hallowed custom and contemporary consumerism. In a city of dazzling skyscrapers, global financial markets and expensive designer stores, you still find at the base of each soaring tower block a tiny red shrine where joss sticks burn and offerings of paper and food are laid out.

Living in Hong Kong, I treated Qing Ming like any public holiday – a precious extra day off in a place where few employers gave you more than two weeks' annual vacation. News reports of the traffic jams (human and motorised) that built up across the territory as a sizeable chunk of Hong Kong's seven-million-strong population headed out to the cemeteries gave me another incentive to stay at home and watch a movie.

So now I've come back to attend the Qing Ming festival, partly to find out what happens to all those paper objects, but also to observe a festival that demonstrates how we humans reinforce our relationships with the dead, maintaining a connection with them, wherever we think they are.

Once inside the Tin Chau Hong Worshipping Material store, I can't resist buying some of its paper merchandise. First, I select a box set containing a paper gold watch, a pair of glasses, a smart silver cardboard mobile phone and a Louis Vuitton wallet with matching belt (the famous "LV" initials appear as "XV" in the paper version). I've got a pair of those high-heeled shoes, a basket of dim sum and the cardboard electric iron (the neat freak within me insists). Then I collect great handfuls of gold bullion and stock up on cash – wads of those Hell Bank notes. The denominations are impressive (the highest is $100,000,000). If I can't get rich in life, I'll certainly be able to do so in death.

Many people dismiss the notion that you can take material goods with you into the afterlife – my father, for one. He also held that obsessing about possessions while alive was a thoroughly bad idea. Possessions, he always said, were dispensable. "One day you have something. The next you don't," was his philosophical response to the removal from our house by burglars of a lovely antique French mantel clock (although he was very sad to lose it).

Fa relished the idea of giving everything away after his death. To divide his possessions up fairly, he announced one day that he'd be placing stickers on every item in the house. More valuable or interesting items would have, say, five stickers, while less desirable ones would only have one. When he died, he explained, we'd all have a quota of stickers and take turns choosing the things we wanted. For something more valuable or desirable, we'd have to forfeit more stickers.

What he didn't explain was how he was going to put out the stickers once he was dead. However, true to his philosophy, towards the end of his life, he started giving away things – fishing equipment, binoculars and the like – to people he knew would appreciate them. I have a few of the tools of his trade, including his tape measure, a beautiful object encased in leather with brass fittings. As an agricultural surveyor, he never went anywhere without it. I love to pull out the canvas tape with which he measured so many fences, walls, doors and windows.

I've tried to adopt Fa's dispassionate attitude towards things – not always successfully. I once managed to remain calm when my Renault 5 disappeared from the place I'd parked it the previous evening. I later found out it had been towed, but at the time, I assumed it had been stolen. "Once I had a car. Now I don't," I said to myself, thinking how proud Fa would be of my Zen-like approach to the whole affair – until I realised I was late for a dinner party and had no cash for a taxi. Then I completely lost it.

While I was very fond of that little car, it wouldn't have occurred to me to take it to my grave (although I suppose like Ed Kienholz, I could've saved it as my coffin). Yet, some people like to keep the more portable things they've acquired in life with them in death. For as well as getting relatives to burn goods for you in the afterlife, you can also be buried with them.

We all know the old saying, "You can't take it with you", but the funeral industry is helping us do precisely this. Among the features of the caskets manufactured by Batesville Casket Company, the giant US coffin manufacturer, is the "MemorySafe Drawer", which has a velvet interior in which, says Batesville, you can house "cherished keepsakes" or "private mementos" such as Bibles, crosses, signet rings and photographs of the family – perhaps even a mobile phone.

For if Ghanaians like to be buried inside giant wooden cell phones, a lot of people now want to be buried *with* their mobile devices. John Jacobs, a criminal defence attorney who died in 2005, was not only buried with his mobile phone – his wife Marion Seltzer put his number on the gravestone in the cemetery in Paramus, New Jersey. She continues to pay the monthly charge so that, although the phone's batteries are as dead as their owner, callers can still leave voicemail for the former lawyer. "He would love this," she told reporters. "He liked attention."

Being buried with favourite possessions is not a new idea, of course. Providing the dead with grave goods, as they're known, is a practice dating back to the world's earliest civilizations. In southwest France, a bison leg with the flesh still attached was found in the tomb of a Neanderthal man who lived roughly seventy thousand years ago. Archaeologists think the leg was intended to leave the dead person with something to eat.

Anglo-Saxon kings also provisioned themselves richly. In 1939, excavations of a grassy mound in Suffolk, England, revealed a ninety-foot wooden vessel containing priceless treasures. The Sutton Hoo ship was the burial tomb of Raedwald, King of East Anglia, one of the country's first monarchs. The king had himself buried with weapons, drinking horns, silver dishes, shoes, buckles, belts and priceless jewels in gold and silver. The most famous item in the stash – now a star exhibit at the British Museum – is the king's helmet. This magnificent mask-like object, decorated with pictures of warriors, has a moustache, eyebrows, holes for his nostrils and black eyeholes through which the ancient king seems to be staring out at us.

However, it was in 1974, when a farmer in northwest China was digging a well, that the most astonishing example of grave goods was unearthed, after more than two thousand years below ground. What the farmer found was the life-sized clay head of a warrior, the first clue to one of the greatest archaeological discoveries of the twentieth century. That terracotta head belonged to an infantryman who was part of a seven-thousand-strong imperial army that included horsemen and charioteers, complete with bronze chariots made up of three thousand separate pieces.

The man who commissioned this army was Qin Shi Huang, the first emperor of China, who lived between 259 and 210 BC. As well as shoring up his post-mortal military strength, the emperor had servants, acrobats, administrators and officials fashioned from terracotta and buried with him. Pets were recreated, too, for bronze birds have been found in the burial pits. Perhaps most remarkable is the individual workmanship on the soldiers, each with different facial features, clothing, armour and body types. These figures weren't conceived as public art or pieces of sculpture. They were practical tools, essential for battles in the next world.

These grave goods may represent just a fraction of what lies beneath the huge mysterious mound east of the city of Xian. The tomb itself has not been excavated yet, but it's thought to be at the heart of an immense underground metropolis covering an area about the size of Manhattan, with lavish palaces whose chambers contain treasures of untold richness. Writing a century after the tomb was constructed, Han historian Sima Qian describes how more than seven thousand men from all over the empire were brought to the site to work on a project of breathtaking ambition – an entire imperial infrastructure, all for the emperor's convenience in the afterlife.

In 2008, the British Museum managed to secure a loan of twelve terracotta soldiers, as well as eight acrobats – the largest group ever to leave China. The exhibition was a hit. Opening hours had to be extended until midnight to cope with the crowds. When I tried to book a ticket a month in advance, none were available so I turned up early one morning hoping to get one of the five hundred tickets released every day. After queuing for an hour and a half, I secured an entry – at 12.10pm precisely, I was told.

Once inside the dimly lit dome of the museum's magnificent Reading Room, temporarily converted to house the show, the atmosphere was tomb-like. Hundreds of people huddled around the displays of gold, bronze and ceramic objects. Visitors were so tightly clustered around the exhibits that without joining the slow, shuffling queue, it was impossible to see anything, so I headed into the second half of the exhibition to view the soldiers themselves.

I'd seen them before. On a 1986 trip around China, I visited the site in Xian. Looking down at ranks of the clay figures from a wooden platform, it was the sheer numbers that had impressed me. Here in the British Museum, it was their humanity. I was on the same level as the individual figures, staring them in the eyes, scrutinising their features, their hairstyles and their uniforms – every detail created for an existence in the afterlife.

I couldn't help wondering what Qin Shi Huang would have thought had he known that, centuries after his death, some of his soldiers would end up thousands of miles away, a trip that would take them via Beijing on a series of jumbo jets to London, where they would be loaded into trucks, delivered to the exhibition halls of the British Museum and positioned beneath high-tech lighting.

More than 850,000 people visited the soldiers in London, while another 400,000 or so saw them when the show moved to the High Museum of Art in Atlanta. Newspapers published features about the warriors, postcards and glossy exhibition catalogues were printed and a BBC TV documentary was made about how the show was staged. The emperor Qin Shi Huang had badly wanted to live on. And perhaps he really is out there in the afterlife, conquering new territories with his terracotta army. But if not, his wish for eternal life has still been fulfilled – albeit in a way he might not have predicted.

Otto von Bismarck, the nineteenth-century German aristocrat statesman, was unequivocal in his assessment of the life beyond. "Without the hope of an afterlife," he famously proclaimed, "this life is not even worth the effort of getting dressed in the morning." As an energetic and influential politician, Bismarck's belief presumably did allow him to get dressed every morning, and perhaps he was happier for it. Studies have found that confidence in the existence of an afterlife – at least of a pleasant one – is associated with better mental health, although the authors of such studies admit that happier, more positive people are those more likely to embrace such belief.

As an optimistic atheist, my father needed no such reassurance in order to get dressed every morning. Quite the contrary – he was an extremely early riser and loved to boast about how many years he was adding to his life by waking a couple of hours earlier than the rest of the family. My approach to life is similar. If this is all there is then, as the song goes, "let's keep dancing". Let's enjoy every last moment of it, get up as early as possible and go to bed way too late (although it helps to take a nap in the afternoon).

Still, in our lack of faith in an afterlife, my father and I seem in the minority. In the UK, just over half of the people surveyed by Theos, a think tank, said they believed in some form of life after death, whether physical or spiritual. Few Americans doubt its existence. In a survey of people over the age of fifty, three-quarters of respondents agreed with the statement, "I believe in life after death," according to the AARP, which conducted the survey in 2007. About half said they believed in the existence of ghosts or spirits, while almost nine in ten respondents confirmed that they believed in heaven. Two-thirds claimed their confidence in life after death had strengthened with age. Even Woody Allen once remarked, "I do not believe in an afterlife, although I am bringing a change of underwear."

So if most people hope to reach an afterlife, what do they expect to find when they get there? The answer is, different things. For the Chinese, thoughts of the netherworld call up images of an island far out into the ocean or a haven somewhere in the sacred mountains of the west (although if Hong Kong's paper goods or Qin Shi Huang's terracotta armies are anything to go by, the Chinese afterlife may not look that different from real life).

In the Christian world, heaven is a beautiful paradise; a reward for the faithful and a place for reunion with loved ones. Muslims espouse a similar vision, enriched with promises of milk, honey and, at least for men, pleasures of the flesh that were forbidden on earth.

For some, heaven is not necessarily the first stop after death. Christians may have a spell in purgatory, a temporary condition during which the soul is purified. In eastern religions, you may have to live several lifetimes via the process of reincarnation before you get there. Yet even these secondary lives offer the potential for something better. For India's Hindu untouchables, a belief in reincarnation helps them tolerate life at the bottom of the social and economic pyramid, raising the hope of an improvement in status next time around.

Traditional death rituals are all about the afterlife. What we do at the funeral plays a critical role in helping the dead reach whatever heaven they've been anticipating, for the funeral ceremony sits at the intersection between two worlds – the one the deceased recently inhabited, and the one to which he or she is now heading.

So we send our dead off with handfuls of goodwill, bucketfuls of love and the occasional sigh of relief. But we also burn paper offerings for them, bury them with food, clothes and precious jewels and recite prayers or chant spells. We bind the corpse into a foetal position, sending it out of the world in the manner in which it entered it. We mummify the dead, equipping them with the well-preserved bodies they require in the Egyptian afterlife. We place coins on their eyes to pay the ferryman to take them to the other side.

The dead also need a mode of transport. The Vikings had their ships – symbols of Norse power in life – as graves. Fire, as Hindus will tell you, is also a powerful engine, speeding the soul into the next life amid a burst of flames, whether via cremation in the giant effigy of a Balinese cow or on a pyre by the Ganges in the holy city of Varanasi.

And as with any trip, cash, maps and directions come in handy. Now in the British Museum, the lid of the inner coffin of Hornedjitef, an Egyptian priest, is decorated with a chart of the heavens as a navigation aid. A copy of the Book of the Dead – a sort of guidebook written by a priest on a papyrus roll – helped Egyptian mummies plot a course through the difficult and dangerous passage to the afterlife. The Tibetans have a similar book, which illuminates the paths humans take between death and rebirth.

For the Chinese, money is critical – their journey to the netherworld is an expensive one. Burning those paper Hell Bank notes and credit cards gives the dead the cash needed to bribe the officials they'll encounter on their passage to the spirit world, and with the rest they can make a down payment on a decent place for themselves once they arrive.

Meanwhile, those left behind devise elaborate schemes to prevent the spirit returning by accident. In Balinese funerals, the cremation tower is carried back and forth and spun around so the spirit loses its sense of direction. In the Buddhist death rites of Roi Et Province, in northwest Thailand, all kinds of things are done to stop the spirit returning to earth. The deceased's hair is parted down the middle, from the brow to the back of the neck (believed to help the dead forget the past). Tossing the shroud three times back and forth over the coffin adds to the confusion, as does reversing the ladder leading up to the family home. Much as we hate saying goodbye, we don't always want our dead to come back too soon.

Once the dead person's spirit has successfully left the earth, the next bit of the journey can be long and complex. Bridges must be crossed, gates entered, all manner of monsters battled. In their classic book *Celebrations of Death*, anthropologists Peter Metcalf and Richard Huntington describe how, at the climax of their death rites, Berawan communities in Borneo sing special songs giving the deceased detailed instructions on how to get to the land of the dead. The songs can last eight hours.

Here's what a Berawan soul needs to do: first it must bathe in the river. Then it should dress appropriately and, without looking back, climb into a canoe at the edge of the river and paddle upstream with a vigour that sends spray flying up from the oar. Speeding past longhouses, the soul eventually reaches a branch of the river that leads to a mountain range. Here it must disembark and find some of the betel nut leaves used for chewing in this part of the world. That's when the emissaries from the land of the dead show up. At this point, the Berawan funeral recital ends. The soul is now in good hands.

Of course, long before the funeral, good behaviour in life is considered a reliable way of improving the soul's chances of reaching a happy afterlife. Achievements and sacrifices made on earth are investments whose dividends can be spent in heaven. In seventeenth-century America, the private prayers and public devotions of the Puritans of New England reflected this belief, focusing on the approach of death, the salvation of the soul and the preparation for eternity. Primers and prayer books exhorted readers to be in a state of constant preparation for mortality. Earthly suffering, they explained, was a prelude to the afterlife; death was the final barrier – a glorious gateway to endless unity with Christ.

My father's lifelong view was that there was no afterlife, no heavenly gates to enter, no happy reunion with loved ones. "I have no future," he told me calmly one day, after it had become clear his cancer was terminal. "I have a past – and it's all been marvellous – and a present [which wasn't so great at that point, but he avoided stating the obvious]. But I have no future."

He was right. The only thing that lay ahead for him, as it turned out, was relentless discomfort and a painfully slow decline. Yet even Fa seems in the end to have modified his view of what lay ahead of him. His request to be scattered near his friends' graves in the Dorset countryside was surely an acknowledgment of some form of continued existence, if not for his soul then at least for his biological remains. And perhaps, as mortality approached, picturing his ashes in a beautiful corner of West Dorset gave someone with no belief in an afterlife a delicate but continuing thread with the world he'd loved.

So powerful is our attachment to the idea of an afterlife that we've often sought out hard evidence for it. In her entertaining account of the subject, *Spook*, Mary Roach tells us that during spiritualism's nineteenth-century heyday, mediums appeared to extrude through their orifices a physical manifestation of the spirits. This ectoplasm, says Roach, provided "a link between life and afterlife, a mixture of matter and ether, physical and yet spiritual, a 'swirling, shining substance' that unfortunately photographed very much like cheesecloth."

The quirky exploits of spiritualists and mediums reveal a powerful desire by humans to establish a connection with the dead – a faint voice from the other side; a barely perceptible twitch of the planchette on the Ouija board; a flutter in the wind that tells us Granny's calling. We crave the scantest evidence of this connection because confirmation from those who've made it over there will assure us of the afterlife's existence. Then, O Death, where is thy sting?

For the Chinese, the wall dividing the living from the ancestors in the afterlife is a porous one. After death, the soul flits in and out of its owner's body, so relatives wave its clothes over the corpse to tempt it back into it. Only when it appears finally to have left the building, do mourners pronounce the individual dead and proceed with the funeral. Ancestors are treated as a part of the family long after they've died, with the home shrine stocked with joss sticks and offerings.

In Chinese culture (where doctrines often blend Taoism, Buddhism and Confucianism), the dead have the power to intervene in the affairs of the living – for good or ill. So rather than pondering the fate of the soul, as Christians and others do, the spiritual question of greatest concern to the Chinese is how to encourage the ancestors to bring health and success to their descendents. The magnificent bronze vessels created by the Shang and Zhou dynasties were designed for regular banquets in which food and wine were offered to the ancestors in the belief that they would in turn look after the living.

Providing nourishment is one way to solicit a caring attitude from the dead. Another is to find a decent spot for their tomb. Where space permits, geomancy or *feng shui* can establish an optimum site for the grave. A view of water (representing money) is always desirable. And hillsides are best for neutral *feng shui* – and neutral is good, for energy that's too powerful can, like high-voltage electricity, cause no end of trouble.

At times, living and dead come together in a head-on collision. During the Hungry Ghosts Festival in the seventh month of the lunar year (usually late August), the doors are flung open between the three realms – heaven, hell and the domain of the living – and the restless ghosts return to earth to wander about looking for food and wreaking vengeance on those who wronged them during their lives. To appease them, families burn joss sticks and lay out chicken, pork, rice, fruit and sweets. The wandering spirits are longing for a bit of entertainment, so throughout the month, communities stage lavish Chinese operas.

In Taiwan, a rather unusual method was used to prevent dead spirits from bothering the living – by marrying them off. In traditional Chinese society, women only acquire ancestors through marriage, so a daughter who dies before reaching marriageable age cannot be honoured on the family altar. To provide that line of ancestry, a husband must be found for her – and the matchmaking is done by bald-faced entrapment.

The "bait" is laid by placing money on a road in a small red envelope (used by the Chinese for cash gifts at occasions such as birthdays and weddings). When an unsuspecting male picks up the money envelope, the dead girl's relatives leap out from behind a bush and announce that he must now be the groom in the posthumous marriage of their daughter. Fear of being haunted by the girl's ghost usually encourages the young man to comply, but the offer of a generous dowry provides an added incentive.

The ceremony is much like a real wedding, except that standing in for the bride is a small effigy, which is placed by her ancestral tablet (the wooden representation of her soul on the family altar). With the effigy bride and her real-life groom united, banquets are held at the homes of both families. Then the ancestral tablet is separated from the effigy, the clothing returned to the company that rents accoutrements for such occasions and the remains of the effigy bride are burned. Thereafter, the groom's only responsibility is to place his spirit bride's ancestral tablet on his family altar and supply it with regular offerings, as he would if he'd married the girl in real life. And yes, he can still marry a live woman.

Anthropologist David Jordan, who documented this practice while living in a Taiwanese village in the 1960s, found the bride effigies a little unsettling. In his book, *Gods, Ghosts, and Ancestors*, he describes one. With a narrow strip of wood forming her backbone, "arms were made from padded newspaper and were jointed at the shoulders to allow them to be lifted in dressing her. She wore a pair of trousers and a skirt of white, then a red dress [red being the traditional colour for Chinese bridal outfits], covered over with a white lace outer dress that was considered part of the red dress". The spirit bride also wore red children's shoes. Her hands – white gloves stuffed with newspaper – bore fake gold bracelets and rings, and around her neck was a gold pendant.

Most disturbingly, however, her head was a photograph of the smiling face of a woman cut out of a wall calendar. "A Chinese bride even at that time would not be smiling – she'd be looking rather demure and weeping at leaving her family," Jordan explains. "The smiling bride was not how you did it, and the fact that she was dead made it even creepier." Strange too, were the effigy's three layers of clothing, the traditional burial attire. So while she was being paired off as a bride, the daughter's effigy was also being honoured as a corpse.

Our relationship with death is a schizophrenic one. On one hand, we hide mortality behind a curtain of medical procedures, materialism and euphemism. On the other, we parade it across cinema and TV screens in its goriest incarnations, in what British writer Geoffrey Gorer once called "the pornography of death". For if real death has been buried, the entertainment industry has stepped in to resurrect the body. Crime shows invariably open with corpses – a mutilated cadaver stretched out on a morgue slab or a body in the woods, half eaten by wild animals. Hollywood's menu is replete with foul murders, vengeance killings and battlefield slaughters, not to mention the armies of ghosts and zombies that parade across its screens. Meanwhile, real death has a poor showing.

Thomas Lynch, the American undertaker poet, likens the modernisation of death to the introduction of the flushable toilet, which by quickly removing evidence of the "corruptibility of flesh" has stripped us of the ability to deal with this evidence. "It's the same with our dead," writes Lynch. "We are embarrassed by them in the way that we are embarrassed by a toilet that overflows the night that company comes. It is an emergency. We call the plumber."

It's also tempting to brush death off as something that happens to other people. Not so, says the *Onion*. World Health Organization officials, the satirical journal once reported, expressed disappointment that "despite the enormous efforts of doctors, rescue workers and other medical professionals worldwide, the global death rate remains constant at 100 percent".

In our technological age this is, to put it mildly, frustrating. We put men on the moon, extract living organs from one human and transplant them into another, talk to each other via devices that communicate wirelessly. But we've made no headway in combating what the *Onion* identifies as humanity's top health concern: "A metabolic affliction causing total shutdown of all life functions." Modern death is a failure.

What's also perplexing is the fact that death is at once certain and uncertain. We know we're going to die but we mostly don't know how or when. We can live the healthy life, cut back on drinking, increase our intake of broccoli and stick to the yoga programme, but one day – we've no idea when – we may be felled by cancer or flattened by a bus.

Death has a double anxiety, then, since it's certain we'll die and it can happen at any time. "This means that death is always with us," writes philosopher Todd May in his concisely titled book *Death*. "It haunts us. It accompanies every moment of our lives. We are never far from death, because it will inevitably happen and we cannot control the moment when it will."

And while we try to push it from our thoughts, death is always lurking beneath the surface of our consciousness. "Let sanguine healthy-mindedness do its best with its strange power of living in the moment and ignoring and forgetting," wrote psychologist and philosopher William James in 1902. "Still the evil background is really there to be thought of, and the skull will grin in at the banquet."

It's scary stuff. And the more we try to block out death, the more terrifying becomes its shadow. But we humans are practical beings. When we need shelter, we build a house. When we're hungry, we hunt, farm and cook. So when confronted with the terrifying vision of our impending mortality, we get really creative. After all, there's perhaps no human condition to which more attention has been devoted than death. We've formulated elaborate ceremonies to manage it, erected great architectural and intellectual edifices to honour it. Death inspires music, literature and poetry. Some say the afterlife is just part of this – a human invention designed to assuage our horror of annihilation.

But there's more. One theory claims that the fear of death

("mortality salience", as it's known) shapes not just our visions of an afterlife, but our entire world. The pillars propping up our culture – religion, education, materialism, capitalism, nationalism, the arts, philanthropy – are also cushions that keep us from bumping up against the prickly reality of our ultimate termination.

There's even a name for this hypothesis. With the alarming title Terror Management Theory, a group of academics posits that "mortality salience" has provided the seeds from which the whole of civilization has sprouted. Death, so the theory goes, is not just something that happens to us – it's central to our very being, informing much of what we do, what we believe in and the way we behave.

Developed by Jeff Greenberg, Sheldon Solomon and Tom Pyszczynski, Terror Management Theory has its roots in the work of Ernest Becker, a cultural and scientific anthropologist born in 1924. In his 1973 Pulitzer prize-winning book *The Denial of Death* (a copy of which Woody Allen's character gives to his girlfriend in *Annie Hall*), Becker argues that death awareness is a dynamic force, driving a great proportion of human activity.

Building on his work, the TMT theorists argue that, confronted with unavoidable annihilation, we respond in two ways. First, we construct a "cultural worldview" about the nature of our reality, one offering reassurance that the world is orderly and meaningful and that we're not wasting our time in it. Second, we build self-esteem, which reassures us that we're living up to the values of our particular cultural worldview. So we run the London marathon or run for office, help at the local jumble sale or help the starving – because we want to be *part of something bigger*.

Possession of mortality salience is also thought to be one of the ways in which we differ from other creatures. Of course, there's no way of knowing whether animals perceive death in the way we do (and on encountering their dead, elephants fall silent and fondle the remains ceremoniously as if grieving for a loss). But perhaps it's why cows haven't built their equivalent of the Empire State Building and mice haven't put a fellow rodent on the moon.

While all this may be true, terror management theory seems

a little bleak. After all, the academics don't mention the possibility that we're doing all these things because we want to enjoy life and meet new people, help our fellow humans – or simply because we're looking for something fun to do at the weekend.

Yet, for me, TMT and similar theories make a lot of sense. It seems highly plausible that philanthropic legacies, religious beliefs and artistic and sporting achievements are partly motivated by our wish to cheat death of its finality. Mortality salience theories also go a long way towards explaining why we make our exits in certain ways. Nowhere is awareness of our own death expressed more clearly than in the manner in which we choose to leave the terrestrial world. We fear death's definitive ending, so we do whatever we can to turn that ending into a new beginning.

For Ghanaians, that means going off in a coffin in the shape of plane or a favourite car. For an ancient Chinese emperor, it meant taking along an army of terracotta soldiers. For the Egyptians, it meant consulting a guidebook to the afterlife. Today, it might mean being buried with your mobile phone. In short, the ways in which we leave this world speak volumes about the uneasy relationship we have with our own transience.

On the face of it, eternity sounds like a good thing – an escape from the grim clutches of death. Isn't that what we all secretly hope for, whether we're religious or not? In fact, part of me still thinks my death might never happen – that I may against the odds manage to escape alive. What then? Eternal life would stretch out before me. Yet eternity comes with looming uncertainties that, when you start to consider them, make death actually look like an agreeable alternative.

Many have mulled over this in the past, Shakespearean characters among them. Hamlet fears the "undiscover'd country from whose bourne no traveller returns", as he speculates on the dreams that may come after we've "shuffled off this mortal coil".

Second-century Roman emperor Hadrian, the energetic conqueror and empire builder, also seems to have had misgivings about what awaited him. Shortly before his death, he wrote an intriguing poem musing on his post-mortal fate:

Little soul, little wanderer, little charmer,
Body's guest and companion,
To what places will you set out for now?
To darkling, cold and gloomy ones –
And you won't make your usual jokes.

So if an elixir guaranteeing an eternal afterlife were available, would we really drink it? I'm not sure I would. The prospect of eternity throws up all kinds of tricky questions – what age do you want to be, for example? Assuming you aren't left with your age and physical state at the time of your death (which for most of us would not be how we'd want to spend perpetuity), would you choose the beauty of youth, with all its uncertainty and emotional angst, or an older, more confident you, but one that's tired, frail and sagging in places?

To a control freak like me, the approach of death – the great unknown – is bad enough, without these kinds of questions. Then there's the anxiety that comes with the prospect of heading to an eternity of indeterminable form. What if you get there and the seats are uncomfortable, the food is terrible and you get stuck next to the guy shouting into his mobile phone?

And it's one of life's perversities that the things we most desire lose their appeal if we get them in boundless supply. I learned this lesson as a child when, after badgering my mother to let me eat more Angel Delight (a popular 1970s dessert made from pink powder and milk), she told me to go ahead and have as much as I liked. I eventually threw up. The promise of an end, on the other hand, makes everything far more delicious. Life is (or should be) made precious by the fact that its supply is limited.

And looked at another way, maybe it's actually death that makes us great. For, if we were to live forever, we'd have no need of leaving marks or creating legacies. But faced with an end, we leave behind things we reckon will have a longer shelf life than our patently frail human bodies. So we bequeath money to the local hospital, endow a scholarship, fund a park bench with our name on it, design a building, compose an opera or – in perhaps the most labour-intensive version – produce offspring. And, of course, some of us try to get our work in print.

This was something my father loved to do. In addition to his commentaries on drainage, Fa enjoyed contributing to debates about the Church of England, an institution for which he professed a great fondness, even though he was a non-believer. His letters on local diocesan issues or the church's broader role in society appeared in *Team News*, our parish weekly. Fa's became such a familiar name that the rector once came dashing over to invite him to join the fold, only to be disappointed to find a man unwavering in his atheism. But while he never joined the church, Fa kept writing his letters and articles.

Money can also extend the human spirit's reach that little bit further. And while large financial bequests often spark family rifts or lengthy lawsuits, the best ones are those helping the people surviving us to have a good time when we're gone. One friend, Tom Schuller, was surprised to receive a letter one day from the executors of the will of his godmother, a woman he'd not known well. The letter was brief and it ran along the following lines: "Miss Barbara Vincent-Jones has indicated in her will that £200 should be given to you 'for a fine dinner'. Please let me know where the check should be sent."

More than three centuries earlier, Oliver John, a surveyor who helped rebuild London after the great fire of 1666, devised a similar scheme, leaving money in his will for an annual roast meat dinner for the boys of the Blue Coat School at Christ's Hospital, Newgate. And today, Merton College, Oxford, is known for superb cuisine since an old Mertonian left an endowment specifically to feed the students.

This sort of scheme appeals to me. For although I envy those with a belief in the afterlife, nothing can wipe out my persistent conviction that when I die, that's it – no more games, no more parties, no more fine dinners. But other people can still play the games, hold the parties and eat the dinners. In fact, there's something reassuring about the idea of planning something fun for others to do after you're gone. You can't be there, of course. But in a way, it's something to look forward to, giving you that delicate but continuing thread connecting your future dead self with the world of the living.

I've yet to decide what that might be. A big party, perhaps, or a slap-up meal – alternatively I could invite all my friends to get together to set fire to my paper high-heeled shoes, my cardboard iron, the tissue paper dim sum set and those huge wads of Hell Bank notes.

Today is Qing Ming. It's one of those warm, soggy Hong Kong afternoons that hit you like a wet sponge. Armed with an umbrella, I'm heading to one of the territory's largest cemeteries. I once passed this graveyard every day on my way to work when my home was Shek O, a village on the island's far southeast coast.

In Shek O, I lived amid a motley collection of tin-roofed houses in what, as I enjoyed telling friends, was officially termed an "illegal erection". Planted on top of another building and with windows all around, I slept with the sound of the sea in my ears. Everything about living there was an adventure. To get to my house, I followed a tiny passage past a noodle stall, a Chinese temple where old men played mah-jong, and across what was essentially someone's backyard – a small courtyard where a family would eat dinner while a brown hen tethered to a brick pecked feverishly at a bowl of rice. Directions for my visitors therefore included the unusual phrase: "Go past the chicken on a string."

To get to the cemetery from Shek O, you take the number nine bus, a blue-and-cream Leyland Victory double-decker. Get on at the tiny terminus and, if you have nerves of steel, choose the front seat on the top deck. From the terminus, the bus makes an impressive three-point turn, heads up the hill and winds around a series of terrifying coastal curves where glorious views open up across the azure waters of the South China Sea. At a certain point, you'll catch a glimpse of a series of grey stone structures set on terraces that cling to the mountain slopes. This is the Chai Wan Chinese Permanent Cemetery.

It's a tranquil spot. Far from honking horns and hammering construction sites, Hong Kong's daily roar is reduced to a low hum. Trees rustle in the breeze. Dragonflies dart around (you can hear the buzz of their wings). Thousands of grave terraces – each numbered – cover several of the mountain's slopes, hugging its curves, leaving no space wasted. Like hillside rice paddies, they rise in steps up to the summit, where a thick fringe of sub-tropical foliage looks ready to pounce down over the cemetery wall.

Every grave is like a mini temple, featuring a tiny courtyard (the worshipping platform) and a small roof sheltering pictures of the deceased, captured in black-and-white photographs on ceramic tiles. As you clamber up the steep steps past row after row of graves, each with the faces of their occupants visible, you might sense a sound; a sort of murmuring. Is it your imagination, or is it the voices of the thousands of souls whispering to you from the afterlife? As always, in Hong Kong one is rarely alone.

The view from the top is spectacular. Beyond the grave terraces lies a shimmering landscape of tower blocks framed by sea and mountains. Urban drama has replaced what was once a rural valley of fishing villages and rice paddies known as Sai Wan. Now, clusters of tall public housing blocks compete in height with a mountain range behind. It's a battle between mixed concrete and natural rock as to who'll reach the heavens first.

Today, though, the main battle is getting to the cemetery. During Qing Ming, the Hong Kong Transport Department goes into overdrive. On its website, the list of arrangements runs for several pages, with details of traffic re-routings, extra buses, parking suspensions and closure of roads to large vehicles ("except hearses"). Meanwhile, at Chai Wan station, like ants fleeing the anthill, people pour out from Hong Kong's efficient subway system. I'm swept along with the crowd through the Hing Wah Shopping Centre and out again at the entrance to a steep road leading up to the cemetery.

Police officers with megaphones arrange and rearrange barricades to accommodate the flow of people. They stop the crowd every so often to let double-decker buses through. On one side of the road, hundreds of people are walking up the hill, swinging capacious red plastic sacks full of paper treasures. Meanwhile, on the other side of the road, visitors descend empty-handed – their goods are now well on the way to the afterlife.

At the entrance to the cemetery, notices posted by the Food and Environmental Hygiene Department (the agency responsible for public cemeteries), exhort worshippers to burn offerings only in the incinerators provided. It's not surprising such warnings are needed. Already, as I approach the rows of graves, I can smell burning cardboard and the thick perfume of incense. Fragments of blackened paper drift through the sky and smoke wafts up the hillside.

The cemetery slopes are crawling with families. The yellows, reds and blues of fleeces and raincoats combine with the pinks and purples of the paper offerings to create an explosion of colour against the dull grey of the grave-covered hillside. The old women employed to keep the cemetery clean (identified by their eccentric headgear of wide-brimmed straw hats covered in bin liners) ferry around big rusty tins, the incinerators. People chat loudly on mobile phones. Bored teenagers play with their Game Boys. It's a family day out.

The grave terraces are not the only place to visit the ancestors. Many more reside at the cemetery entrance in a large tower – the Cape Collinson Columbarium. Lack of burial space in Hong Kong has created a new type of high-rise building: the multi-story mausoleum. In columbaria across the territory, more than three hundred thousand niches store the cremated remains of dead individuals. And even these mortuary skyscrapers are filling up. On the "Available Niches Lookup" section of the Food and Environmental Hygiene Department website, the words "No Vacancy" come up in a search under the "New Niche" option in five of the six columbaria listed on the site.

Stylistically, the Cape Collinson Columbarium is undistinguished. Its octagonal form with an open centre represents the *bagua*, a Chinese cosmological symbol, but inside municipal efficiency prevails, with white tiled walls and a distinct absence of decoration. Two staircases with steel railings spiral up in opposite directions to the upper floors where, on every level, concentric walls following the building's octagonal format house neatly ranked grave niches, six layers high, each covered by a marble plaque of about nine inches by ten.

At the base of each wall, troughs to accommodate plant joss sticks and food offerings, while miniature vases attached to the front of the niche tablets hold tiny flower arrangements. Gold and red text engravings in the marble mark the names of the occupants who, as on the hillside tombs, stare out from small black-and-white photographs.

According to my calculations, this columbarium must contain almost sixty thousand niches, most holding two sets of ashes. As do the living in Hong Kong, here in this funerary skyscraper, the dead live cheek by jowl.

In front of one niche, an older woman squats below the pictures of her parents. With her hair in a chignon, she's dressed in a smart red jacket, black trousers and high-heeled shoes. At her feet are bowls of rice, piles of oranges and a clutch of joss sticks. The ancestors look down impassively at their daughter. But she's not paying attention to them. She's too busy tapping the keypad on her mobile phone. With a look of deep concentration on her face, she's oblivious to those in the domain of the spirits. They're being elbowed out by the technology of the terrestrial world.

By now, the industrial fans that ventilate the columbarium are fighting a losing battle. Like the vast mouths of terrifying gods, huge incinerators on every floor gobble up the offerings being thrust into them. Smoke from the joss sticks and paper conflagrations pours down the corridors. It's like being in a burning building, except it's not the building that's going up in flames – it's reams of paper money and cardboard TVs.

My eyes are streaming with tears and I'm starting to cough violently. Everyone around me is clutching tissues to their eyes. It looks like a mass mourning ritual except that no one seems remotely unhappy. Between sniffs and splutters, teenagers send each other text messages and families catch up on gossip. With all the chattering and phone rings, the atmosphere is more like a cocktail party than a ceremony honouring the dead.

I wander around the smoke-filled corridors for a while until the smoke gets too much. Turning to leave, I see the woman in the red jacket again. She's still squatting in front of her family niche, still tapping into her mobile phone.

But I was wrong about her – she's not ignoring her parents. She's not making a call or sending a text. Now I see what she's doing. She's flipping through the photographs stored on her phone. Finally she finds the one she wants. It's the smiling face of a chubby baby and, once it's on the screen, she turns it towards the sepia snapshots of her dead parents on their ceramic tile. With a great beam of pride on her face, she addresses them, chattering excitedly as she introduces them to their new great-grandchild. Paper goods are going up in flames all around. But in front of this niche, it's a mobile phone (not one made of cardboard) that's providing a connection to the afterlife.

6

RAISING PIGS

A Get-Together in the Philippines

If you happen to be strolling through Sagada at dusk, you'll notice a fragrance that feels dangerously potent. It comes from Angel's Trumpets, extravagant tubular flowers whose pendulous pink blooms have hallucinogenic properties. Every evening in this remote mountain village, they open their petals to release a heady perfume. In the Amazonian rainforest, Angel's Trumpets are prized for their ability to induce dreams foretelling the future and revealing the causes of death. But not in Sagada – here, death isn't lurking in the flowers. It's hidden in the mountains.

Sagada sits five thousand feet above sea level in the craggy Cordillera Mountains that cut through the Philippine province of Northern Luzon. Its settlements – known as *barangays* – drift across a valley at the upper end of a tributary of the Chico River amid forests of Benguet Pine, glassy lakes, clear waterfalls and limestone caves. Not far away, at Banaue, are the two-thousand-year-old rice terraces that Filipinos like to call the "Eighth Wonder of the World".

Lying about two hundred miles north of Manila, Sagada's spectacular landscape is home to the Igorots, a fiercely independent people whose language is Kankana-ey. Bubbling away like one of the cheerful brooks that tumble down the slopes around them, its gentle tone belies the fact that the Igorots once drove spears into their enemies and brought home the heads as trophies.

Today, Sagada is a peaceful place where everyone knows everyone and the town motto is: "We share what's good." By the standards of rural areas of the Philippines, it's relatively affluent. Neat homes have pitched tin-roofs painted green or red and balconies and terraces. Hillside gardens burst with nasturtiums, red hibiscus, blue petunias and pure white lilies.

But there's another presence in this idyllic domestic landscape – the rock itself. Jagged boulders sit uncompromisingly in the middle of vegetable patches. Needles of limestone jut up unexpectedly in front of a porch or next to a bedroom window in what seem like attempts by the mountain to thwart the domestication of its slopes. And if the rocks invade the living space of humans, humans have penetrated the mountain's deepest crevices – for this is where the people of Sagada bury their dead.

These days, some locals opt for the tranquillity of the Christian cemetery near the Church of St Mary the Virgin, a handsome if rather stout granite structure with two huge rose windows that has provided a vigilant presence over the valley since the early 1900s. In its cemetery, whitewashed gravestones, their backs turned towards the lower slopes, clamber up a steep grassy hill as if struggling to reach the heavens.

It's a bucolic resting place. But even so, many of Sagada's citizens still want to be laid to rest according to local custom – wrapped in ceremonial blankets, tied in the foetal position and carried down into the valleys. There, they're placed in wooden sarcophagi that are left hanging on cliff faces or lodged in the fissures and caverns of Sagada's jagged forests of stone.

Intrigued by tales of coffins in caves, I'm heading to Sagada. It's true that in weighing up burial options, this is not one I've so far considered. But while I doubt I'll settle on a final resting place in a coffin on the side of a Philippine mountain, I want to see what this highly unusual form of interment looks like.

From Manila, the Philippine capital, the first leg of my journey is a dramatic flight to Baguio, the mountain resort that's the starting point for long-distance buses to Sagada. After an hour winding up the Halsema Highway in a GT Trans Company bus (signs warning that this is an "Accident Prone Area"), we emerge into mist-shrouded mountains sliced at every opportunity by layer upon layer of terraces. On the lower slopes, they were planted with neat rows of vegetables but up here they're covered in dazzling green rice plantings. Small settlements cling precariously to the edge of the road as if the tarmac has some special magnetism preventing them from tumbling into the ravines below.

Between hairpin bends, random snippets of life flash into view – chickens peck the dirt enthusiastically, satellite dishes bristle on top of tin roofs and laundry flaps in the breeze. A concrete tomb surmounted by an iron cross sits in a garden. A giant billboard displaying all Ten Commandments casts its authority across the valley. I see fleeting glimpses of human dramas, too. On a stoop, a young woman sits crying, her hair covering her face. Next door, two men are engaged in a fierce argument that seems to concern a rusty cement mixer. What's the dispute? What's the girl's trouble? I'll never know. The bus moves on.

By the time we shudder to a halt in Sagada, it's late afternoon and my legs feel in desperate need of a stretch. I have the names of two people who know about cave burials, so after securing myself a room at the Saint Joseph Resthouse (a former seminary surrounded by a lovely garden), I call one of them, Siegrid Bangyay, to see if we can meet. Siegrid is a potter who supplements her income by working as a guide. She agrees to meet me tomorrow to take me through Echo Valley, the canyon where many of the coffins hang.

Then there's Villia Jefremovas, a Canadian anthropologist recommended to me by Lucy, an English friend living in Manila, and Neal, a photographer I called up to ask for advice for my trip. I don't have an address or phone number, but that's not a problem. When I stop in at the Log Cabin restaurant, owner Dave Gulian says that of course he knows Villia. Following his directions, I head through town and, next to a small provisions store, I clamber up a steep lane. Reaching a glass door, I hesitate. After all, it's not often in this era of e-mail and mobile phones that one turns up unannounced at a stranger's house. Seeing three people inside sitting around a circular wooden table, I worry even more about intruding. I knock gingerly.

From within come the words: "Is that Sarah?" I'm astonished. How can it possibly be that in this isolated mountain village, someone is expecting me? "Yes?" I answer, puzzled, as I push open the door. Stranger still, once inside, I know none of the people around the table. Then Neal, the photographer, introduces himself. Ah, now I recognise his voice. But what on earth is he doing here? Only yesterday, we'd spoken by phone in Manila. Neal says he was given a last-minute assignment in Sagada and, with time to spare before heading back to the city, he decided to visit Villia. Just before I arrived, he was telling Villia and her friend Tessie that a writer called Sarah Murray might be contacting her.

This is extremely fortunate. For Villia explains that she often turns away strangers because they're usually tourists wanting to see her home. And no wonder – she lives in what must be one of the most spectacular houses in the Philippines. Perched on the outcrops of limestone cliffs, everything is constructed around the rock face with furniture, fittings and a state-of-the-art steel and granite kitchen all accommodating the stone, rather than the other way around. As evening draws in and the light dims, the floor-to-ceiling window becomes a giant mirror reflecting the rocky back wall, turning the place into a cave.

But it's what's outside the window that interests me, for the house has a breathtaking view over Echo Valley, the deep gorge in whose cliffs are lodged many of the hanging coffins I've come to see. The light is fading, so it's impossible to make any out now but, as the setting sun spreads a flush of pink across the grey rock face, I get my dramatic first glimpse of these intriguing burial grounds.

Villia invites me to sit and hands around cups of cappuccino (made, she says, with the milk of local water buffalo). She's a tall woman with long grey hair, three earrings in one ear and two in the other and she wears a deep indigo-dyed kaftan from Senegal. Without pausing for breath, she speaks passionately about everything you care to mention. She's like a wind-up toy that only needs the key cranked a notch or two to set it sallying forth ("You may have noticed, I talk a lot," she tells me later).

But in Villia's stream-of-consciousness storytelling is a rich seam of information. After claiming to know little about death rites – "That's not my field," she tells me brusquely – she proceeds to explain in detail everything from all-night vigils to ritual pig slaughtering.

Soon Tessie, who was born in Sagada, joins in, matching Villia's descriptions with memories of funerals she's attended over the years. She remembers that an old woman from Sagada died recently – Mrs Batnag, who once ran a local shop. The vigil is on Saturday and if I'd like to, she says, I can go along. The whole community attends funerals around here, so it's no problem for a stranger to turn up, particularly if they bring gifts. Cognac and cakes are best, explains Tessie, and money, too.

By now, my mind's reeling – barely an hour after arriving, I've been greeted warmly by strangers who seem to know me; I've caught my first glimpse of Echo Valley; I've tasted water buffalo-milk cappuccino; and I'll be here for the all-night vigil of Mrs Batnag. I came here simply to see coffins hanging in caves, but I suspect that in this small mountain town I'll encounter much more.

Then Villia hands me a photograph. It's a shocking image. It shows a man strapped to a chair with a band across his mouth and his hands tied together in what looks to me like a hostage situation. What's worse, the man appears to be suffering from some terrible skin disease, for his arms are covered with large blisters.

This, Villia explains, is the death chair and it's part of the *sangadil*, the traditional way of preparing people for burial here. The deceased is placed in a chair and tied up in a sitting position. In order to keep the head upright and prevent body fluids from leaking out, a band of bark is strapped across the mouth and fixed to the back of the chair. Cotton is wedged into the nostrils and ears. The corpse remains this way for several days and, since it's not embalmed, it may start to shrivel, bloat or blister.

Surprisingly, Sagadans find neither the sight nor the sickly-sweet stench of a rotting corpse upsetting. They treat the body in the chair as temporarily in the living world and visit it as they might a friend or neighbour. And it's probably easier to have a conversation with a person who's sitting up, rather than lying in a coffin. This is important because in Sagada friends, relatives and neighbours come not only to pay their respects but also to talk to the dead person, exchanging last greetings, passing messages to the ancestors and even – I like this part – venting their anger by having a good yell at the corpse.

I don't remember the last thing my father said to me. But a conversation we had near the end of his life sticks in my memory. It took place one morning after a terrible night during which, consumed by illness and drugs, he seemed to have lost his mind. By morning, he was himself again, if terrifyingly weak. But he clearly couldn't stay at home, so we got in my Renault 5, the smallest but most comfortable of the family vehicles, and headed to the Joseph Weld Hospice. When we arrived, I sat in the car with him, while Sam went to the reception desk to ask for a wheelchair.

Fa and I chatted quietly about this and that. But what I remember most clearly is that he congratulated me on the drive there. Fa had always loved driving and he often told me he liked the way I drove. But for some reason, at that moment, it made me insanely proud to know that, in the midst of extreme pain, discomfort and helplessness, he'd been noticing the way I was driving.

Grief, it seems to me, is often bound up in unfinished business – remorse for bad behaviour or regret for the things we never got to say to those we've lost. When it became clear Fa's illness was terminal, I thought a lot about whether I needed to tell him anything, something I'd wish I'd said after he'd gone. I could find nothing.

Of course, I desperately wanted him to be around for longer so that we could continue the conversations and jokes. But there were no grievances to be resolved; no dark secrets withheld.

Except for one thing – something I knew I had to do with him before he died: to watch a film. It starred Walter Matthau. Fa had videotaped it years earlier and had often tried to get us to watch it. He didn't exactly sell it to us, saying merely that it was a "courtroom drama" (it's called *The Incident*, I found out later, and in it Matthau plays a small-town lawyer who, during the Second World War, defends a German prisoner accused of murdering the local doctor). "How about the courtroom drama?" he'd say every time we'd decide to flop in front of the TV for the afternoon. "It's brilliant, you know." And every time, we'd roll our eyes and choose something else. Eventually, not watching it became a family joke.

One afternoon on a visit home during his illness, I told Fa straight out, "I can't let you go to your grave without watching that film." He laughed (he liked it when we didn't tiptoe around the subject of his impending death) and went off to find the tape. He and I watched the movie from start to finish. The plot, it turned out, was gripping, with unexpected twists. The drama was well paced and Matthau was superb. "You see, wasn't I right?" he said, smiling triumphantly when he saw how much I'd enjoyed the movie. "Absolutely," I replied. "And I'd never have forgiven myself for failing to watch it with you after all these years."

Remorse over unfinished business can be a destructive force – and often the business concerns more than a movie. Remorse, writes E.M. Forster in *Howards End*, is a wasteful emotion. "It cuts away healthy tissues with the poisoned. It is a knife that probes far deeper than the evil." He's right. When we feel we've failed them, we spend our time longing to talk to the dead, going over and over the things we'd say to them. If only we'd told them we loved them one more time, or made up after that terrible fight. If only we could have one last chance to sort things out, clear the air (or watch a movie), before saying goodbye forever. Well, in Sagada, thanks to the death chair, you have that chance.

I meet Siegrid at 8am in front of the Saint Joseph Resthouse for our tour of Echo Valley. She's a remarkable individual. A small, self-possessed young woman, she has jet-black hair cut in a bob and bright, intelligent eyes. After working for several years at an insurance firm in Baguio, she returned to Sagada in 2001 for the funeral of her grandmother, who was killed in a bus crash on her way back from a wake. Although it was this double tragedy that precipitated her return, once back home, Siegrid decided to stay, preferring the clean air of the mountains to city life.

These days, when she's not trekking around the valley as a guide, she works on her ceramics in a studio that sits on a pine-covered hill. Apart from its simple corrugated iron roof, the studio is open to the elements. In summer, the breeze keeps the place cool. In storms, the rains crash on to the roof in a thrilling cacophony of sound.

On our way to Echo Valley, Siegrid and I pass the Church of St Mary the Virgin and its cemetery before descending into a verdant landscape of bamboo forests and fern thickets framed by the same strange limestone formations that decorate the sitting room of Villia's house.

After a few minutes, Siegrid points up towards the first coffin on our route. I can barely make it out as the wood has faded to the same pale grey of the stone in which it's lodged, but there it is, sticking out of a narrow crack in the rock. Above, in an arched opening high in the cliff face, is a collection of coffins. Different shaped caskets are piled on top of each other. Most look like what I think of as a coffin – long, narrow boxes. But some are short and squat. These, Siegrid explains, are sections of hollowed-out tree trunks and contain bodies in the traditional foetal position.

We pass through caves where coffins sit in unruly piles and gaze up at limestone cliffs where they cling dramatically to the rock face, supported by pegs driven into the stone. One of these, Siegrid says, was erected only a couple of years ago. She remembers the smell lingering for months after it was put in place. Two of the coffins we see have wooden chairs tied up with them – their death chairs. Several are painted in blue and white, decorated with names of the deceased. One has a wooden crucifix attached to it – signs of Christianity's penetration of these tribal burial grounds.

Anglican missionaries arrived here just before US military forces took control of the Philippines in 1905. In Sagada, the missionaries found a small enclave that had never submitted to Spanish rule or to the Catholic religion of the sixteenth-century colonisers, who sometimes literally lost their heads trying to penetrate this region of fiercely independent tribal warriors.

In 1904, the Reverend John Armitage Staunton, the "engineer-priest", established a mission in Sagada to "civilise" what one of his chroniclers, William Henry Scott, describes as "a population only three generations removed from raw head-taking paganism". It was Staunton who built the Church of St Mary the Virgin. Its cross, writes Scott, "was to rise like a beacon above the heads of pagans seeking a better goal, and whose tower clock was to symbolise the changes that would accompany the process".

Whether Sagadans saw it quite like that is another question. But like an extra spoon of sugar in a cup of tea, Anglicanism slipped into the way of things here. This was partly because early missionaries accommodated existing traditions. Soon after arriving, Staunton visited the biggest of the burial caves, Lomiyang, and gave it his blessing (Siegrid jokes that luckily the missionaries could tell locals how Jesus, after his death, also spent time in a cave).

Yet Christianity penetrated Igorot culture incompletely, for tribal traditions remain strong – and nowhere more so than in death and burial. What's more, explains Siegrid, the painting and naming of caskets is a new phenomenon. "We don't visit our dead," she tells me, "so we don't need to name their coffins."

This becomes clear when she tries to take me down a less well-trodden trail leading to a place where she knows there are more coffins. When we arrive, the path is so overgrown that we have to turn back.

Perhaps Sagadans don't visit their dead because they don't need to. Since they can intervene in the fortunes of the living, bringing wealth or illness, the spirits of the dead are called upon at all ceremonies. And, explains Siegrid, it's not only friends and relatives who are acknowledged – the spirits of dead enemies are also invoked. Their remains may be hidden in the thick undergrowth or perched on an inaccessibly high cliff ledge, but in Sagada, the dead are constantly present. They remain influential members of the community.

In some cultures, remembering the dead is limited to specific times or places – prayer sessions, church services or graveyard visits. In others, the ancestors are constantly present, as for the Chinese, who place their effigies on altars in the home. But even in the west, we're finding ways of keeping the dead with us, particularly when deaths have been tragic.

Take roadside monuments, floral tributes on bridges or memorials on school lockers. Then there are Ghost Bikes, part of a global movement in which bicycles painted white are locked to street signs or railings near a crash site; reminder of a tragedy. These improvised memorials put the dead directly into our lives in ways that weren't possible when their only marker was in a graveyard on the edge of town.

So are the dead influential members of my community? In some ways, they are. For one thing, I've yet to erase deceased friends from my contact book, although at some stage I suppose I should. The dead pop up in other ways, too. My grandmother comes to my mind whenever I add capers to a dish of pasta or fish. In her later years (she lived to one hundred), I'd give her a jar of capers every Christmas because she loved them, and because what else do you give an extremely thrifty nonagenarian? (In her late nineties, she turned down my mother's offer of a new pair of shoes, saying, "I'll never get the wear out of them.")

And though he has no memorial plaque or gravestone, Fa appears in my consciousness whenever I hear a piece of music he'd have enjoyed or come across a book I'd have bought for him. They're sad moments that sometimes take me by surprise. But they're sweet moments, too, because they keep me connected to my father.

Of course, the memories gradually blur and we're left with shadows, approximations of a person, names in an address book, jars of capers, faded flowers on a bridge. Like copying an original drawing over layers of tracing paper, we track the marks of those we've lost as closely as we can. But while the outline may become distorted and veer off in places, the essence of the image remains.

Most of Sagada's householders raise pigs. You see them snuffling around in the gardens and yards of the *barangays*. But don't be misled. The motive for swine farming here has nothing to do with the popularity of pork or financial dependence on trade in livestock. It's ceremonial. Most occasions in Sagada – marriages, births, breaking ground on a new house – require the sacrificial slaughtering of pigs. You need a good supply of hogs to keep up.

Death is particularly expensive in porcine terms, precipitating the slaughter of more than twenty animals over a period of a year. Advances in swine husbandry and use of fast-maturing, non-native pigs means the whole thing can be wrapped up in less time these days, but that's still a lot of pigs – and after the death of wealthy individuals you need an even greater supply.

You also need a good head for detail. An astonishing array of rules govern death in Sagada – on everything from how many pigs to butcher (the number of animals killed is referred to as *limina*), the dates and times at which each butchering should take place and when to distribute the meat among relatives and neighbours (*bingit*). Variations in these procedures arise, depending on the age, gender and social status of the deceased, and local divergences mean a family in Central Sagada might follow different rules from one just across the valley in Eastern Sagada.

The rules on death clothing are complex, too. For a man, there's a black-and-white striped vest with orange patterns on it, a seven-foot-long piece of fabric making up the lower garment and a dark blue headband. For women, a wrap-around skirt of three pieces of dark blue cloth has red eye-shaped designs on it, while a long-sleeved blouse in white is decorated with black designs. Women also wear the blue headband.

The subtle variations are mind-boggling – it's a wonder anyone manages to remember them all. And getting them wrong can lead to dire consequences. Failing to dress the dead in the traditional mortuary clothes, for example, may prompt their spirits to return to earth, causing an illness to occur in the family.

Fortunately, there's a book that can help. In 2004, Dinah Elma Piluden-Omengan, a native Sagadan, documented the rules of local funeral rites in a book called *Death and Beyond: Death & Burial Rituals & Other Practices & Beliefs of the Igorots of Sagada, Mountain Province, Philippines*. Browsing though its pages gives you an idea of the complexity of dealing with the dead in Sagada. And though it records the funeral customs of just one tiny mountain community, it runs to more than two hundred pages.

Rules on how to respond to mortality are among the most carefully defined of cultural conventions. Today, many have disappeared. And, in some cases, that's no bad thing. It seems astonishing, for example, that in Victorian Britain, widows were obliged to wear mourning dress for two years – and not just any old black. For the first year, the fabric had to be parramatta, a silk blended with wool or cotton to give it the special dullness deemed appropriate for the widow's gloom. For the next nine months, it was black silk trimmed with crepe (a silk with a crimped texture – also not attractive). For the last six months, the widow could (yippee!) add in a little grey or lavender.

Even in Bali, where cremations are spectacular, joyous events, the courtly hierarchy has a darker side. Anyone violating local regulations and religious obligations may be expelled from the *banjar* (the local committee that arranges rites such as cremations) and barred from worshipping at temples or using the cemetery for burial and cremation. Anthropologist Carol Warren cites the story of a man who repeatedly failed to join in the communal tasks required at cremations. When it was his turn, the *banjar* members kept picking up and dropping his bier until the cremation tower broke and his body fell out. In Bali, disruption of death rites is a serious matter, for the fate of the body governs the soul's ability to reach the afterlife.

Death can also trigger an unfortunate change in status for those who are left behind. In Sagada, a surviving spouse is considered something of an outcast. While this practice is fading, it's still reflected in mourning rituals, since for a certain period of time, the widow or widower is supposed to remain inside, in one corner of the house.

Often, of course, it's the women who suffer most. In India, the Hindu rites performed by a widow on her husband's death reflect her diminished standing. First, she must break the dozens of glass bangles she's accumulated on her arms. Then the red vermillion spot – the *sindoor*, worn on her forehead since her wedding day – is wiped off. In poor rural areas, widows may still be expected to shave their heads, sleep on the ground and remain unseen by men for the rest of their lives.

Happily for Indian women, the practice of *suttee* is now outlawed. But in the Rajasthani city of Jodhpur is a chilling a reminder of a time when this tradition required the widow to throw herself on her husband's cremation fire. On the wall of a gate at Mehrangarh Fort is a series of handprints representing the fifteen wives and concubines of Maharaja Man Singh, women who in 1843 committed suttee on his funeral pyre. Several of the prints are clearly those of young girls.

If it hasn't actually precipitated forced suicide, the requirements of some death rituals make Sagada's pig slaughtering obligations look positively benign. In Fiji, according to early anthropologists, mourners would cut of the tops of their fingers for the dead. "So common was the practice of lopping off the little fingers in mourning," noted anthropologist Sir James George Frazer in 1913, "that till recently few of the older natives could be found who had their hands intact."

And you might think that the carpeting of a grave with *thotho* (grass) sounds romantic – that is, unless you happen to be the wife of a Fijian chief, in which case it once meant being strangled and used as *thotho* to create a cushion for your dead husband's body. Sir James, who described this grim practice, found that the same was not true for a husband after his wife's death. "The great truth that all flesh is grass appears to have been understood by the Fijians as applicable chiefly to the flesh of women," he writes curtly. Death demands its pound of flesh – quite literally in some cases.

Some of the old rules might not be life threatening, but just seem outdated. When my friend and fellow writer Diane Daniel's mother died, she was appalled at the black outfits of the undertakers who, at four in the morning, came to pick her up. "I couldn't believe what the two youngish guys from the funeral home were wearing," she told me. "Full-on suits and starched shirts – right out of the Munsters. It was so incredibly ghoulish. I wanted to scream, 'Get out of those ridiculous costumes!' I'd rather have seen them in medical scrubs if they had to dress up."

If death brings together the community, it also has a way of forcing us to dig deeply into our pocketbooks. While Piluden-Omengan applauds the comfort Sagada's communal death rites bring the bereaved, she also notes that these rituals can be costly. "The expensive death practices are a serious burden for Sagada folk," she writes. "The family concerned spends beyond its meagre income just to comply with the excessive and elaborate rituals and practices that are prescribed by tradition."

But Sagada's rituals are nothing compared to the money lavished on funerals in some places. In the United States, of course, Jessica Mitford accused the funeral industry of perpetrating "a huge, macabre and expensive practical joke on the American public". Today, the average cost of a US funeral runs six or seven thousand dollars.

Still, beside Ghana's citizens, Americans start to look positively thrifty in their funerary spending. Like weddings in India, funerals in Ghana are huge community parties, often attracting hundreds of guests, who all expect to be fed, watered and entertained with live music, drumming, DJs and dancing. Funerals, more than any other ceremony, are opportunities for Ghanaians to display their wealth. In a country where many citizens live on a few dollars a day, families shell out thousands of dollars on funerals – sometimes re-mortgaging their homes.

To bide time while amassing funds for the party, the body is kept on ice. This can also play into a game of one-upmanship, with a long mortuary stay for the corpse indicating that elaborate planning is going into the funeral, suggesting a lavish event. The high prices charged by mortuary managers add to the family's prestige.

In fact, fees for holding dead bodies help keep many Ghanaian hospitals afloat, according to anthropologist Sjaak van der Geest. At one private health centre, the Agyarkwa Hospital, he found that, after investing in the necessary equipment, the hospital could accommodate up to three times as many corpses as living patients. Storing the dead was more lucrative than treating the sick.

Money is what anthropologist Marleen de Witte calls the "social glue" behind death in Ghana. Guests, she writes, donate money to the family, which in theory covers the cost of the whole affair. And it's all very public – a table and donation box are placed prominently at the funeral ground, with staff assigned to count the cash as it comes in, to record names and amounts, to issue receipts and to announce the arriving donors and their gift amount through a loudspeaker. Managing funeral finances is a tricky balancing act, though – spend too much and invite too few contributing guests and, instead of money left over, you'll be stuck with a sizeable debt.

In Mitfordian tones of outrage, commentators in Ghana's newspapers regularly berate the public for excessive spending on funerals, accusing families of investing more in the dead than they do in the living. Even international financial institutions have advised the Ghanaian government to persuade its citizens to spend less on death rites. Others, however, claim that the commercialisation of funerals in Ghana has created jobs for carpenters, caterers, seamstresses, musicians and others.

The "dismal trade", like any other, has innovators and entrepreneurs. It has successes as well as excesses. But while the funeral industry is often criticised for making money, we seem happy to accept the profit motive in other businesses. Most of life's rites of passage – baby showers, births, christenings, weddings, bar and bat mitzvahs – precipitate shopping sprees that are less frequently questioned. And anyone who finds the plethora of funeral paraphernalia on the market today a little *de trop* should look at the many ways the baby-care industry has found of selling a stroller.

Death is, for some reason, different. It's a rite of passage many feel should be left in the hands of God, not Mammon. Yet, why shouldn't we be able to spend on funerals as readily as we do for christenings and weddings? Certainly, those who want cheap, simple versions should be offered them. But if someone really wants a lavish send-off in a coffin decked out in the Mets team colours – or, indeed, one shaped like the Empire State Building – shouldn't they be able to buy one?

Traditional death rites can be harsh or overly pricey. And yet, without any ritual, we seem lost. A friend recently confided her dilemma about how to approach a colleague who'd lost his wife to cancer. "Should I talk to him about it? Should I e-mail, phone or send a card?" she asked me. In the absence of guidance, she chose the worst path – she did nothing. Meanwhile, bereaved friends have often told me how isolated they've felt after hearing nothing from acquaintances or noticed people crossing the street rather than having to talk to them. "I don't care if they blurt something that's totally inappropriate," one told me. "I just want my loss to be acknowledged."

It's true, rituals can seem awkward or artificial. But they do give us a framework with which to get through difficult moments – hooks on which to hang our behaviour. Ritual and action step in when words fail.

Emily Post, the American writer and great authority on etiquette, knew all about this. She called etiquette "the science of living" and in death, it was the "time-worn servitor, Etiquette", she wrote in 1922, who "decrees that the last rites shall be performed smoothly and with beauty and gravity, so that the poignancy of grief may in so far as possible be assuaged".

Perhaps, even the dress code has something to be said for it. Some of my friends would agree. Debbie Hartley, who was born in a Greek community in Australia and now lives in New York, wore black for a month after her father died. She remembers the striking effect it had on friends. Back in Sydney for the funeral, she went out with her mother and sister-in-law – both also dressed in black – to buy a new pair of shoes for her father to wear for his burial. On the way, they ran into an old family friend, also from Sydney's Greek community.

The friend initially smiled at seeing Debbie in town. Then she noticed the three black outfits. "Her face turned," Debbie told me. "Within seconds she knew something was up and when she came up to us, she immediately asked who had died. That's when my mother broke down. But the fact that someone from twenty feet away from you knows your personal situation – there was something very powerful about that."

Sarah Callaghan, a British friend, also wore black for a month after her mother died. "It was a way of paying respect to her, and it was a personal thing that I think helped me though my grief," she told me. When the month was up and Sarah donned more colourful clothes, she was struck by the feeling, marking the passage of time after her mother's death. "The morning I put on a change of colour, it was as if something lifted from me," she says. "I realised that she wasn't coming back and I felt refreshed. I didn't feel guilty – just the sense that it was okay to move on."

Different coloured clothing plays an important role at funerals in Ghana, too, with red distinguishing close relatives from acquaintances and friends dressed in black. As the funeral moves from one ceremony to the next, the colours change, explained Patrick Awuah, who I met while commissioning my coffin in Accra. "On Saturday, you wear black and red," said Patrick, recalling his father's funeral. "Then on Sunday it changes to fabric in black and white. And for me the colour really mattered. The white was so light after the heavy red and black of the day before. Even the conversation seemed different on the Sunday – by Sunday, it was more of a thanksgiving than a mourning."

Like the drumbeats of the funeral march, ritual procedures and mourning codes keep us moving through our grief. First, they give us something to do. They also imbue seemingly meaningless loss with reassuring significance. But most importantly, familiar procedures that are known to all in the community bring a degree of social order to the chaos that's sparked by a death.

So in the absence of these rules, with no pigs to slaughter, and no special clothing to arrange, how do we manage grief and dignify death? In Britain, those without a faith to guide them can have a humanist funeral. A humanist funeral, explains the British Humanist Association, recognises no afterlife, "but instead uniquely and affectionately celebrates the life of the person who has died". The association has produced a book called *Funerals Without God*, giving practical advice on how to structure humanist ceremonies, including a selection of prose and poetry.

In the United States, the New York Society for Ethical Culture – which describes itself as a "humanist religious community" – takes a similar approach. The society was founded in 1876 by Felix Adler, a Jewish intellectual who felt the need for a new religion that focused on ethics rather than doctrine, one open to diverse forms of belief. The society conducts ceremonies on behalf of members and non-members, including funerals. "People who've grown up without a more traditional religion still want to mark this moment somehow," says Anne Klaeysen, one of the society's leaders. "And ceremonies play an important role. Their job is to give you a good footing on which to carry on in your grief."

And even in faith-based ceremonies, we're introducing more personal elements into the proceedings. Where the presence of a member of the clergy was once at the heart of the service, today the eulogy – where friends and family speak about the deceased, reflecting on their achievements and character – takes centre stage.

With the help of videos, photo displays, treasured possessions and favourite pieces of music, more time is spent remembering the lives of the dead than reciting the liturgy or praying for their souls.

Some people are finding even more creative ways of saying goodbye to their dead. Take the family of Katie, my friend and hairdresser in New York. Her great aunt had always been fascinated by Viking history, so when she died, one of her relatives built her a model Viking ship. The family attached messages and photographs on to the sail and took it down to the edge of a lake, where everyone placed a handful of ashes into the hold. Then setting the vessel on fire, they launched it out on to a lake in Minnesota.

And like the clients of Ghana's fantasy coffin makers, some are using the iconography of their lives to shape their final exits. Harry Ewell, whose business in life was selling ice cream from trucks around Rockland, Massachusetts, arranged to have his old ice cream van lead the funeral cortege to the graveyard, where ice cream was served to the mourners. Malcolm McLaren, the "godfather of punk", was sent off in a coffin emblazoned with the words: "Too fast to live, too young to die". As he'd requested, many fans held a minute of mayhem – rather then the traditional minute's silence – in his memory.

So what's happening here? As we struggle to redefine our relationship to death, it seems we're yearning to rediscover some meaning in rituals (our own meaning). We're rescuing death from the clutches of the dull anonymity and professionalised mortuary services that began with the funeral reformers of the late nineteenth century. Out with the suits and starched shirts of the mortuary men; in with Viking-style send-offs, funerary ice cream vans and minutes of mayhem – it's death, Jim, but not as we know it.

On Saturday night, Siegrid and I go to Mrs Batnag's vigil. We arrive at the house at about 9pm. I leave a cash donation for the family, a gift of loaves of sweet bread (I couldn't find any cake) and a bottle of cognac. It's rather like the Ghanaian system, where contributions to the family help cover the costs of the funeral. So does gambling, I notice, for in a yard at the back of Mrs Batnag's house, dozens of men are gathered around a game of cards.

Siegrid and I sit for a while under a tarpaulin erected over the courtyard to keep the rain off the visitors. Friends and relatives sit four rows deep with others perched on a pathway to the side. Most are older people. The women wear an assortment of headscarves and woolly hats (it's a chilly night by Filipino standards).

As warm, sweet tea is handed round, everyone sings quietly, alternating between the traditional tribal dirge – the *baya-o* – and renderings of Christian hymns delivered in quavering voices (*How beautiful to walk in the steps of the Saviour* is being sung as Siegrid and I arrive). In between the hymns and dirges, people chat and joke. A few of the older members of the party have fallen asleep. In an adjacent shed, an old man in a cowboy hat tends the flames of a fire that's boiling water for the tea being passed around and that will later roast the sacrificial pigs. Another will be butchered at midnight.

Siegrid and I go inside to see the coffin, which is in the main room. Wood planks line the floor and walls painted in an arresting shade of green have an assortment of objects hanging on them – a map of the Philippines, a pair of deer antlers, a triangular black velvet souvenir flag from Amsterdam, a clock with an ornate gold plastic frame, a picture of Christ wearing the crown of thorns and a promotional calendar from D'Rising Sun Transport System Inc. On the wall above me, a couple of dusty laminated photographs depict Mrs Batnag and her husband, who's still alive. A green plastic rosary hangs between the images of husband and wife.

Siegrid and I sit down on a bench beside the coffin. There on the floor in front of us is Mrs Batnag, in a plain wooden box with angled shoulders and sides that taper towards the end – a classic toe pincher. To keep away the flies and mosquitoes, an old woman waves a fan of torn strips of newspaper on a stick over Mrs Batnag's face. White cotton fabric lines the coffin – a modern addition, as traditional coffins have no lining – and two large candles flank a carved wood crucifix that's watching over the corpse. Covering the body is the death blanket, in white with blue lines on it: tribal tradition again meets the trappings of Christendom.

The room is filled with friends and relatives, all packed on wooden benches against the walls. In here, too, some people are dozing. Siegrid tells me locals joke that it's important to make sure at least one person stays awake during the vigil. If not, when they awake, the dead person may have disappeared.

I'm taking a close look at Mrs Batnag. Hers is the first dead body I have ever seen, unless you count mummified corpses. At first, I find her presence shocking. Then, as I get used to the fact that I'm inches from a cadaver, I start wondering whether, after I die, I'd want my body laid out in a room full of everyone who knew me. The answer is no. While for some, a recurring nightmare is appearing naked in public, mine is finding myself surrounded by crowds of people who've been watching me while asleep. In these dreams, I always tell the onlookers to go away and leave me alone – something I wouldn't be able to do if I was dead.

Still, Mrs Batnag doesn't seem perturbed by the presence of an audience. She died several days ago but, unlike the blistered corpse in Villia's photo, she's been embalmed, since the family had to wait for some of its members to travel back to the Philippines from overseas before holding the funeral. Her face looks strange. The skin is greyish brown and her lips are a disturbing purple-black colour. Her eyes are tightly shut. But, unlike those dozing opposite her, she doesn't look like she's sleeping. She's unmistakably dead.

Which is why my heart starts racing as, at one point, I think I can see her breathing. Siegrid says she noticed the same thing. Perhaps it was a breeze moving the blanket, she ventures. We both agree that it was uncanny. Still, no one else in Mrs Batnag's sitting room seems to have registered the fluttering movement. With the matter-of-fact calm of people waiting for a bus, family, friends and neighbours have all gathered to watch over the dead woman through the night.

With such a high demand for ceremonial pigs, Sagada's town motto, "We share what's good", comes into its own after a death in the village. Friends and neighbours from the barangay bring food for the bereaved family and assist with chores, such as planting or finishing the rice harvest. Those who've helped neighbours out can turn to them for assistance when they're in need, particularly when it comes to pigs for slaughter. It's all part of a system known as supon – you slaughter my pig, I'll slaughter yours.

The whole village shows up at the burial, too. Once the deceased has spent its allotted time on the "death chair", the relatives

– no doubt trying to ignore the smell of the rotting corpse – untie it and wrap it in the traditional blanket. Young men compress the body, breaking bones in the process, until it's in a tight foetal position. Securing their bundle with cord, they set off through the *barangay* and down the mountain slope towards the caves.

Everyone battles to take a turn handling the body, which is tossed roughly from one person to another along the way. This is partly a show of respect for the deceased. But there's another reason friends and family all want their moment with the corpse – any blood or bodily fluids that fall on to the bearer are thought to bring extremely good luck, and anyone marked in this way refrains from washing for twenty-four hours afterwards. With all the jostling to grab the parcel of human remains, these ceremonies have acquired the name "basketball funerals".

As the cortège approaches the cave, children run ahead, rattling wooden clappers or banging on tin cans to let the ancestors know someone else is coming to join them. Once at the cave, the unpacking begins. The men lower the body gently into the coffin (which arrived earlier), chattering loudly in the process. But they're not discussing the weather or where best to place the coffin – they're talking to the corpse, explaining what they're doing in the way a nurse might to a patient. "We'll lay you out," they say. "You have a blanket so you'll be warm. You'll be comfortable now."

Once this communal way of death was taken for granted. Take the drinking at Irish wakes. This arose because refreshments were needed to keep people entertained, since it was thought the corpse should never be left alone. In traditional societies, the bereaved did not "move on", go straight back to work or "keep busy", as we're often encouraged to do. They abandoned the rice harvest. They kept all-night vigils. They sang songs. They drank. They gambled.

In the west, community participation in death survives most vibrantly in the Jewish tradition of sitting shiva. This seven-day mourning ritual observed by the closest relatives is part of a long series of ceremonies leading up to the one-year anniversary of the death, when the headstone is placed on the grave. Jewish rituals, like others, mark different stages of grief, but shiva is considered the most important, giving mourners time to move from shock and intense emotion to a state in which they can return to normal life.

J. Leonard Romm, a New York rabbi, compares it to a pinky ball (the rubber interior of a tennis ball). "When you squeeze one of those things, it contracts and when you let your fist go, the ball springs back," he told me. "That's like the Jewish ritual – you're contracting and then gradually expanding back out."

The process starts immediately after the funeral when the family returns home and remains there for the seven days of shiva. The first meal after the funeral, which is prepared by friends and neighbours and consists of eggs and bread rolls – round objects that imply an endless circle, a reference to the continuity of life.

Everything, from domestic arrangements to habits of the mourners emphasises the fact that this is an intense period of grieving. First, mourners sit on low stools. "Sometimes the funeral home gives you these little corrugated boxes," says Rabbi Romm. "In the old days they'd give you wooden benches and some places have folding chairs where the legs have been shortened. But when you're mourning you feel low, so you sit lower than the people who've come to comfort you."

All mirrors in the house are covered. Some say this practice originates in an ancient fear that the soul might see the reflection of family members in the mirrors and steal them away, but other interpretations suggest that, like many shiva traditions, it's a discouragement of vanity at a time of mourning. Moreover, Jewish tradition stipulates that prayers must not be said in front of mirrors, and during shiva mourners recite the kaddish, a beautiful prayer that is an affirmation of faith.

As in so many traditions, clothing is important. Jews in mourning wear the *kriah*, a garment or piece of ribbon that's torn by siblings, spouses, parents or children at the funeral (a tradition rooted in early lamenting practices, where mourners would tear at their clothes). For bereaved parents, the *kriah* is worn over the left side of the body (over the heart), while others wear it on the right. Mourners wear no leather shoes. They're prohibited from working or having sex and, beyond taking a shower a day, they're not supposed to shave, to wear any make-up or to cut their hair.

Most importantly, mourners are rarely left alone. For a start, the kaddish can only be recited in the presence of a minyan – a group of ten adult males (in less orthodox households, women can be included). "That's another time you've got community coming to the house," explains Rabbi Romm. "So during the week of shiva, there's a lot of people coming over."

But mourners never play host to their visitors. Traditionally, arriving guests should not greet the family but wait for them to speak first. And during shiva, it's visitors that bring food and supplies or help the family do the cooking. They may bring news of what's happening in the outside world, but discussions often focus on the dead person, their life, achievements and character. It's a time for exchanging memories.

"I know someone who described the process of sitting shiva by saying she felt as if she were wrapped in cotton wool," says Diane, Rabbi Romm's wife. "She said it was a point in her life where she felt very fragile and the community came and enveloped her in cotton wool. I thought that was a good image."

What if there's no one left to gather around your coffin all night or sit shiva in your memory? An alarming number of people die alone every year, with no relatives or friends to organise their funeral. Demographic shifts tell the story. In America, according to the US Census Bureau, the proportion of households consisting of "one person living alone" rose from 17 percent in 1970 to 26 percent in 2005. That figure is rising. And since they produced far fewer children, baby boomers are more likely than the previous generation to end up alone in old age.

Eric Klinenberg, a New York University sociology professor, has tracked the evidence of a society where more and more people are dying alone. In the research for his 2002 book *Heat Wave*, he found that, of the hundreds of people who died in the Chicago heat wave of July 1995, one hundred and seventy people initially went unclaimed by relatives or friends. Even after the Public

Administrators Office conducted an extensive search programme, about one-third of the cases were never resolved. Their personal possessions still sit in cardboard boxes at the County Building.

There are places for the unclaimed dead. They're called potter's fields, a term used for the burial grounds of paupers, indigents, strangers orphans, illegitimate children, unknown individuals and those unwilling or unable to pay for a funeral.

The term is thought to originate in the Bible. The book of Matthew tells of the thirty pieces of silver paid to Judas Iscariot for betraying Jesus in the Garden of Gethsemane. When a penitent Judas returns the money to the temple, the priests use it to buy a plot of land, owned by a potter, which lies outside the walls of the city of Jerusalem. The plot is turned into a cemetery for foreigners.

In the United States, the biggest potter's field lies just east of New York City on Hart Island, a one-hundred-acre tract of land in the waters of the Long Island Sound. There the unclaimed dead are buried. Access to the island, which is owned by the city and run by the Department of Correction, is barred to all except those with relatives buried there. But, in the early 1990s, photographer Joel Sternfeld produced a series of images of the island. His photographs show a hauntingly lonely place; a scrubby grassland whose friendless monotony is broken only by abandoned buildings – a stable, a laundry, a butcher's shop (where knives and saws still hang in boxes) and a warden's house; shadows of the island's former incarnations.

Even when these buildings were occupied by the living, it was by the world's unwanted. Hart Island has over the years been home to a lunatic asylum, a women's charity hospital and workhouse for delinquent boys and a prison. During the yellow fever epidemic of 1870, it was where the sick were quarantined. During the Cold War it was a base for Nike missiles. An attempt to build an amusement park on the island in the 1920s was abandoned.

The city purchased the island in 1869 and that April, the first civilian burial took place, of the unclaimed body of Louisa Van Sluke. Photographs from the 1890s by Jacob Riis show a desolate stretch of flat land into which large rectangular pits have been dug and simple pine coffins are being laid, one butting up against the other. Today, inmates from the prison on Riker's Island build the coffins and bury the dead – about fifteen hundred adults and a thousand infants every year.

Once a year, those who are buried on Hart Island receive a visit. Every May, a group affiliated with Saint Benedict's Roman Catholic Church in the Bronx goes there on Ascension Thursday to pray for the dead. Occasionally, individuals make it to the island, since the Department of Correction permits a family to take a final trip to see a relative who's been confirmed as being buried on the island. However, no gravesites can be visited and no maps of the graves exist. Like the dead of Sagada in their caves, only disturbed when another cadaver arrives, the individuals lying beneath the ground on Hart Island are left alone. But, unlike the Igorot ancestors, these individuals have no one to invoke their names at ceremonies. They remain, for the most part, forgotten.

After I die, chances are there won't be an all-night vigil with groups of villagers singing tribal dirges and Anglican hymns for me. No pigs will be slaughtered at my death. No one will sit shiva in my name. Do I mind? Not really. Because to have a community funeral, you need a community – and much as I'm drawn to Sagada's quiet pastoral idyll and the collective participation in life's important moments, I feel the limitations of being part of a close-knit society would outweigh the benefits. For me, the greatest of life's pleasures is freedom and the chance to travel, to meet new people, to gaze across an unfamiliar metropolis or stick my toe into an undiscovered ocean. And if that means making my own funeral arrangements, that's a price I'm prepared to pay.

On the other hand, funerals are also for those left behind. So if after I'm gone, my relatives and friends want to gather to drink, gamble, dance or whatever, I won't (unlike my father) raise any objections, even if I could. In any case, trying to prevent people from commemorating your death can prove a futile exercise. The attempt by Thomas Hardy, a confirmed atheist, to avoid a funeral didn't work out too well – in the end, the nineteenth-century English novelist was given the equivalent of a state funeral in Westminster Abbey, with ten pallbearers, including the prime minister.

Like Hardy, my father didn't want any kind of gathering to take place after his death. Unlike Hardy, he got his way. But while I respected and understood his feelings, I felt it was important to do *something*. My father was a man who engaged and entertained so many people. I was sure they'd want to celebrate his life. My mother and sister agreed. So instead, we decided to send out a simple white card announcing his death and suggesting that, at 6pm on January 15 (which would have been his eightieth birthday), everyone should raise a glass in his honour.

Getting the wording on the card right wasn't easy. Sam and I had a moment of horrified hilarity when we realised we'd left out the essential phrase "wherever you happen to be" before the instructions to raise a glass. We quickly added that in, lest the card look too much like an invitation to cocktails and, come January 15, everyone pitched up at our house in what would have been the precise opposite of what Fa had wanted.

Of course, it wouldn't have been that easy. These days friends and family are dispersed more widely than ever. Yet, as humans, we're hardwired to form communities and get together at significant moments. In our globalised world, what we need are new ways, metaphorically speaking, of lining up our pigs for slaughter.

And perhaps we can do that virtually. Adam Cohen learned of the death of his college friend Luke Cole in a car accident in Africa on Facebook. "After Luke died, his Facebook page became an online gathering place for his hundreds of Facebook friends," he wrote in a *New York Times* article. Friends exchanged updates on Luke's Wall and included photographs, reminiscences as well as a poem by Rainer Maria Rilke. In a report on the cremation ceremony in Uganda, explains Cohen, "the post said Luke was sent off with Madagascar chocolate, root beer and a small 'environmental justice' note tucked in his pocket".

Like Cohen's friends, others are gathering online to announce a death or remember a life. Website postings are starting to replace the newspaper death notice and, even better, allowing friends to send in messages, to post photographs and to exchange memories. The funeral industry is stepping in with technology allowing live webcasts of funerals to be broadcast globally via high-speed internet. Meanwhile, collective mourning is now possible on social networking sites such as MyDeathSpace.com, as well as through online organisations with names like Virtual Memorials, Remembered Forever, Tributes.com and SadlyMissed.com.

For my father, the snail-mail version seemed more appropriate. So soon after Christmas, we sent out the cards. I was still on my trip to India. Working on a travel writing assignment, I was comfortably lodged in the Imperial Hotel, a grand old Delhi institution with twenty-four king palms flanking its entrance and a turbaned Sikh at the door. On January 15, at 11.30pm (6pm Greenwich Mean Time), I made my way to the hotel's Daniell's Tavern. There, surrounded by the slightly soulless décor of a recent refurbishment, but in the company of a friendly barman, I toasted Fa with a glass of Indian red wine from the state of Maharashtra.

Back in London, Kate was in the kitchen of her flat, a child in one arm and another on the way, breaking off briefly from stirring pureed vegetables to take a quick sip of wine. For both of us, the setting was entirely appropriate – Kate as the mother she had always longed to be, me out and about in the world again. Fa would have been amused and pleased.

For my mother, the card was a wonderful thing. In the weeks after it went out, friends and relatives sent her letters recounting their favourite stories of my father. They were letters of condolence, but people also described where they'd been the moment they raised their glasses, some adding that for the occasion they'd opened a special bottle of wine. Rather like a postal version of sitting shiva, reading through the many letters helped Sam navigate her grief in the knowledge that, at 6pm on January 15, an entire community – albeit a geographically dispersed one – had raised their glasses and celebrated my father's life.

7

FOREIGN FIELDS

Far From Home in Calcutta

If ever Tears deservedly were Shed
If ever Grief was due to Virtue Dead
Thy Merit Martha, and thy spotless Ways
Claim Tears from all, for all allowed them praise.

So runs the first stanza of the tombstone poem of twenty-three-year-old Martha Goodlad, who died on March 21, 1789. Martha's grave sits among the eighteenth- and nineteenth-century tombs of South Park Street Cemetery, a bucolic burial ground running wild with bougainvillea, oleanders and other flowering shrubs. With its ancient trees, rampant greenery and elegiac tomb inscriptions, South Park Street Cemetery is the most English of resting places. Except that it's not in England – it's in Calcutta, the chaotic capital of the state of West Bengal, part of Bharat Ganarajya, or the Republic of India, an independent nation once ruled by Martha's compatriots.

Among the emotional, social, legal and familial problems death presents, the most immediate one is physical – what to do with the body. And with the "what" comes the question of "where"?

If the family cemetery is nearby, then perhaps the answer is easy, for in most societies the desire to be buried at home is the strongest one. But what about those who die far from home? And for some – expatriates, immigrants, those who've married into another country or culture or globetrotters like me – there's a bigger question: where is home?

No doubt Martha Goodlad thought of India as home. After all, when she was alive, Calcutta sat on British territory. Until the administration moved its headquarters to Delhi in 1911, the city was the dazzling capital of a colossal empire stretching from Canada to Australia, taking in everything from Caribbean islands to African savannahs. British bureaucrats governed more than a fifth of the planet's population. In Calcutta, the Brits erected mansions, hotels, cathedrals, banks, railway stations and courthouses that wouldn't have looked out of place on the grandest of London's streets. The scale of these buildings says something about the state of mind of colonial planners – they were in India for good.

A long-stay mentality governed the approach to death and burial, too. South Park Street Cemetery is filled with pyramids and obelisks, oversized Roman sarcophagi, Greek tombs and Palladian mausoleums the size of small houses topped with all manner of cupolas, rotundas and pediments. They were built to last for eternity – one in which the ground sheltering the bodies of the British dead would forever remain British soil.

Rudyard Kipling was disdainful of this show of sepulchral stone. "They must have been afraid of their friends rising up before the due time that they weighted them with such cruel mounds of masonry," he wrote of the cemetery in *The City of Dreadful Night*, part of a series of 1888 articles.

Today, the mounds of masonry don't look so cruel. Time, decay and dappled sunlight soften hard edges and fill the place with an air of romantic melancholy. With pathways, moss-covered tombs and marble gravestones – many of them shipped out from Liverpool as ballast – the South Park Street Cemetery conjures up images of that "corner of a foreign field, that is for ever England", of Rupert Brooke's famous First World War poem *The Soldier*.

But is it really forever England? Outside the cemetery walls lies Kipling's "City of Dreadful Night", where poverty, pollution, heat and noise assault the senses. Government House – a creamy neo-classical mansion modelled on Kedelston Hall in Derbyshire – still stands in Dalhousie Square. But Dalhousie Square has been renamed Binoy Badal Dinesh Bagh and the neo-classical mansion is home to Gopalkrishna Gandhi, governor of West Bengal and grandson of Mahatma Gandhi, the man who freed India from British rule. Majestic colonial domes still shape the skyline, but from the porte-cochères of Victorian villas and the gothic arches of the High Court, small livelihoods stream out on to pavements like rivers with no banks to limit their flow – *chai* sellers, shoeshine boys, knife grinders. The buildings are there, but the Brits have gone.

The irrepressible energy of the new India may eventually triumph at South Park Street Cemetery, too. In some ways, it already feels like a place under siege. Just outside its high walls, traffic thunders down Lower Circular Road. Ugly tower blocks peer down into its tranquil terrain. Meanwhile, year after year, monsoon rains attack the crumbling surface of the colonial stones while pollution, heat and humidity slowly undermine their foundations. A charity looks after the cemetery, but it says extra funds are needed to maintain it. Martha and her compatriots rest here in the city that was their home – but for how long?

In the months before he died, my father clearly made a mental transition. From seeing his remains as "organic matter" to be disposed of hygienically, he started considering them as a part of him, a part he wanted left somewhere – or at least that's what his final instructions imply. As to what took him on this intellectual journey, I can only speculate. However, when it came to deciding *where* his remains should be left, the answer was easy – in the "beautiful Dorset landscape".

West Dorset was not his birthplace, but he'd lived there for more than a quarter of a century. It's one of the most beautiful parts of England. Ancient woodlands cluster around the base of rolling hills. Tiny churches and thatched cottages sit comfortably in verdant valleys. Yet the countryside has a grandeur that puts it beyond the realms of the picturesque. Ambitious Roman roads cut through rural curves in dead-straight lines – reminders of a long-departed foreign superpower – and a Jurassic coast marked by strange cliff formations adds a note of drama. Fa knew every hillock, lane and pebble beach of this particular corner of England. He made friends with all the farmers; raised two daughters there. It was his home and the natural choice as a location for his remains.

But what will his West Dorset landscape look like hundreds of years from now? The hill and the little churchyard of St Mary Magdalene, where he requested to have his ashes scattered, lie within a couple of miles of the coast – so it's possible that as global warming pushes up the level of the oceans, his fleeting wish for a sea burial could actually be fulfilled.

We think of gravesites as sanctified grounds, places that should be left untouched. But the world moves on, often with little heed to the homes of the dead, many of whom lie beneath skyscrapers, shops, highways, playing fields, hospitals and military facilities.

Sometimes we stumble upon them – as happened in 1991 in Lower Manhattan, when work on the foundations of a federal office tower uncovered a burial ground where archaeologists and historians think up to twenty thousand people of African descent were buried in the seventeenth and eighteenth centuries. A memorial now marks what was the graveyard.

Also in Manhattan, Bryant Park and the Waldorf-Astoria both stand on old burial grounds. (Since 1852, however, no Manhattanite has had the option of being buried "at home". Fearing the spread of epidemics, the Common Council of New York City passed a law banning all burials on the island.)

The gravesites we know about constitute a fraction of those that have existed. Around the world, tens of thousands of burial grounds go undiscovered, leaving most of the world's dead voiceless, silenced by the pavements and fields on which we walk.

Sometimes, it's remarkable how long graves have remained undisturbed. In the Persian Gulf, the kingdom of Bahrain is home to thousands of Bronze Age burial mounds dating from about 2,500 B.C. to A.D. 500. Here, bodies of an ancient civilization were buried in the foetal position along with possessions such as knives, personal seals and ceramic pots. Today, however, pressure for this oil-rich state to develop its land is threatening these resting places. Many were lost in recent decades, as petrodollars powered high-rise urban developments. The question is whether conservationists can win the battle to preserve the rest.

Just as places move on, so do people. Newark, New Jersey, was once home to America's fourth largest Jewish community. Immigrants started to settle in Newark in the 1840s; by the middle of the century about sixty families, mainly from Germany, had put down roots there. "Most of them were peddlers, who carried their goods in baskets or bundles from house to house and often went far out into the surrounding country," write the authors of *A History of the City of Newark*, published in 1913.

By that time, around fifty thousand Jews were living in Newark, with many from Eastern Europe and more than half coming from Russia. As they prospered, they erected homes, shops, Hebrew schools, hospitals, synagogues, temples – and burial grounds.

Newark's graveyards dramatise the story of these early Jewish communities. They're arranged in sections grouping congregations, health and welfare societies and *Landsmanshaftn* – benefit societies with names such as Linitzer, Gombiner and Robeshower that sprang up in the 1880s to support immigrants from the same town or region. Marsha Dubrow, a local cantor and musicologist whose family came to Newark from Odessa, describes the cemeteries as "patchwork quilts" of different sub-communities. "This is a walkway of the diaspora from Eastern European and Russia," says Dubrow, as she and I wander through one of the cemeteries on Grove Street.

However, that diaspora has moved on. As the Jewish communities became more affluent, they relocated to suburbs such as Clinton Hill, Weequahic, Irvington and Ivy Hill – leaving their dead behind them. As a result, the cemeteries fell into disrepair, their lawns left un-mown, trash accumulating, stones falling over with no one to re-erect them and the small gates to each community section leaning more alarmingly as each year went by.

Today, a few efforts are underway to reverse the damage and Dubrow is among the most passionate about this mission. With the money given to her by an uncle, she established a fund that recently re-erected about seventy headstones in one section, and she hopes to raise more to help restore the cemeteries in their entirety. "It's gotten better – but this upsets me," she says, gesturing towards some fallen stones and picking up an empty plastic bottle lying near the graves of her husband's parents.

Yet it's not only neglect that has left the cemeteries in an altered state. The surroundings have changed, too. What was once rolling countryside (Jewish cemeteries were typically located on the outskirts of cities) is now an urban sprawl that's home to communities that are largely African-American, not Jewish. While trees and bushes once clustered around the cemeteries, the burial grounds now rub shoulders with the Aisha Hair Braiding salon, the Sand Pit BBQ Bar and the Heaven Belongs to You Ministries.

At its lowest point in the 1960s, the area was plagued by poverty, unemployment, corruption, crime, racial tensions and police brutality. Tension came to a head in the summer of 1967, when riots erupted. In one week of violence, twenty-six people were killed, hundreds were injured and tens of thousands of dollars' worth of property was destroyed. The cemeteries did not escape unscathed.

Things have improved dramatically since then, with a wave of urban regeneration sweeping through the area. However, on High Holy Days when a diminishing band of relatives returns to the cemeteries to pay respects, recite the mourners' kaddish and place stones on the graves, local officers from the Newark Police Department are still deputised to provide security and reassure visitors who remain wary of setting foot in a district they now feel is foreign to them.

Once inside, the cemeteries have a warm, familial atmosphere, with their "patchwork quilts" of communities. The stones tell poignant stories, too, of lives that started in one far-off country and ended in another; of lives cut short, with severed tree trunk gravestones symbolising deaths of those "young in years". Through granite and marble, they send us messages across time – memories that refuse to die. In places, graves are packed closely together, for the cemeteries were developed when money to purchase real estate was in short supply. Today, however, looking in from outside, the proximity of the stones seems to reflect something else – the need to huddle together for protection against the unfamiliar world that now surrounds them.

"If one who attains honour and wealth never returns to his original place," runs one Chinese proverb, "he is like a finely dressed person walking in the dark." This is particularly true for the Chinese dead, whose spirits cannot reach the afterlife until their bodies have been returned home, where relatives can visit them on grave sweeping days such as Qing Ming.

It appears that in China at one time, professional corpse walkers were employed to walk bodies back home for funerals. In his interview with the retired professional mourner Li Changgeng, Liao Yiwu says he's heard that these corpse walkers were paid to travel hundreds of miles in order to deliver the dead back to their homes. Liao wants to know if this is true. "Correct," begins the old man. He explains that they travelled in pairs at night, one in front, the other at the back, with the body suspended on the walker's shoulders by its arms, its feet trailing the ground. "Like carrying a sedan chair, and they pulled the body to walk along, as fast as the wind," says Li. "The would utter in unison, 'Yo, ho, yo, ho.'"

Of course, being walked back to your homeland is not an option when there's an ocean in the way. In the nineteenth century, as Chinese immigrants poured into America, this worried them greatly. During the gold rush, one of the first things Chinese workers would do on arrival at "Gold Mountain", as they called California, was to make arrangements for the twenty-thousand-mile passage home in the event of their death. They did have one advantage – the fact that their death rites included exhumation and secondary burial of the bones. They could therefore be buried in America and sent home once funding for the passage could be arranged.

So bodies were interred in shallow graves, giving them more exposure to air, which speeded up the process of decay. When sufficient time had passed for the flesh to fall away, individuals with titles such as "Chief scraper and gatherer of the bones of dead Chinamen", as one account records it, would exhume the remains. The bones would be cleaned and counted, sealed in a zinc-lined box and put on a ship bound for the Far East.

Organisations such as the Sam Yup Benevolent Association used membership dues to cover the costs of repatriating the bones of deceased compatriots who'd been interred on "foreign soil". Tracking down the remains could be a challenge. When in the 1870s, the association set out on a mission to rescue the remains of dozens of fellow citizens, the account records how, in search of a Mr Wong Sei, who was buried near Idaho's Salmon River, the exhumation team "had to hire horses and mules to take them there. They travelled by day and rested by night, sleeping outdoors in the wild, risking attack by wild beasts. The whole trip took them more than fifty days".

In Hawaii's Manoa Valley, the Lin Yee Chung Society Chinese Cemetery was established not only to ensure that Chinese burial rites were adhered to but also as a temporary resting place for the bones of migrant workers who came to Hawaii in the nineteenth century. A building on the cemetery's ground still contains jars, suitcases and boxes of remains that never made it home.

For Native Americans, it's legal rather than logistical battles that have been fought in order to return ancestors to their homelands for burial – ancestors whose remains (tens of thousands of them) have been stuck in the cabinets, drawers and display cases of museums around the United States.

The struggle to control ancestral remains emerged at a politically charged moment in the history of the American Indian civil rights movement. In the 1960s, prominent individuals started to put American Indian concerns in the spotlight. In 1969, Vine Deloria, a writer, activist and son of a distinguished Sioux family, published *Custer Died for Your Sins*, in which he attacked everyone from government bureaucrats and missionaries to members of Congress and the Bureau of Indian Affairs. He reserved his most searing criticism for the "anthros", whom he accused of reinforcing racial stereotypes and of treating Indian people as objects of observation, "like so many chessmen available for anyone to play with".

In 1971, anger against the "anthros" erupted when a group from the American Indian Movement disrupted a dig in Welch, Minnesota, claiming archaeologists were desecrating their ancestors' graves. In Los Angeles, another group of Native Americans occupied the Southwest Museum in a bid to remove human remains and cultural artefacts from the museum's displays, claiming the ancestral right to bury their dead in their homelands.

Recognition of the rights of American Indians to control the removal of archaeological material on their land came in 1979 with the passing of the Archaeological Resources Protection Act. However, it wasn't until 1990 that they were given the kind of protection enjoyed by all Americans when it comes to the sanctity of the grave. The Native American Graves Protection and Repatriation Act (NAGPRA) stipulates that, among other things, museums receiving federal funding must return human remains and cultural items such as funerary art to their descendants.

The issue still sparks debate. Some claim the protections offered by NAGPRA don't go far enough, while scholars argue that research will be hampered by loss of these items. Others suggest that tribes may have motives beyond the spiritual, since a reclaimed object can establish rights to land. However, thousands of human bones have now been returned and reburied, and many have hailed NAGPRA as a piece of civil rights legislation.

So how important is it where you're buried? Friends often tell me that, as far as they're concerned, they really don't care. I'm not so sure. While I don't need my body returned to my birthplace in Dorset, I still feel that it's important to end up somewhere meaningful; in a place with which I have a connection.

Philosophers might see such a sentiment as a futile attempt on the part of humans to shape from their lives some kind of narrative, with a beginning, middle and ending, when the reality is that none exists; life – and death – is random. My father's view on this was similar. "One is born, one lives, and one dies," Fa wrote at the end of the living will he asked me to sign a few years before his death. There's nothing more, nothing less, is what he seemed to be saying.

Well, it may be futile, delusional even, but I want my life to have a narrative – and, like any good novel, that includes an appropriate ending in a suitable location. Yet my thinking is slightly different from that of the Chinese, Native Americans and others who want to be returned to their homelands. Their choice implies a movement backwards, a return to a place of origin (ashes to ashes, dust to dust). I want something else from my final resting place – a means of going forward.

If you're travelling anywhere in the world and you happen to see a sign with the letters CWGC on it, stop and have a look. Regardless of whether you're in North Africa or Southeast Asia, whether surrounded by sub-tropical creepers or desert sands, you'll find a cemetery conjuring up images of an English country churchyard. The lawns will be pristine, green and neatly clipped – unmistakably English; unmistakably England.

CWGC stands for Commonwealth War Graves Commission, an organisation that marks and maintains the graves and cenotaphs of the hundreds of thousands of individuals from Commonwealth countries who died in the First and Second World Wars. Yet none of these graves rests on home turf.

The Commonwealth War Graves Commission was founded by Sir Fabian Ware, then commander of a mobile unit of the British Red Cross, and was established by Royal Decree in 1917. While its mission was unarguably noble, its formation did not come without controversy. For a start, the commission decided to bury the war dead without a nod to rank, status or religion, an extremely unorthodox notion at a time when class distinctions were woven into the very fabric of British society, particularly the military.

Also revolutionary was the practice of commemorating the dead no matter what the circumstances of their death, whether they were shot at dawn for desertion or slain heroically in battle. "We didn't care whether you'd won the Victoria Cross or whether you fell off your bicycle drunk," says Peter Francis, who's worked with the commission for more than a decade. "You were still serving with the Commonwealth forces so you deserved to be commemorated."

Most contentious, however, was the commission's proposal not to repatriate any of the bodies. There were practical reasons for this. The sheer numbers of dead in the First World War were overwhelming. Taken together, the death tolls for battles of the Somme and Verdun alone represented a fatality rate of nearly five men every minute. Transporting so many bodies home would have been impossible.

But there was another, more philosophical, reason behind the decision. The commission founders believed repatriating the dead would have led to discrimination, since the cost of sending corpses home would have separated rich from poor, creating divisions within an army that had been united in its fight to defeat the Germans.

The proposed ban on repatriation sparked fierce opposition. "It caused a bit of a fuss," says Francis. "But luckily, our chairman was Winston Churchill, and not a bad speaker." Churchill's mighty oratory did the trick. In a parliamentary debate in 1920, he spoke of a fellowship in death that crossed all social, racial and economic boundaries. The cemeteries, he said, would for thousands of years "preserve the memory of a common purpose pursued by a great nation in the remote past and will undoubtedly excite the wonder and the reverence of future generations". The opposition caved. The motion of non-repatriation was passed.

So no bodies were sent home for burial. Instead, dead from the two wars lie near to where they fell. In Cairo, they rest in a palm-fringed enclosure near the River Nile. In sub-tropical Hong Kong, they're overshadowed by the giant tower blocks that have arisen on the northeast of the island since the cemetery was built. In Thailand, their home is Kanchanaburi, a town at the confluence of two rivers that flow into the Mae Klong, where Japanese prisoners of war built the famous bridge over the River Kwai.

Notwithstanding a few adjustments for climate, topography and culture (Muslim graves align with Mecca; Hindus were buried after cremation), the format for the cemeteries is replicated in more than twenty-three thousand sites around the world.

In each one, inside a porch just past the wrought iron gate is a brass door on one wall reading "Cemetery and Memorial Register". Behind this door, tucked into a small recess, is a book listing the individuals buried in the cemetery. Inside – it's guaranteed – are modest gravestones, the same height, evenly spaced, identical in shape, carved from Portland limestone and neatly arranged to resemble soldiers on parade, with generals and officers buried next to infantrymen and military engineers. Shrubs and flowering borders soften the military precision of the ranks of graves.

A hundred years earlier, in the aftermath of the Battle of Waterloo, things were very different. While the bodies of high-ranking military officials might have made it home, ordinary soldiers were shovelled into pits near where they fell. Some were later exhumed, not for reburial but by scavengers who knew the value of the remains. In Victorian England, as dentistry advanced and false teeth became popular, alternatives were sought for ivory, which deteriorated quickly. Real human teeth were in great demand. War provided the supply.

By contrast, the commission ensured that the war dead were well looked after. And while no casualties of the First and Second World Wars were returned home, relatives could send a personal message to be engraved on the tombstone. Contacting the relatives of each soldier or officer it buried, the commission collected names and dates of birth, asked whether the family wanted a religious symbol such as a cross carved on the stone, and invited them to compose a few lines to be engraved on it.

On the headstones, powerful sentiments and sad histories are encapsulated in a handful of words. The father of Private Albert

Ingham, a twenty-four-year-old soldier who was executed in 1916 for desertion, requested the lines, "Shot at dawn, One of the first to enlist, A worthy son of his father". Others are delightfully creative. The family of Hugh Gordon Langton, who was killed at Passchendaele, Belgium, in 1917, wanted to reflect Langton's skills as a musician so requested a bar of musical notes.

I first saw a Commonwealth war graveyard in Italy. I'd spent the day with friends in a medieval town called Bolsena, about an hour north of Rome. After visiting its churches, we relaxed for a couple of hours in a local trattoria over some pasta and red wine. It was a hot August afternoon. The hills around were yellow and scrubby; the horizons dominated by olive groves and cypress trees. It was the Roman countryside at its summertime best.

On the way home, we spotted a sign with CWGC on it, stopped the car and entered the cemetery. Suddenly we were in a different country. It was unmistakably England. It was unmistakably English. There, at the entrance, was the brass door reading "Cemetery and Memorial Register." Behind the door was a book containing a long list of names. Simple, uniform gravestones were neatly laid out in ranks, like soldiers on parade. And the cemetery lawns were pristine, green and neatly clipped.

These days, the availability of jets and refrigeration technology makes getting a body home a relatively minor logistical exercise. So today, America's war dead are flown home (something that's become more public since an eighteen-year ban on media coverage of the returning coffins was lifted in 2009). And for civilians who die overseas, commercial airlines have business lines in shipping corpses. Handled by their cargo divisions, these shipments are growing as globalisation creates a mobile world whose inhabitants often want to be returned home after their death.

More than four thousand Brits die outside their homeland every year. Six thousand American civilians do so. And since the United States is so culturally diverse, hundreds of bodies leave its shores each year, many of them of Latin Americans, who make up more than half of the country's immigrants. And of course, many are on domestic flights, returning from retirement centres in Florida, Arizona and California to other parts of the United States.

Angie Berwald knows all about these cargos. She's president of National Mortuary Shipping and has been working for more than two decades with funeral directors to help families retrieve their "out of town" relatives. Her company is a sort of travel agency for the dead. "We contact the airlines and make all the arrangements," she says. Even when people have the funeral in their most recent place of residence, in the place where they're perhaps best known, many still want to be returned to their hometown afterwards. "They still want to be buried with their other family members," says Berwald.

This cargo was once handled in a desultory manner. No centralised operations existed at airlines for handling human remains. Funeral directors had to negotiate with each cargo facility and had no special units designed for handling human remains. "There were just caskets and of course the planes were also limited in their capacity to handle a casket," says Berwald.

On one occasion, an Irish friend told me, this led to a rather unusual scene at the airport. She remembers a cousin recalling the repatriation of her brother's body by plane from America. The family, she says, simply stood by the luggage carousel at Shannon Airport waiting for the coffin to come out on the conveyor belt.

Today, corpses rarely travel in caskets, let alone on luggage conveyor belts. They travel in an air tray or a "combo unit", a wooden and cardboard box designed to transport remains. The remains are placed in a hermetically sealed container, but since most bodies are embalmed before departure, decomposition en route isn't a problem. In any case, the air trays are designed to prevent leaks. (One ad for air trays in *American Funeral Director* magazine shows a man holding an upturned one above his head on a stick. "You wouldn't use our lead-resistant cremation tray as an umbrella," runs the headline, "but you could.") When the remains arrive at their destination, the funeral home provides the coffin.

Post-mortal repatriation is not cheap. In the UK, the cost of an "inbound" flight can be up to three times higher than a cheap ticket out of the country, according to BRITs (Beat Repatriation Inequality Together), a campaign to lower the cost of bringing home citizens who've die abroad. In the United States, the price of a final trip home can be up to ten thousand dollars.

This has prompted the birth of some inventive financial services businesses, many designed for Latino immigrants, whose families often struggle to find the cash for the passage back south. Los Angeles-based Servicios Especiales Profesionales is one. To the sound of a jaunty song called *Tu Tierra en Tus Manos*, or "Your Land in Your Hands" (the lyrics speak of Mexicans travelling north illegally only to end up dying there), the company's website explains that, for fifty dollars, you can buy a "certificate" covering the cost of repatriating a body for up to five years. Another company, Mexpro, has a package called *"Tus Brazos Hermanos* [your brother's arms] Repatriation Insurance", covering everything from legal paperwork and administrative assistance to collection, packing, shipping and transfer of mortal remains.

The airline industry has its own euphemisms for these transfers, such as "specialty shipments" and "special care" cargo, as well as acronyms – HRs (human remains) and HUGOs (HUman remains must GO, according to one online forum). At American Airlines, customers looking for these services evidently need to ask for the "Jim Wilson desk", named after the person who established the division. He's no longer alive, but his name lives on since the American Airlines "Jim Wilson Service" is now a registered trademark.

For the airline industry, repatriation of corpses generates a modest but tidy business. "It's not a major commodity for us," a Continental Airlines' cargo division executive told the *Journal of Commerce*. "But it's one we like to focus on because of the dollar return that we receive from moving these types of shipments."

At one point, the battle for the "dollar return" on these shipments became fierce enough to prompt airlines to devise marketing schemes similar to those offered to passengers. Through airline loyalty programmes, funeral directors could keep the "frequent dier" miles accrued by their clients' shipments. On Delta Airlines, for example, funeral directors could, according to the *Wall Street Jour-nal*, save air miles by paying through their credit cards, while Jet-Blue offered a return ticket to any funeral director who purchased about fifteen shipments for bodies.

These days, says Berwald, cost cutting means airlines have reined in such benefits. "And they've cut back on a lot of their larg-er planes, which creates a problem for us," she says. "In a smaller plane, the length of the unit won't make the turn through the door."

Still, as cash-strapped airlines look for additional sources of revenue, many are investing in equipment and trying to win more of the business, boasting about "bringing cargo to a better place" and stressing the "care and sensitivity" with which they treat their specialty shipments. You might call it "stiff competition".

Amid the few short instructional paragraphs Fa left for us – tanta-lising glimpses into his state of mind as he approached his death – he briefly explained why he'd chosen the spot where he wanted us to scatter his ashes. The reasons, he said, were simple – it was a "very beautiful place", but also, he wrote, "I have my very oldest friends there already (Jim and Dood Anderson)".

My father met Jim and Dood through Sam's family, when they were her mother's neighbours in West Sussex. After they moved to Dorset, some years later, Jim and Fa became very close. Consid-erably older, Jim became something of a father figure to Fa. The two were fellow anglers, spending long afternoons in waders in the middle of some quiet river where the conversation counted for more than the weight of the trout at the end of the line. Jim and Dood lived in a cottage near the church of St Mary Magdalene. When they died, they were buried in its small graveyard. For these friends, it seems, my father was prepared to put aside his atheist principles and leave his remains in a Christian burial ground.

What a lot we can learn about people from the choices they make in death. The means by which we elect to mark our departure from this world reflect hopes, fears, values and beliefs. And in the decisions about the body we must leave behind, we also reveal our feelings about love and friendship.

Since the earliest times, families have wanted to be buried in the same tomb or next to loved ones. A beautiful example of this appears on a late sixth-century BC. Etruscan casket known as the Sarcophagus of the Spouses. With their remains housed below, the couple appears in a sculpture on top of the teracotta tomb, where they recline together in an elegant, relaxed pose. With graceful hand gestures and smiling faces, they appear to be in the middle of animated conversation. United in life, they remain so for eternity.

Sometimes, the dead were buried in several locations to be joined with their various loves. In medieval Europe, women who'd married more than once could be divided up so they could end up near all their husbands. In the case of Eleanor of Aquitaine, the rich and powerful twelfth-century queen, a three-way burial was motivated by the desire to allow her influence to be spread to the broader population. She had a "visceral tomb" for her entrails in Lincoln Cathedral, while her heart was buried at Blackfriars in London and the rest of her body went to Westminster Abbey.

Burial decisions give us glimpses into the nature of friendship and love. When strolling through the chapel of Christ's College, Cambridge, the late gay activist and historian Alan Bray came across a seventeenth-century double tomb containing the remains of Thomas Baines and John Finch. Linking their marble portraits was a knotted cloth. Curiosity took Bray to other such double burials, such as the memorial plaque in Rome of John Seton and Nicholas Morton, documenting their wish to be buried together. The tombstones led him on an exploration of the centuries-old intimacy that existed between men before homosexual activity came to be viewed as a form of sexual deviance – an intimacy expressed in burial choices.

On the other hand, graveyard preferences can divide families. When Christine Hudson, a British woman from the village of Long Bennington, reserved a place in the same grave as her lover of twenty-five years, Alfred Nocquet, who died in 2007, it sparked a bitter row. Nocquet's three children by an earlier marriage vehemently opposed the plan, claiming Hudson's relationship with their father had broken down five years before his death and that they would not want to visit the grave if she were in it. The case went to ecclesiastical court, where the judge ruled in favour of Hudson and called on the family to settle their differences. "This would be the best way," the judge said, according to a report in the *Daily Mail*, "that the memory of Alfred Nocquet could be honoured by those who loved him."

The price of a post-mortal place next to the right person has a monetary as well as an emotional cost – and you have to wonder at what some are prepared to pay. For a Marilyn Monroe fan, the price was $4.6 million. This was the sum achieved for a crypt looking directly on to the actress's resting place at Westwood Village Memorial Park in Los Angeles when in August 2009 Elsie Poncher, who wanted to sell her late husband's crypt to pay off the mortgage, put it on eBay.

The bidder later backed out of the deal, so other buyers had to be sought. But there's another story here, too. Like rings handed back, houses sold or life insurance policies cancelled, the exchange of funereal real estate is another sign of a broken marriage or a love affair gone sour. Richard Poncher had bought the crypt in 1954 from Joe DiMaggio when Monroe was divorcing him on the grounds of mental cruelty. Joltin' Joe softened, though, when Monroe died in 1961; for twenty years after her death, DiMaggio had six red roses sent to her grave three times a week.

Of course, if you want to be certain of ending up next to someone, you need to do more than book the spot. You should make sure distance does not keep you from them. In the fourteenth and fifteenth centuries, this was a serious concern for the more mobile among the nobles of Europe. Often, the wills of husbands and wives provided for a joint burial at home, along with arrangements for the return journey.

Cecily, Duchess of York, the mother of two English kings, was careful to leave sufficient funds for a burial alongside Richard, her husband, who was killed in battle. When she died in Hertfordshire in 1495, the duchess made a seventy-mile posthumous trip – accompanied by a large retinue of householders and clerks – to

Fotheringay in Northamptonshire, where she joined her "most entirely best beloved lord".

For Fa, people and place coincided. To reunite him with his friends Jim and Dood in his chosen corner of Dorset, all Sam and I needed do was to hop into the car and drive through a few country lanes in the company of his ashes. But whether we're laid to rest after a short car ride, a long journey accompanied by a medieval retinue or a flight managed by the Jim Wilson Service, "home" doesn't necessarily have to be our place of birth – it can often be wherever our loved ones are.

So what about Martha Goodlad? In 1785, as she lay dying in Calcutta, did she contemplate sending her remains back to England for burial in the family churchyard? Probably not – in her day, transit to Britain by steamship from India meant a three-month journey. In the days before refrigeration, that would have left her corpse in a shocking state by the time it arrived on the docks in London. Calling up the Jim Wilson desk was not an option for Empire's citizens. So Martha was laid to rest in the place where she'd lived, a place whose connection with her native home now exists behind the dusty covers of British colonial history books.

The Park Street Cemetery is not the only "corner of a foreign field" where Europe's colonial bodies lie. Between 1600 and 1947, when India gained independence from British rule, about two million Europeans (most of them British) were buried on the subcontinent, according to the British Association for Cemeteries in South Asia. South Africa, Sudan, Iran, Hong Kong and other parts of the world once ruled by Europeans also house colonial cemeteries in various states of dilapidation.

The chances of Britain's empire builders dying were high, particularly in a place like India. On the plains, the heat was unbearable and if you didn't expire from cholera, malaria would get you. There were poisonous snakes and deadly scorpions. You slept under a mosquito net. You kept a mongoose at your house to fend off the snakes. You banged your shoes together before putting them on to make sure no that scorpions were lurking in the toes.

The memories of those who were born or lived in colonial India – their oral histories were recorded by Louisiana State University in the 1990s – paint a picture of an existence in which death was always around the corner. "You had to be very vigorous and tough to live," recalls G. N. Jackson. "The place was full of bilharziasis. There were Baghdad sores, terrible thing, great holes in your skin that wouldn't heal, dysentery all through the hot weather. Cholera. You had to be tough, you had to take care of yourself."

Many were unable to, particularly in the eighteenth and nineteenth centuries. Their stories – in compressed form – appear on the stones of cemeteries such as the one at South Park Street Cemetery. They tell of those who died "young and fair", in the "vigour of life", the "season of innocence". These long-gone imperialists died from illnesses that were "long and tedious", "lingering and painful" or, as we learn from Martha's tombstone, ones that brought a "most agonizing pain". Small wonder then that, as Kipling noted, at parties in the fall, "those who were alive gathered together to felicitate themselves on having come through another hot season".

For those who didn't make it, the end was brutal and sudden, even in the twentieth century. Living in India during the Second World War, Margery Hall remembers the death of "little Tommy Rushton" during a monsoon. "He was playing in the garden in the morning, at eleven. He was buried at six that night. It was as quick as that," she recalls. "He was buried in a downpour, where the grave was full of water. They just dropped the coffin into a lake."

In a climate where, as Hall puts it, "you went bad so quickly", burial had to be swift. Fergus Innes remembers the time the deputy commissioner of a remote district in what's now Pakistan was taken ill with a high fever. With no doctors near and the prognosis bleak, the assistant commissioners decided to get a coffin ready. However, the patient rallied and next morning had his bed carried out on to the verandah to get some fresh air. "As he lay there, what did he see but the man working," recalled Innes. "And he said, 'Who are you and what's that?' And the man turned round and said to him, 'The box has come for Your Honour.'"

With people around them dropping like flies, the Brits tried desperately to make India feel like home. When the summer heat of Calcutta got too much, they headed to the slopes of the Himalayas at Simla, shifting the machinery of government more than seven thousand feet above sea level every year at a time when mule carts were the best India had to offer in transportation logistics.

On the slopes of Simla, they surrounded themselves with the familiar, building mock Tudor cottages and Scottish baronial lodges decked out in chintzes and with names like Annandale or Mount Pleasant. "You had more or less ordinary English furniture," remembers Major-General William Odling. "You took your own pictures, and china, and silver, and glass, and linen, and those sorts of things." They engaged in amateur dramatics and held fancy dress parties, observing social distinctions more rigidly in India than in England. They were, recalls Philip Mason, expected to "keep up a front" and "dress for dinner in the jungle".

But in spite of the crockery and tea cozies, the Brits still felt of India that they were "strangers by her streams" as Mary Leslie, a colonial poet, put it in 1858. They might build Gothic Revival mansions, but they couldn't stop the troops of monkeys gambolling across the tennis lawns.

Indian nature interfered with the British way of death, too. At the 1916 funeral of Sir Alexander Pinhey in Hyderabad, writes Jan Morris in *Stones of Empire*, the bees nesting under the roof of the residency's portico were "so angry to be awoken by the strains of the harmonium that they sent the gun-carriage horses bolting down the drive".

Of course, some Brits thrived on the difference, and the chance to live bigger lives overseas than they could have done on their small, rainy island. But many longed for home. "Dear, dear England!" declared Susanna Moodie, a British-born Victorian author who described with passion her life as a settler in the Canadian wilderness – and her feelings of homesickness. "What heinous crime had I committed, that I, who adored you, should be torn from your sacred bosom, to pine out my joyless existence in a foreign clime? Oh, that I might be permitted to return and die upon your wave-encircled shores, and rest my weary head and heart beneath your daisy-covered sod at last!"

Perhaps, then, Martha Goodlad felt more like she was living "in a foreign field" than in somewhere that was "forever England". And if, like Moodie, Martha and the occupants of Park Street Cemetery had hoped one day to return to the "wave-encircled shores" they called home, their wishes were not granted. What's more, in an era when mail took up to six months to reach India, family back in England might not receive word of their deaths until some time after the fact, so would continue corresponding long after the funeral. A special place was established in Calcutta to manage this undeliverable mail. It was called the Dead Letter Office.

After her mother died in 1997, my friend Sheila was thinking about an appropriate place to scatter her ashes. She knew her mother had wanted to be cremated and that no flowers should be sent (her mother had always hated cut flowers – she saw them as dead things), but a suitable location for her remains didn't immediately spring to mind.

Widowed twenty years earlier, Sheila's mother spent the last eighteen months of her life in a nursing home, sad and depressed. Her happiest times had been the years just before the Second World War, when she and her husband, then newly married, lived in a flat in London's Maida Vale opposite the Warrington, an imposing Art Nouveau pub. "She used to speak fondly of Sunday afternoons, when they would stagger home from the pub with their friends, and she would try to slice the runner beans for lunch with an inexpert and unsteady hand," says Sheila.

After the war, the couple moved out to the suburbs and never visited the Warrington again. Sheila, however, happened to live near it, and opposite the pub was a large roundabout, which she'd pass every morning around 7am on her way to the swimming pool. It was always imaginatively planted with shrubs, herbs and grasses. This, Sheila realised, would be a perfect spot on which to scatter the ashes – it was within sight of the place where her mother had been so happy and she'd be amid living, growing plants.

"Knowing I'd have to be discreet, I stopped one day and scattered her ashes on the roundabout, where, as luck would have it they'd just planted rosemary, for remembrance," says Sheila. "The ashes were remarkably granular, and some of them lodged in the turn-ups of the rather natty trousers I was wearing that day. I still use that route regularly and I metaphorically tip my hat to her as I pass the roundabout. The rosemary has long gone, but the memory lingers on."

Whether your spiritual home is next to Marilyn Monroe or on a London roundabout, the task of getting your remains there becomes a whole lot easier if it doesn't involve a corpse. As cremated remains, the dead are highly portable. They can take flight – sometimes literally.

From Seattle, Aerial Missions operates an airborne ash scattering service across the coastal waters, rivers, lakes and mountain peaks of the Pacific Northwest. Jim Howard, a commercial pilot, and his wife Wendy, a licensed notary, launched the business after scattering Jim's father's ashes in the Adirondacks in New York State. "He loved it there," says Jim on the company's website. "I remember travelling the lake by boat and scattering his ashes at many of his favourite spots and areas along the lake … It felt to me like we were setting a human soul free, to drift on the currents of the wind and water."

The International Scattering Society has taken this concept and run with it globally. Calling itself "the travel agency for the deceased", the Missouri-based company can release your ashes over destinations such as Venice, the Swiss Alps, Cancun beach, Stonehenge and even Mount Everest.

Some have planned even more ambitious post-cremation journeys – trips into outer space. Since, 1982, a Houston-based company called Celestis has been arranging for small portions of human ashes to boldly go where no ashes have gone before. The service which piggybacks on commercial or scientific satellite launches has attracted celebrities, the most appropriate being Gene Roddenberry, the creator of *Star Trek*, whose ashes, or at least a handful of them, went into orbit in 1997.

The portability of ashes opens up all kinds possibilities. Volleyball athlete Misty May-Treanor has been taking small pots of her mother's ashes with her to sporting events. At the 2004 Summer Olympics in Athens, she sprinkled some on the court before the beach volleyball semi-final where she and Kerri Walsh won the match. She did the same thing four years later in Beijing, where her mother's ashes also worked their magic. "We can't leave her home alone," she told reporters after the match.

Send-offs for ashes are becoming quite theatrical, too. Perhaps most spectacular is the conflagration arranged by Angels Flight, a Californian company that loads cremated remains into modified shells and explodes them in the sky in a fireworks display.

Since they're in no danger of further decay, the cremated dead enjoy a more relaxed time schedule than a regular corpse. They can wait around until relatives find an appropriate slot in their diaries to get together for a scattering – or until the seasons change. Sam and I waited for five months before we scattered Fa's ashes, hoping that May would bring us a warm, sunny spring day with conditions that were, as he'd suggested, "calm, with no more than light winds".

Cremation gives the dead mobility. No longer tied to sanctified burial grounds, their options for final resting places become far more interesting. We may decide to return home. On the other hand, we could find a spot next to those we loved. Perhaps we'll end up in a favourite lake or on a mountain peak. Of course, many "cremains", as they're known are simply buried, or even left on the funeral director's shelves. But once our bodies have been freed from the shackles of weight, volume and putrefaction, decisions on where to make a "home" for our remains become less practical and more romantic and philosophical.

So where does that leave me? If I'm cremated, I can choose from an infinite selection of destinations. If friends are not available or willing to do the scattering, I can call upon the services of companies such as Aerial Missions or the International Scattering Society.

But if the "how" of my final ending is now easier to organise, the "where" is a question that continues to perplex me. I'm a child of globalisation. I've matured alongside it – when I first started travelling, communicating with family and friends meant collecting letters from the Poste Restante sections of post offices. Now my computer goes everywhere with me and I connect with people online, often without revealing where I am at any given time. Home is often my in-box.

I've also learned to call home wherever I've been happy – and that includes many places. There's Dorset, where I was born. There's the tiny 1860s terrace house in Edinburgh near the Victorian bathhouse where, as students, my flatmate and friend Lucinda and I would book adjacent cubicles and spend whole afternoons submerged in piping hot water in the huge ceramic tubs installed at a time when homes didn't come with bathrooms.

I've had many flats in London, as well as my "illegal erection" in Hong Kong. There was Cape Town, where in the house I borrowed one summer, I was followed everywhere by the owners' posse of affectionate dogs. There's the apartment in Hanoi, where each morning I woke to the sounds of women selling fresh bread as they yelled down the alley, "*Bahn mi!*" ("Good bread here!"). And now, of course, there's New York, where my apartment houses a coffin I commissioned for myself in the shape of the Empire State Building.

How can I choose from among these places? Is any one more my home than another? But do I even have to leave my remains at home? On my travels over the years, there've been times when, looking across a valley in the Himalayas or wandering through street market in Mexico, I've experienced a rush of exhilaration; a feeling that I could happily drop dead there and then. Wouldn't one of those places make a suitable home for my remains?

The day has come to scatter my father's ashes. My mother and I are in The Hut. Sam put the urn in here, no doubt because it was a convenient place to store it. However, it suddenly strikes me as appropriate that his remains have been lodged here. Some of his possessions have gone, but his computer is still sitting on the desk, watching over the proceedings – the computer on which he typed out the instructions we're now doing our best to follow.

"Listen, darling," says Sam in her no-nonsense voice. "I know how to do this – I've done it with soap powder." With a pair of kitchen scissors, she snips away at a thick plastic bag so its contents, tightly packed inside a steel pot, can flow out more freely. I'm worried that if we open the bag too wide, what's inside will spill out in a rush. Sam, however, is in household-chore mode. She's convinced her method will work – and, as usual, she's right. Suddenly our task is much easier. But before we can go on, we find ourselves on the floor, weeping with laughter at the absurdity of what she's just said. For, of course, the dust we're decanting isn't from the inside of a vacuum cleaner or a cereal packet. This dust was once a living, breathing human being: my father.

The reason Sam and I have embarked on the strange task of decanting my father's ashes is that we soon realised they'd be impossible to scatter from within the thick plastic bag stuffed inside the urn. We're going to put them into something else first. Fa's letter specified that a "polythene bag will suffice" and, as it turns out, a plastic bag is what he gets – two of them, in fact. One is from Fortnum & Mason, the posh London department store; the other from the less pricey but thoroughly British chain Marks & Spencer.

The idea is that when we start scattering the ashes, we won't attract attention (we didn't, as my father suggested, secure "prior approvals" as we thought this might complicate matters unnecessarily). It was Sam who devised the plan: we'll carry the ashes in the bags, and when we're ready, we'll snip the corners and stroll around casually, letting the contents trail out on to the ground. I feel sure Fa would appreciate the ingenuity of our little scheme.

My sister Kate is not with us. She's in London but she asked us to let her know when we'd be carrying out Fa's scattering. We telephoned her in the morning and she's happy with our plan so Sam and I set off in the car.

It's May and hedgerows are thick with cow parsley, blackberry brambles, wild garlic and curling ferns, all jostling for position in their gloriously crowded habitat. At this time of year, Dorset's narrow lanes – many of them dug deep into the earth – become dark tunnels of green pierced by pale shoots that reach up to catch the rays of sunlight.

The route we're following takes us past all our old Dorset homes and family landmarks. First, Spickhatch, the rented house in West Milton in which my parents lived at the time I was born. When we moved to Pear Tree Farm, a couple of miles away, our cat Porgy – perhaps driven by a homing instinct similar to that of America's early Chinese immigrants and Native Indians – would often return to Spickhatch. Whenever he went missing we'd find him prowling around the garden as if he still owned the place.

As we continue on our route, I notice that one of the bags containing Fa's ashes is pressing against my leg, gently moulding itself around my ankle. Is that my father at my feet, creating this cushion for my right limb? He would have almost certainly dismissed the idea. Nevertheless, I feel a certain comforting presence in the crushed bone dust nestling at my feet – a protector against any number of ferocious farm dogs.

We reach a junction in the road. At this point, in the days when Pear Tree Farm was home, we would have taken a left-hand turn down a steeply sloping tree-covered lane, which takes you to the hamlet in which we lived for several decades – Loscombe, a collection of houses and farms so small and hidden that, whenever a car passed our house, we'd rush to the window to see who was in it.

Today, instead of taking this road, we continue up the hill. Near the top, we stop at the entrance to a field. Sam and I get out of the car to take in the view of Loscombe and of our old house. It looks little changed at this distance, although Sam and I know that the present owners have in fact done a great deal to it. My father bought Pear Tree Farm in 1964 from a local farmer. It came with two fields, a barn and a cowshed. I still think of the little valley surrounding it as "ours".

It's about now I realise that, while we hadn't planned it this way, we're on a sort of tour of Fa's life in Dorset. More than

orty years of his existence are bound up in these narrow lanes and
muddy fields. As a surveyor and agricultural consultant, he's trodden most of this ground. He knew all the farms and their farmers.
Now after several years of being grounded by illness, he's out and
about again, surveying his territory – for I still can't help feeling
he's here with us, a tangible presence on the floor of the car.

At the church of St Mary Magdalene, we park and walk up a
narrow path towards it. The setting and tiny scale of the church is
utterly charming, while a gothic spire distinguishes its otherwise
modest form. A bright yellow sign tacked on to a telephone pole
at the churchyard entrance reads: Danger of death, and shows a
simplified image of a man being hit by an electric current.

Fortunately, once we get inside, the only danger appears to be
a large black male sheep, accompanied by a smaller white female
one. They're there, we suppose, to keep the churchyard grass cut.
They look ancient – and rather threatening. Still, they merely stare
passively on at our arrival. Also in attendance are five magnificent
pheasants and their hens. My father always admired these birds. In
remembrance of his shooting days he'd sometimes, on seeing one,
raise an invisible gun and pretend to fire. In the company of this
curious bestial gathering of onlookers, I let a few grains of ash trail
around the edge of the graves of Jim and Dood.

Okay, so it's not exactly what my father had specified, which
was to be scattered in the churchyard itself. However, the amount
of ash left by my father is not insubstantial (the average cremated male leaves behind seven pounds or so), and I was worried it
would damage the graveyard grass, so we separated off a tiny portion, which we decanted into the Fortnum & Mason bag, to sprin-
kle around his friends' graves. The rest, we're going to distribute
nearby.

Sam and I head back to the car. We want to find somewhere
appropriate to scatter the rest of the ashes. We drive down a muddy lane towards the bluebell wood. Every year in this enchanted
glade, for a brief but glorious couple of weeks, a blue mist rises
around the base of the trees; an ethereal cloud of colour that hovers
mysteriously just above the ground. I have a photograph of Fa in

this wood, his walking stick in hand, gazing ahead at this magical phenomenon. Sam thought we might scatter his ashes here. But sadly, the bluebells came early this year and we've missed the best of them so we head back up the hill.

Reaching a curve in the road next to a hillock, I have an idea. "I think this is where he took his 'X marks the spot' photograph", I tell Sam. We get out of the car to have a look. From the hillock, you get a perfect view of the church and the surrounding landscape. Standing with the photograph in my hand and the vista ahead of me, it seems that this must have been the place from which he snapped the image of what was to be his resting place. It even feels like my feet are planted on the exact spot where he stood, camera in hand. In any case, he's given us a certain license to improvise. "From my own point of view, however," his document states, "if none of it happened, as set out, it would not matter!"

I run back to the car to get the Marks & Spencer bag. Standing on the hillock, Sam takes the scissors and snips the corner. I start swinging it to release its contents. Suddenly, the wind takes the ash and sprays it wildly in all directions. The gusts taking hold of Fa's ashes are stronger than the "light winds" specified in his instructions. I can hear his "I told you so" voice as I try to control the direction of the flow – in vain. Some of his dust ends up in my shoes and across my legs. A fragment gets lodged in my right eye, causing it to stream with tears.

Sam is as usual ready to make the best of the situation. She says the wind is actually helping, since it distributes the contents of the bag, preventing it from falling into large mounds in one place. She's probably right, as I'm sure Fa would have grudgingly conceded. And in fact there's something spectacular about seeing the dust of my father become a swiftly flowing stream of grey-white smoke that's disappearing into the clear, fresh Dorset air. This is where Fa belongs.

8

Dem Bones

A Chapel in the Czech Republic

The toe bone connected to your – neck bone,
The neck bone connected to your – arm bone,
The arm bone connected to your – ankle bone …

Hang on a minute – what I'm looking at turns the lyrics of the old spiritual, *Dry Bones*, upside down and inside out. Here in a Bohemian chapel near the Czech town of Kutná Hora, someone has connected human bones to each other in ways that defy anatomical logic. In fact, this unlikely bone jigsaw seems to be challenging the whole relationship between human remains and the individuals to whom they once belonged.

Hanging from the chapel's ceiling is one of the world's most unusual chandeliers. Fringes of femurs dangle from its arms. Candles nestle in rosettes of pelvic girdles, their holders made from the most iconic of bony remains – skulls. Mandibles empty of their teeth join forces in unlikely chains. Sacra become finials topping the whole thing off. Strung between the chapel's stone arches like grisly Christmas decorations are festoons of human remains, with arm bones as spacers and skulls as the beads punctuating the swags. Dancing embellishments turn the ghoulish into something oddly festive.

The theatre of the macabre plays out in other decorations around the chapel's dingy interior. In an arched wall recess is a huge chalice. Topped with a rim of skulls, its bowl is formed from femurs sprouting up from pelvic girdles, while its stem is a complex assemblage of patellae and vertebrae. More pelvic girdles splay out at its base. In another recess, a large monstrance features a sunburst made from what look like tibias interspersed with sacra. At its centre, in the place normally reserved for the Host (the sacramental bread of the Catholic Eucharist), a single skull stares out at onlookers.

This is Sedlec Ossuary, a home for bones. And what a surreal storage facility it is. While most of the bones sit in four large pyramids, each in its own side chapel, others have prominent roles in the ornamentation. The chandelier alone is said to represent every bone in the human body while collectively the chapel decorations are thought to represent about forty thousand skeletons. Here in Sedlec, the remains of countless individuals have been pieced together to create something extraordinary.

Lying about forty-five miles east of Prague, the Cistercian monastery at Sedlec (pronounced "said-lets") was a major destination on medieval Europe's map – a destination for the dead. The monastery became a rich and powerful religious centre after the discovery of silver ore in the tenth century. By the thirteenth century great ecclesiastical edifices were rising nearby. Then something happened that was to raise Sedlec's status to even greater heights.

During the Crusades, in 1278, the Bohemian King Otakar II sent Henry, abbot of the monastery, on a diplomatic mission to the Holy Land. Before setting out for home from Jerusalem, Abbot Henry scooped up a handful of earth from Calvary and put it in his satchel. Once back at Sedlec, he sprinkled it over the cemetery, turning the graveyard into a de facto outpost of the Holy Land.

Almost overnight, Sedlec became one of Europe's most desirable burial grounds. Soon, people were sending the remains of their dead from all over Bohemia and Central Europe to be interred in the grounds made sacred by Abbot Henry's handful of earth.

Plenty of bodies needed to be buried. This was the time of the Black Death. Thirty thousand victims of the 1318 plague were buried in the cemetery at Sedlec. After the Hussite revolutionary wars of the fifteenth century (among the first in Europe to make effective use of gunpowder), many more corpses arrived at its gates.

In 1511, with the cemetery filling up, a monk took on the task of unearthing bones from the graveyard to make way for new arrivals. He turned the bones into six twenty-foot tall pyramids, where they remained until 1784. That was when the Schwarzenberg family bought the monastery and had the ossuary chapel remodelled. Seventy-six years later, in 1860, the family commissioned a woodcarver called Frantisek Rint to create something artistic from the millions of bones piled up in pyramids.

After bleaching and disinfecting the bones, Rint got to work. Dismantling two of the six pyramids, he had an ample supply of material to work with so he chose only the best, most uniform pieces for his masterwork, burying the rest in the cemetery outside. By 1870, with help from his wife and children, he'd finished his unusual commission. To honour his patrons, Rint recreated the Schwarzenberg coat of arms in bone. In it, a crow pecks at the eye of a skull (fashioned, of course, from a skull) with a plumed headdress – a reminder of the family's victory over the Turks in the late sixteenth century. Using bone fragments, he dated his work and signed his name: "1870, Frantisek Rint" of "Ceska Skalice".

This is all we know about Rint. Apart from the letters spelling out his name and hometown (a settlement on the Czech-Polish border), no records exist to give us further clues about his life. What we're left with is his work – a resting place for the dead. And of all the resting places in which human beings have ended up, Rint's bleached bone installation must qualify as one of the most bizarre.

The relationship between a living person and the body they leave behind is puzzling. Just how much of an individual resides in a pile of bones? Exactly which bit – if any – of the human self is left behind after flesh and blood has dried up, rotted off or been incinerated? What exactly are we after our heart has stopped beating – a person, or an object? "Organic matter," would have been my father's answer, at least at one time. For his request to have his ashes scattered in a churchyard near his Dorset home seems to indicate that ultimately he thought otherwise.

Fa's ashes had arrived back from the Weymouth & Portland Borough Council crematorium in a cardboard box. Inside was a squat classical urn, made of what seemed to be toughened tin or steel, with a surface finished to mimic darkly polished brass. It was a plain enough object, although I'm sure it wouldn't have been plain enough for him. As he'd written in his final instructions, "no brass casket to contain the ashes is needed; a cardboard box, or polythene bag will suffice". Oh dear. Well, at least we got the cardboard box bit right.

During the months before we scattered the ashes, they (he?) sat on a wooden shelf in The Hut. On one side was the assortment of plastic models of jet planes I'd collected for him on my travels. On the other was an Egyptian brick, a rectangular block of sand-coloured clay with rows of tiny hieroglyphs imprinted on one side. His father, who'd been a military doctor, brought the brick back to England in the 1930s after a trip to the Middle East.

I'd spent a lot of time wondering what exactly was in that faux-brass urn. How much of my father was amid the grey-white granular particles in the thick plastic sack that was the innards of the urn? I asked Sam whether she thought of the material stored in The Hut as Fa. "Yes, I suppose I do," she said. "Well, it's his bones. But I don't think of his spirit as out there – it's really just his bones."

I wasn't sure what I felt. My rational side (the one I acquired from Fa) told me he was gone. But I couldn't help thinking that some element of my father was in there, keeping company with a few plastic airplanes and an ancient Egyptian brick.

In scientific terms, the urn contained mostly calcium phosphate. Our bones are made up of about 70 percent mineral matter and 30 percent organic matter. The mineral component is what gives bones the rigidity needed to hold up our fleshy bodies. The organic parts, which decompose after death, are like shock absorbers, giving the body the flexibility needed to sustain physical impacts. Most of the organic matter is formed by collagen, while small crystals make up the mineral portion.

But while bones may be mere minerals, we can't seem to shake off the association between those minerals and the individuals of whom they were once part. Even the granules and dust that make up cremated remains, crushed beyond recognition, seem to retain their personalities. We keep them on the mantelpiece or in a box in the basement. We sometimes continue to include them in our lives, as one American woman I know does. Every year on her mother's birthday, she takes her ashes down, places them at the centre of the dining table, bakes a birthday cake and invites the family to eat it sitting around the urn.

We even pay money to see the remains of the dead. Body Worlds, the show displaying real human bodies stripped of skin developed by German anatomist and physician Gunther von Hagens, has attracted more than thirty-one million visitors since it first opened in Tokyo in 1995, pulling in crowds in locations from Prague to Pittsburgh (and has people lining up to donate their own bodies to the project). The exhibit consists of plastinate bodies (whose fluids and fat are replaced with substances such as epoxy and silicon rubber) in a variety of lifelike poses. Von Hagens insists that the show helps visitors to understand how muscles, organs and vascular systems interact to keep us alive. But my guess is that's not the only reason the crowds are there.

Human remains are potent symbols, often used in religious rites. The early Mayan people carved human bones into ritual objects. Tibetans fashioned femurs into horns for use in exorcism rituals or ceremonies invoking good weather (their sound is supposed to scare off evil spirits while pleasing deities). Human bones have been used as drinking cups and daggers. Teeth have found their way into necklaces. So while, scientifically speaking, bones are merely pieces of inorganic calcium phosphate, their significance extends far beyond their mineral composition.

Whether it's a femur trumpet, a necklace of teeth, plastinate corpse or a chandelier in a Bohemian chapel, human remains can be much, much more.

On the night train to Prague, my accommodation is a high-tech version of an old-fashioned sleeper carriage. Doors shut with an antediluvian clunk but open with a plastic key card. Inside, a blue mock-granite washbasin is cleverly concealed in a small cupboard, the outer bulge sticking out, as if a miniature flying saucer has become lodged in its doors. I last travelled through the Czech Republic in the 1990s, when visiting some American friends living in Prague. Together we'd toured the countryside for a few days and one of our stop-off points was the Sedlec Ossuary, where I remember being astonished by the chapel decorations. I still have the tiny folded souvenir pack of photographs I bought there at the time. Ever since, I've been curious to revisit the place.

As the train enters the Czech Republic, my mobile phone beeps. In today's European Union, there are no midnight passport checks conducted by frontier guards boarding the train with flashlights and rough voices. Instead, a text message from the phone company telling you the service provider has changed is all that indicates a border crossing. Soon, the train is passing through towns with names I can't pronounce – Prackovice, Litchovice, Lovosice. Medieval castles perched on rocky peaks rise above densely forested countryside. The romance intensifies on arriving in Kutna Hora itself, where splendid medieval squares and postcard-perfect cobbled streets sit in the shadow of spectacular Gothic cathedrals and medieval palaces.

The district surrounding Sedlec Ossuary benefits from none of this historic charm. Today, the ossuary is at the edge of a suburb dominated by public housing and approached via a nondescript road. I don't remember these utilitarian surroundings from my last visit and I'm wondering if this is the right place. Then, seeing a line of tourist coaches parked outside a church, I know I'm on the right track. I enter the gates and follow a path through the graveyard to the chapel behind the main church.

After paying for my ticket, I head down the steps and into the lower section of the chapel, which houses the ossuary. There, the place is crowded with visitors chatting loudly and cooing at the bone decorations. "Just think, all these people died, and I bet they never thought for a minute they'd end up in this," says a British woman gesturing with one hand and shaking her head disapprovingly. "What a cool place to be on Halloween!" exclaims an American man in blue shorts and a T-shirt.

Two big tour groups arrive – a party of schoolchildren and a cohort of student photographers equipped with tripods and long lenses. A high-pitched electronic alarm goes off as a photographer pokes his zoom through the bars towards one of the bone pyramids. The schoolchildren don't seem at all disturbed by the dismembered skeletons. They're too busy throwing coins up at the skulls, trying to get one lodged in an eye socket – death and its symbols reduced to a game of skill.

Soon, however, everyone files out. Children, photographers, cameras and tripods all disappear. Like a railway station platform after the train has left, the chapel is empty and silent, marked by the absence of what went before.

Suddenly alone, I feel like an intruder – this, after all, is the domain of the dead, a club that has not granted me membership (at least, not yet). And now I'm alone, my imagination begins to work. I can hear a faint chorus of sound calling out from distant centuries. I'm reminded of a scene from Samuel Beckett's Waiting for Godot in which Estragon and Vladimir, the two tramps, are discussing "all the dead voices", how they whisper and rustle – or do they murmur?

Vladimir: What do they say?
Estragon: They talk about their lives.
Vladimir: To have lived is not enough for them.
Estragon: They have to talk about it.
Vladimir: To be dead is not enough for them.
Estragon: It is not sufficient.
[Silence.]

Children often imagine their toys coming out to play while they're sleeping. Is that what happens to the bones in this chapel? Once the tourists have gone, do the dead turn up to inhabit their bleached remains, dance around before reassembling themselves into a garland or a candlestick, ready for the next tour group?

From empty sockets, the skulls stare blankly out at me. Who were these people? What did they eat? What did they wear? What were their hopes and fears? What was it like to be alive when one in three people were dying around you? How did you carry on tilling the fields after you'd buried a wife and six children? The lives of these people seem so remote from mine. And yet, when flesh, fashion, mobility and speech are gone, we'll all look pretty much the same. Memento mori – "Remember you will die." That, at least, is the message the bones here seem to give me; a scrap of intelligence from beyond.

In medieval Europe, it was common to dig up long-buried bones and store them in charnel houses and ossuaries to create space in the churchyard for fresh corpses. Bones ended up in great piles or, like those in the ossuary of Wamba in northern Spain's Church of Santa Maria, Valladolid, were simply stacked up. Others were neatly arranged. At the English church of St Leonard's, Hythe, two thousand skulls and eight thousand thighbones are laid out on shelves as if awaiting some rush of morbid shoppers.

While these bone accumulations are the result of practical measures to prevent cemetery overcrowding, those responsible for them often decided to do something creative with their charges. In Rome's Capuchin Crypt, the artist – possibly an eighteenth-century monk – arranged bones according to their shape, turning pelvic bones into rosettes, vertebrae into garlands.

In the sixteenth-century Capela dos Ossos in Evora, a Portuguese town not far from Lisbon, the bones of an estimated five thousand individuals, thought to be soldiers and plague victims, are embedded decoratively in the chapel walls.

The skeletal festoons and swags at Sedlec are the most daring of Europe's ossuaries decorations, but they're certainly not unique.

One of Europe's biggest bone collections lies beneath the streets of Paris at Denfert-Rochereau. Known as the Empire of the Dead, these catacombs lie sixty-six feet below the Fourteenth Arrondissement (lower even than the Paris Metro and the city's sewerage system). There, roughly six million bones and skulls are piled up against the walls of several miles of subterranean corridors.

The Paris catacombs were born of a burials crisis. In the late eighteenth century, the city's cemeteries were bursting at their seams – literally. In one instance in May 1780, a communal grave running along the Rue de la Lingerie split open, disgorging its contents into the cellars of neighbouring houses. Similar spillages occurred in other parts of the city, too, sparking public outrage.

Soon after, Alexandre Lenoir, lieutenant-general of police, devised a plan to construct new catacombs in the abandoned limestone quarries that then lay on the city outskirts. Once the catacombs were completed, the bones from several Parisian cemeteries were transferred down to the dingy caverns. To avoid distressing locals, hundreds of cartloads were shifted at night shrouded in black cloths. Along the way, priests chanting the Office of the Dead accompanied this morbid cargo.

It's a strange sort of resting place. But as at Sedlec, it's an ornamental one. While much of what is lining the walls could be mistaken for neatly stacked logs of wood, some of the bones decorate the surfaces, forming crucifixes or heart shapes. And the catacomb designers certainly knew how to play up the drama of their dungeon for the dead. An ominous sign at the entrance tells visitors: "*Arrête! C'est Ici L'Empire de La Mort*" (Halt! This is the Empire of Death).

Throughout the winding passages, a series of quotations from French writers such as Racine, Rousseau and Lamartine, and ancient scribes such as Homer, Horace and Virgil play their part in a gloomy drama. "*Croyez que chaque jour est pour vous le dernier,*" is one from Horace, translated from the Greek, which in my very loose translation runs something like this: "Live every day as if you're going under a bus in the afternoon."

But skeletons don't always need poets and philosophers to pass on their messages. Some of the remains housed across Europe tell us about the medical history of the people whose living bodies once relied on them. In the Sedlec ossuary, as anthropologist Charles Merbs has pointed out, the bird's wing in the Schwarzenberg coat of arms is made from the hand and wrist of someone with arthritis so severe that the bones fused together forming a single piece.

At the ossuary in St Leonard's Hythe, the benefits of a sugar-free diet are evident in a collection of teeth that, though worn, show few signs of decay. More worryingly, however, holes in some of the skulls indicate that their owners underwent trepanning, an agonising medieval therapy in which the cranium was perforated with a saw. Other details emerge in the skulls at St Leonard's. In many of them, a high cephalic index (the ratio of the widest point of the head to its length), something that was not an English trait, may indicate genes passed down through intermarriage during the Roman occupation of Britain.

Our bones have tales to tell. They speak of hideous wounds, primitive medieval surgeries and natural deformities. But others, like the skulls housed at St Leonard's with their unexpected shape, tell a bigger story about the ethnic shifts in a society. History, demographics, migration patterns and geopolitics – they can all show up in the curvature of a cranium.

Medieval Europeans dug up bones for purely practical purposes – to create more space in the cemetery. But exhumation and reburial can be important ceremonies in their own right. Anthropologists call them "rites of secondary treatment", and they usually mark the spirit's departure for the afterlife, representing a vital stage in the leave-taking of the living from the dead.

Double burials are practiced in a surprisingly diverse range of places, from Bali, where the corpse is unearthed for its cremation, to Vietnam, Borneo and Greece – parts of the world with radically different languages, cultures and beliefs, yet united in the practice of digging up and reburying the bones of their dead.

Robert Hertz, an influential French sociologist born in 1881, was fascinated by double burials and how they reflect a changing relationship between the body, the soul and the survivors. Drawing on well-documented practices found in Borneo, he argued that as the "wet" body deteriorates, it loses its status as a member of the living community, and hovers temporarily on the threshold of society. As the corpse gradually separates from its bones, the soul is forced to wander in a sort of limbo. Once the "dry" bones are free of flesh, the soul's "liminal" phase ends and it can enter the land of the dead.

In Greece, traditional death rites in rural villages also involve digging up remains. Loring Danforth describes these rites in Potamia following the tragic death of Eleni, a young girl from the village who died in 1974 in a hit-and-run accident. After an all-night vigil with her mother, Irini, Eleni is buried in the customary Greek outfit for women who die unmarried – a white bridal gown and a wedding crown. (Links between death and marriage often appear in death rites. After all, in different ways, weddings and funerals are both occasions for saying goodbye.)

For Irini, the exhumation is a painful experience. "The chorus of laments could not mask the sharp ring of the shovels against the earth, nor could it blot out the increasingly violent cries and shouts of Irini and [her friend] Maria," writes Danforth. When the skull is uncovered, Irini cradles it "as she would have embraced Eleni were she still alive". Eleni's bones are placed in a box in the village ossuary. Looking down at the empty grave Irini sighs wearily. "Eleni, my child, you have gone away," she says. "But you will never come back."

For Irini, it's the end of a prolonged and highly emotional relationship, for during the year after her daughter's death, she left the house only to visit the grave, where she talked to her, wept and sang mourning songs.

Between death and exhumation, the relationship between the living and the dead can continue in other ways, too. "Women in mourning," explains Danforth, "frequently report dreams in which the soul of a dead person appears to them with a request that some service be performed." It might be for food, water or clothing, but once the requests have been fulfilled and the bones have been exhumed (the final service performed for the dead), the dreams tend to stop.

Astonishingly, this phenomenon appears in yet another, very different, part of the world – Vietnam. One story I heard suggests an uncanny connection between living and dead in the period between burial and exhumation. After the burial of her father, Nguyen Thi Thuan, a Vietnamese teacher living in Hanoi, started experiencing terrible headaches, accompanied by vivid dreams in which her father would talk to her. Night after night, he would appear, agitated and desperately trying to tell her something. Thuan could not work out what he was saying.

When the day came for her father to be exhumed, the family went to the cemetery. As soon as they uncovered the bones, Thuan knew the cause of her father's agitation – growing through his skull was the root of a tree. They removed the root, retrieved the bones, cleaned them, arranged them in the proper order and placed them in the clay pot designated for his re-burial. That night Thuan had no headaches or unsettling dreams and she has had none since.

While science and rational thought might tell us otherwise, human remains have a funny habit of living on. Even after the death certificate has been signed, we persist in attributing thoughts, sensations and feelings to the dead. Throughout history, people have endowed corpses with all kinds of special powers, whether political, medicinal or spiritual. Corpses could contaminate or cure, give life or take it away, curse or bless, wreak revenge or deliver wealth and happiness. They refused to do what they were supposed to: lie down and keep quiet.

In the early seventeenth century, treatises such as Dr Heinrich Kornmann's *De Miraculis Mortuorum* described corpses that could laugh, cry, speak, jump and scream. It was also once believed that the body parts of decedents had curative properties. According to Philippe Ariès, a woman with dropsy (build-up of fluid between the tissue cells) could be cured if she were to rub the warm hand of a fresh corpse across her abdomen. Bones worn around the neck or sewn into clothing prevented disease. The finger of a dead comrade could help a soldier emerge from the battlefield unscathed.

Cadavers can even play detective. It was once believed that the corpse of a murder victim would start to bleed at the approach of its killer. The superstition appears in Shakespeare's *Richard III*, when, at the funeral procession, Lady Anne cries out that the murdered Henry's wounds "Open their congeal'd mouths and bleed afresh!" It is, she says, a "deed, inhuman and unnatural / Provokes this deluge most unnatural".

As well as producing a "deluge most unnatural", bodies could also stand up for themselves in court (well perhaps not stand). In one of the more bizarre episodes in the Catholic Church's history, a ninth-century pope, Formosus, was yanked from his grave in Rome for a macabre trial – the "Cadaver Synod" – in which the rotting papal corpse was accused by his successor, Stephen VI, of usurping the papal office. Dressed in vestments propped up in a chair, the unfortunate and no doubt malodorous cadaver was found guilty. Three of his fingers were cut off – those used for blessings, so symbols of his authority – and his body was hurled into the Tiber.

The potency of the corpse has inspired other posthumous acts of violence. During the French Revolution, while aristocratic heads were being sliced off, the remains of dead kings and queens were also punished when the tombs at the abbey church of St Denis, used as a royal necropolis since the Middle Ages, were desecrated and the bodies summarily dumped in nearby pits.

And so powerful was the Andean cult of the dead that when the Spanish conquistadors arrived in Peru in the sixteenth century, they felt it necessary to destroy the royal mummies before they could convert the people they'd conquered to Catholicism. For the Andeans, the destruction was devastating. They considered the mummies sacred living potentates (every year they'd take them out of their tombs and display them in Cuzco's main square, where they offered them food, drink and prayers), and as they could no longer feed them, they imagined them suffering terrible starvation.

Jeremy Bentham, the English philosopher and social reformer, believed that, through his remains, he might continue to influence the affairs of the living. In his will, Bentham, who died in 1832, requested that his skeleton (along with the "soft parts" of his body) be preserved, dressed in a black suit and placed inside a case, seated "in a chair usually occupied by me when living". The case, he continued, should occasionally be taken to the chamber in which his friends and disciples met and "stationed in such part of the room as to the assembled company shall seem meet".

His request was fulfilled, although the preservation of his head went horribly wrong and it's a wax version that now tops his be-suited skeleton. Today, the "Auto-Icon", as he called it, sits in its cabinet at the end of the South Cloisters of the main building at University College London. Legend has it that he's still wheeled in to join College Council meetings, where he's recorded as "present but not voting".

For me, the Cadaver Synod or Bentham's creation of his Auto-Icon are the acts of a species gripped by an inescapable bond – that between a living and a dead individual. We just can't let go. For some, double burials succeed in severing the link. Yet others insist on anthropomorphising, assigning abilities, motives and emotions to lifeless flesh, and even using this as an excuse to wreak revenge on their late enemies. Whether driven by hate or by a desire to retain influence over college council meetings, I wonder if this isn't simply another way of persuading ourselves that there is indeed some form of life after death.

Poke around a bit in any of Europe's churches and cathedrals and you'll probably find in a side chapel on an altar small caskets that are deeply carved, elaborately decorated and heavily gilded, with glass sides that permit a glimpse of what lies within. This is usually something that looks decidedly grim – a blackened finger bone, a piece of what you're told is an elbow, a finger or, if you're lucky, a whole skull, often resting on beds of dusty cotton wool. These are pieces of dead saints and martyrs. Since the dawn of Christendom, they have been placed in reliquaries and venerated as holy objects.

Europeans are not alone in their reverence for sacred remains. A Muslim pilgrimage shrine in Srinigar, India, houses a whisker believed to have come from the beard of the Prophet himself. The whisker is displayed on important Islamic religious days in a glass casket inside the Hazratbal mosque on the banks of Lake Dal.

Possessing far more powerful properties than your average cadaver, these fragments have for centuries inspired pilgrims to make long and arduous journeys to pray and prostrate themselves before them. They still do. When in 2008 the body of Padre Pio – the controversial Catholic saint known for his stigmata (palm wounds resembling those of Christ on the cross) – was exhumed and displayed in a glass casket on the fortieth anniversary of his death, a million or so people visited the shrine, many hoping to be cured of disease and disability.

The healing properties of saints' relics even extended to those with no wish to be cured. One story has it that in the medieval city of Tours, a couple of beggars – one blind, the other a cripple – heard that the body of Saint Martin was to be paraded around the town to heal the sick. This was unwelcome news for the beggars, for their disabilities were critical in attracting alms. But while trying to make their escape as Saint Martin's body approached, they got caught up in the crowds and, against their will, had their ailments removed (along with their earnings potential).

But the fascination with relics is about much more than healthcare. These pieces of human remains also draw their potency from the legends and miracles that were associated with their owners in life. In relics, the morbid is endowed with something extraordinarily mystical. Most importantly perhaps, relics are a strange mixture of this world – a genuine piece of a human being – and the world to come, providing a bridge between terrestrial life and the afterlife.

Given the power of relics, people often wanted to possess their own, as we learn from a short story by nineteenth-century French writer Guy de Maupassant. *The Relic* takes the form of a letter to Abbé Louis d'Ennemare from his friend Henri Fontal. Fontal had given his fiancé Gilberte, the abbot's cousin, a sheep's bone, claiming it was a saint's relic he'd stolen from a cathedral (he in fact bought a genuine one on a trip to Germany but then lost it). "Just note this," writes Fontal, "I had violated a shrine; violated and stolen holy relics, and for that she adored me, thought me perfect, tender, divine."

Unfortunately, when Gilberte visits Cologne, she finds the cathedral from which her lover "stole" the relic does not exist. Realising he's fabricated the whole story, she breaks off the engagement, saying she'll only forgive him if he brings her a real relic. Thus the unhappy Fontal finds himself writing to the abbot to beg for an introduction to a cardinal or prelate who might help him to procure one (Maupassant doesn't tell us whether or not Fontal is ultimately successful).

Getting your hands on a relic was easier if you were wealthy and powerful. Spain's sixteenth-century Hapsburg King Philip II, was a particularly enthusiastic collector. He had hundreds sent to him from all over Europe. In fact, there was something of the trainspotter in Philip – he wanted in his collection a relic from every single Spanish saint. In his austere palace-monastery near Madrid, the Escorial, he would kiss his favourites each night before retiring to bed. Throughout the illness of his later years, he'd have corresponding relics – one of Saint Alban's ribs perhaps, or a bit of Saint Sebastian's knee – applied directly to the parts of his own body that most ached.

In 1598, when the monarch lay on his deathbed in the Escorial, his obsession helped his daughter keep him awake so he could – as she believed necessary for the salvation of his soul – greet death with his eyes open. Watching him around the clock, whenever he drifted off, she'd cry, "Don't touch the relics!" as if someone had entered the room and was laying hands on one of the precious bone pieces. This had the desired effect – Philip's beady eyes would pop open to make sure no one was tampering with his beloved collection.

The cult of saints' relics became so well established that they acquired hierarchical categories. First-class relics were the bodies or body parts of saints. Second-class relics were objects touched by a saint, such as a piece of clothing, while third-class relics were objects that had touched either a first-class or a second-class relic (and, of course, there were fakes). Amazingly, the miraculous power of a saint's relic didn't diminish with the size of bone fragment. A tiny splinter, a fingernail or even a single hair was just as good as the whole body.

This was fortunate for the early Christian church. Since relics could convert pagan sites into holy ones, they became powerful tools in spreading the religion to far-off places. But demand for sacred remains far outstripped supply, so the saintly were sliced and diced and shunted around the religious centres of Europe. The relic's journey was known as a *translatio*, or translation, and along with the pilgrimages made to visit them, they created bonds between members of the new church across Europe. In a pre-internet era, relics were the nodes linking a web of religious connections, giving the lonely faithful, who were so widely dispersed, something tangible – something they could see and touch.

Relics travelled in richly decorated biers, accompanied by religious ceremonies and all-night vigils. When they arrived, grand pieces of architecture were waiting to house them (Sainte-Chapelle in Paris, built by Louis IX, was designed in the shape of a giant reliquary). And while great cathedrals were sometimes built on the graves of the divine, such as St Peter's in Rome, it was cheaper to take the relic to the church than the church to the relic.

Some relics are extremely well travelled. The relic of St Francis Xavier, the sixteenth-century Jesuit missionary to India, has been hauled across several continents. In 1614, he lost an arm when it was sent to Rome as evidence in the case for his canonisation (it's still there, in the Church of the Gesù). His humerus, or funny bone, is in Macau. And when in 1975 his body was processed around Goa, India, in the ten-yearly "exposition of the relic" (a tradition initiated in the nineteenth century), a few toes and other bits were also reported as missing.

St Thérèse of Lisieux, the French Carmelite nun who died of tuberculosis in 1897 at the age of twenty-four, is even more of a globetrotter – she's so far visited more than forty countries. In 2002, her remains were sent to Baghdad in the hope that they could avert war in Iraq. In 2009, she visited twenty-eight destinations around the United Kingdom. Some of her relics have even been propelled into space to orbit the Earth.

Another celebrated nun, St Theresa (the one Bernini depicted in the midst of sensual rapture in his marble masterpiece at St Peter's, Rome), had her body exhumed many times after she died in 1582 at the Spanish convent of Alba de Tormes (the corpse was said to be as fragrant as lilies), and various parts were removed each time. Her hand ended up with General Franco, the Spanish dictator, who kept it beside his bed at all times. But the most important piece of her, the heart, is displayed in a resplendent gold, silver and glass case in the convent at Alba. Here is "organic matter" at its most sacred and spectacular – a recognisable piece of a human body, an organ that once kept that body alive, transformed into a holy shrine.

Relics were also kingmakers. A *translatio* came to symbolise the transfer of power, and in the early medieval struggle for supremacy among Europe's great cities, metropolitan rulers used relics to boost their civic stature, secular identity and religious authority. Among the most desirable, of course, were the remains of the four evangelists, Matthew, Luke, John and Mark. And if you didn't have a relic to hand, you needed to get one from somewhere else.

In the ninth century, this is what the young city of Venice was bent on doing. The doge, Venice's ruler, reckoned the body of Saint Mark would do nicely, legitimising the city's position on Europe's fast-evolving map. But the way Venice secured the apostle's remains was far from legitimate. Some call it the greatest heist in Christendom. The city didn't have much of a claim to the relic in the first place. After all, at the time when the great saint was working on his gospel, Venice was still a marshy bog. And the trouble was, the evangelist's body lay where he was martyred – in Alexandria, a city then under Muslim rule.

There are several versions of the story of Venice's audacious theft, but my favourite is one I heard at a lecture given by an art history professor who clearly enjoyed telling the tale. Here's roughly how it went:

Spreading rumours that Muslims were planning to desecrate Saint Mark's relic, two Venetian merchants set off in a trading vessel to "rescue" the evangelist's body from Alexandria. Their plan was to start a series of fires on arrival to distract the authorities while they retrieved their precious quarry. The first bit of the plan worked like a dream. But as luck would have it, news of their action escaped and, with their ship about to depart, the merchants learned that customs officials were on their way to search the hold.

One of the two, a quick-thinking fellow, ran down to the local market and purchased a job lot of pork bellies, which he hauled back to the ship and packed around the saint's body. When the officials arrived, the merchants waved their arms graciously in the direction of the hold, saying: "Go ahead and search the vessel. We won't stop you." Taking one look at the pork-packed hold, the Muslim officials thought better of it and sent the Venetians on their way. Back in Venice, the merchants presented the relic to the doge, who immediately installed it in his private chapel.

The story doesn't end there. St Mark's presence in Venice transformed the city's fortunes. Because the saint's remains were kept by the doge – not the pope, local bishop or any other religious leader – he was able to free the city from the heavy hand of Rome's papal influence. Instead, he formed an inner circle of his own, appointing clerics to perform the city-state's religious and administrative needs without interference from external ecclesiastical powers.

Similar authority is bestowed by one of the Buddhist world's most important relics, for it's believed that whoever possesses it has a sacred right to rule the land. This holy object – the tooth of Buddha, and supposedly the only relic left after his cremation – is in Kandy, a lush leafy Sri Lankan town in hilly tea country. Housed near a royal lake inside the Dalada Maligawa, or Temple of the Sacred Tooth, it's displayed to the public every five years.

When I visited Kandy in the 1980s, I waited for several hours under the burning sun along with hundreds of Sri Lankans to get a glimpse of this most significant incisor. In the temple's inner sanctum, the tooth sat in a glass case surrounded by gold and silk decorations. It was, I remember, surprisingly large and rather yellow.

Perhaps the close relationship we have with human remains stems from our difficulty in accepting the vacuum created by death and the disappearance of a person's materiality. We are left with "a gap you can't see", says Guildenstern in Tom Stoppard's 1966 play *Rosencrantz and Guildenstern Are Dead*, "and when the wind blows through it, it makes no sound". As we struggle to fill that gap, we hang on to any scraps we can find.

The Victorians loved to keep tokens of the people they'd lost near them. Creating plaster death masks and hand casts was one way to do it. Photographing the recently deceased was another, with the subjects of these morbid portraits lying in their coffins or sometimes posed to look as if they were alive.

But the most tangible way of remaining close to a loved one was to keep part of their remains – a lock of hair. As a memento, hair has practical advantages. Consisting of filaments of protein that grow through the epidermis, hair stops living when it's left the scalp, so once it's cut it doesn't deteriorate further.

Hair jewellery was popular as early as the seventeenth century. In his poem *The Relic*, John Donne hopes that if he and his loved one are ever exhumed, the "bracelet of bright hair about the bone" will persuade the gravediggers to leave alone a couple who thought that:

> *... this device might be some way*
> *To make their souls at the last busy day,*
> *Meet at this grave, and make a little stay.*

The Victorians loved keeping hair in jewellery. The practice took off when Queen Victoria turned grieving into a national art following the early death of her husband, Prince Albert, in 1861 The inconsolable sovereign took to wearing black and, among the signs of her perpetual sorrow were lockets and other pieces of jewellery in which she kept curls of her beloved Albert's hair.

Hair work soon became a popular memento among her citizens. To their precious lockets, they could add further strands as other family members died. Mourning lockets started being mass-produced, and hair work became an art. Encased behind glass or crystal in tiny pendants and brooches, hair was shaped into intricate designs using cross-hatching, weaving, netting, plaiting, feathering or curling. At wealthy high-society funerals, hair work trinkets might be given out to guests. In the budget version, families could send out commercially printed mourning cards with a locket of hair sewn on to them.

Around the same time, Americans also started seeking solace in mourning jewellery. Soldiers departing for the Civil War would leave a lock of hair with their wives in case the worst should happen. If the soldier died in battle, the widow would transfer the hair from one locket to another – a black one for mourning. Memorial rings or bracelets of twisted or woven hair allowed the bereaved to be in constant physical contact with a lost loved one. Pliable, durable and portable, hair personified the dead and provided a focus for mourning. It became an iconic yet corporeal stand-in for the person who was so sorely missed.

If some Victorian practices seem a little morbid, today's funeral industry offers versions not a million miles from their mementos. Gold pendants immortalise fingerprints, footprints, handprints and thumbprints or "Thumbies", as Illinois-based Meadow Hill calls its keepsakes. A British company called DNA 11 creates customised pop art-style portraits (for living and dead) based on lip and fingerprints, and DNA patterns taken from hair. For the dead, they are today's versions of the death mask and the hand cast.

Like the Victorians, we seem to be drawn to the idea of hanging on to pieces of the dead. But instead of hair, cremated remains have become today's memento of choice, with lockets or charms in hearts, crosses or crescents that contain tiny portions of ashes.

Armed with science and technology, the funeral industry can even use human remains as raw material for the jewels themselves. LifeGem, a Chicago-based company, extracts enough carbon from an eight-ounce portion of cremated remains to make a diamond that can be cut, certified and inspected by gemologists. "It's hard for people to accept that the person has gone," says Dean Vanden-Biesen, LifeGem founder. "But having something physical and tangible to hang on to allows them to let go."

Craftspeople who once had little to do with the funeral industry are finding a new market for their work. Neil Richardson, a Welsh potter, fires ashes into a vase using raku, traditional Japanese ceramic technique. A company called Creative Cremains claims to be able to incorporate them in everything from musical instruments to fishing rods and walking sticks. Artist Michael Butler blends cremated ash into the oils he uses to paint pictures of the places where his clients scattered the rest of the remains. Meanwhile, Nick Savage, the Californian entrepreneur behind a company called Memory Glass, puts tiny amounts of human ash into paperweights and pendants. Trails of cremation dust swirl through the glass balls like tiny galaxies in space.

Do these objects help us accept loss, or are we just unable to let go? I'm not sure. Still, they slip easily into our design-conscious world, sitting alongside designer sofas and lava lamps or on Georgian side tables and Victorian desks. Of course, they could also be seen as somewhat mawkish and slightly creepy. Let's face it, few of us would consider displaying a piece of Granny's femur on the mantelpiece or keeping one of Dad's teeth in a glass jar on a shelf in the study. But as paperweights, ceramic vases and oil paintings, the dead fit right in.

That's for the living. But funnily enough, the new art mementos also attract people looking ahead to their own deaths. Dean VandenBiesen told me that what motivated his brother Russell, when the siblings were developing the idea for LifeGem, was that he didn't want his final resting place to be in a cemetery or an urn. "Rusty didn't like his options," said VandenBiesen. "He was worried about being forgotten."

No longer convinced of spiritual eternity, it seems we're starting to look for it on earth, seeking solace in an eternity that's more tangible by leaving behind us biological evidence of our corporeal existence – a human life captured forever in a glass paperweight or stamped into a gold Thumbie.

didn't keep any of Fa's ashes. At first I felt a tinge of regret about that. I even hesitated when, after we'd scattered his ashes, it came to throwing out the urn they'd come in. For some reason, I'd been putting this off; holding on to something, I'm not sure what. Sam said I was being ridiculous and she was, of course, right. Certainly there was no sense in hanging on to a faux-bronze urn. If Fa was anywhere, it was on the hill where we did the scattering – and was he even there? But still, I asked her not to throw the urn out until the next time I was in Dorset.

One morning when I was visiting, Sam said it was time to get rid of the urn. The waste collection truck would be passing the house that morning and she wanted to put it in with the other rubbish. The next question was how to dispose of it. Was it recyclable, we wondered? It probably was, since it was made of metal. But if we put it out on the road along with the tin cans, bottles and jars, wouldn't the dustmen be a little discomfited?

In the end, the planet lost out to our concern over the sensibilities of the dustmen. Sam wrapped the urn in an old cotton sheet to disguise its shape and then tied it into a plastic bag. Pleased with the result, she tossed it up into the air. "There you are!" she said brightly, as if it was little more than an empty piece of Tupperware.

But the incident got me thinking about what might happen to my own remains. Would I want myself trailed around inside a glass paperweight, mixed into an oil painting – or, for that matter, suspended beside hundreds of other human bones in an eccentric ossuary chandelier?

Funnily enough, I don't find that particular idea altogether unappealing. Creating a little ghoulish amusement for tourists might be a tolerable way to end up. I love being useful. Of course, I could be most useful by donating my functioning organs to someone who needs them. Yet that still leaves the rest of me. And as someone who enjoys being intensely productive in life, I'd like to be so

after my death. Having my remains perform some positive func‐
tion would, it seems to me, be one of the best means of living on
Now I just need to find out what that function could be.

About two weeks before Christmas in 1981, the citizens of the smal
El Salvadorian mountain town named El Mozote were going abou
their business – shops were opening up, laundry was being hung
out to dry, children were going to school. By the evening, most o
the town's population would be dead. One woman – thought to be
the sole survivor of the massacre – hid in a tree while US-trained
soldiers rounded up villagers, divided them into groups and killed
them before setting fire to the piles of bodies. Rufina Amaya los
her son, three daughters and husband.

Susan Meiselas, a photojournalist who visited El Mozote after
the massacre described the atmosphere: "A very haunted village
Nothing moving. A plaza with a number of destroyed houses. And
total silence."

For many years, the atrocity – the most violent incident of the
Salvadoran civil war of the late 1970s – was kept secret, denied
by both the government of El Salvador and the US administration
supporting it. Meiselas and the two journalists that reported the
story, Raymond Bonner of *The New York Times* and Alma Guiller
moprieto of *The Washington Post*, came under fierce attack, accused
of talking up flimsy evidence. Almost eleven years later, however
the remains of the dead finally confirmed the truth.

The bodies of those killed that day were uncovered by the Ar
gentine Forensic Anthropology (EAAF, after its Spanish name)
a non-profit organisation that investigates human rights abuses
When bone fragments are discovered, investigators complete an
exhumation and examine circumstantial and other evidence sur
rounding what they've uncovered. The remains are then sent to a
lab for DNA analysis that, by comparison with matching samples
can confirm their identity.

In El Mozote, the bones EAAF unearthed in and around the
town corroborated Rufina Amaya's account. However, the remain

played another even more critical role. For the surviving members of the families, identification of the bones was a way of knowing what had happened to their relatives. The existence of remains meant they could at last hold the funeral.

Here's where the work of the investigators goes far beyond science. "It involves a lot of social issues," says Mercedes Doretti, a senior investigator at EAAF. She and her colleagues tread carefully when asking communities and families how they want to proceed following the discovery of remains. Dilemmas arise along the way. If, for example, the remains are commingled in a mass grave, how far should investigators go in trying to return a complete set of bones? "Should you inform a family, when you may have only a little piece?" says Doretti. "Or do you wait to see if the other parts of the body correspond to the same person?"

When someone dies, we need the evidence – sometimes as proof of a crime but also as a way of accepting the death. Governments, too, want the remains of their dead citizens accounted for. Since the Vietnam War, the US administration has spent millions of dollars on finding those missing in action. In New York, the search continues for remains of the victims of the September 11 terrorist attacks. By 2009, more than eight years later, 1,654 victims of the 2,752 reported missing had been identified.

Advances in technology have helped. Through DNA testing, identification can be ascertained from even microscopic pieces of remains. As recently as April 2009, the remains of a Windows on the World worker, fifty-four-year-old Manuel Emilio Mejia, were identified using new DNA technology that had not been available at the time of the 9/11 attacks. But whether it's a piece of bone or positive DNA identification, somewhere along the line, death demands the existence of remains as a trigger for grieving.

Without these remains, families who start mourning a lost relative can experience a terrible guilt. "Presumed dead" is very different from "confirmed as dead". By saying goodbye before receiving that critical confirmation, they feel they're abandoning the missing person. For this reason, Doretti is happy when she can find even the smallest bone splinter, because it provides the vital evidence of death. "You know that the news you're going to deliver will be terrible for the families at the beginning," she says. "But you also see that in the end, it's a solace."

While working on the El Mozote exhumations, Doretti listened to the story of a man who'd watched as soldiers killed his mother and set fire to her home. That night he returned to the house to recover her remains. All he found were a few charred pieces, which he placed on a roof tile and buried nearby. When EAAF arrived, Doretti asked him why he'd returned to the scene, with soldiers still in the area. He told her he couldn't have left without finding his mother's remains. Eleven years on, the fragments were exactly where he'd put them. The EAAF team exhumed them and he was finally able to give his mother a proper burial.

For most families, holding some form of funeral after the discovery of remains is essential. Even if the ceremony is for a fragment of bone, it marks the passing of the person from one state to the other – from disappeared to deceased. And, says Doretti, "even if twenty years have passed since their disappearance, it's as if the person died the day before".

To my knowledge, Fa's remains did not – unlike those of the medieval saints – work any miracles. Or perhaps they did. For standing on the spot where The Hut once sat is a smart new building where my mother now lives.

Our scheme was hatched soon after Fa died. Sam didn't want to stay alone in the family home, Summerfields. Meanwhile, Kate, her husband Ian and their two small boys, Dylan and Gus, were bursting out of their tiny one-bedroom apartment in London. Unable to find anything else affordable in the city, they were considering moving to the suburbs. The perfect solution seemed for them to take the house in Dorset. We'd build a new self-contained flat next door for Sam. Everyone loved the idea. Fa would, I'm sure, have been thrilled.

Then Melvyn turned up. A successful local businessman, Melvyn started his career as a young architect, working closely with Fa on local development projects and farm buildings. Today, he has a string of companies, from property development firms to golf courses. Dividing his time between his houses in Britain and his villas in Spain, he's now more often in boardrooms than on building sites.

Astonishingly, Melvyn announced he'd like to oversee our tiny four-hundred-square-foot project, and recommended his best contractors for the job. One day, when work was well underway, he stopped by to inspect the progress. Over a coffee in our kitchen, I thanked him for his help. "Ah well," said Melvyn, pausing and glancing at the ceiling. "I know he's up there watching me."

To make way for the construction, however, The Hut had to go. It was a sad thought. It had been Fa's special place and, of course, his temporary reliquary. Then Sam's younger brother Anthony (who accompanied her to Fa's cremation) said he'd like to have it in his yard. Enterprising and energetic, Anthony is astonishingly good at building and fixing things. So when he said he could dismantle and reconstruct The Hut, we believed him.

Anthony drove down to Dorset with a trailer. In a single day, he took The Hut apart, loaded it piece by piece on to his trailer and drove it back to his house that evening ("I did get some funny looks from other drivers on the motorway," he told me cheerily).

Soon after, he sent me photographs of The Hut in its new home, a couple of hours away. It looks exactly as it did in Dorset, except a different set of trees clusters around it. It's got the same irregular shape (Fa had it extended on one side), the same slightly concave roof with its weathered grey asphalt surface. The same faded door still has lichen spreading around the bottom and a padlock securing it shut. I can imagine Fa inside, working on his scrapbooks in the company of the plastic model planes and the Egyptian brick. Of course, The Hut would have never been rebuilt without Anthony's talents. But I can't help thinking that its new lease of life constitutes a miracle – well a small one, anyway.

9

HELLO AGAIN

On an Altar in Oaxaca

I'm looking at a picture of Fa. It's one I took some years ago. In his favourite hat, with his trusty walking stick in hand and a red scarf at his neck, he's standing on a narrow country lane lined with trees stripped bare for winter. I know that lane – it runs alongside the bluebell wood, not far from the hill where we scattered his ashes. I'm fond of this particular photograph. It reminds me of how much Fa loved the West Dorset landscape. He was never happier than when he was trudging through muddy fields, stick in hand.

The photograph is not framed. In fact, it's a photocopy of the original but the paper is just about stiff enough to allow me to prop it up for viewing. I've taken a few moments to decide where to put this picture of him. Next to the tiny plaster figurine of a skeleton sitting at a sewing machine? Or perhaps beside the model of a skeletal sheep wearing a sombrero? Another option would be in front of the large corpse-shaped loaf of bread with a plastic saint's head baked in right where the face should be.

I spend a little longer thinking about it before I finally settle on an appropriate slot. My father is now standing in front of a female skeleton doll in a black and turquoise lacy flamenco dress. Below him is a life-sized sugar skull covered in different kinds of dried berries and another one decorated in coloured tinfoil with green metallic discs in its eyes. I've left a handful of Werther's Originals on the shelf for him. They were his favourite sweets (he always kept a few in his coat pocket). He got me on to them, too, so while I was originally going to leave the whole packet, I've saved a few for myself.

At this point, anyone not familiar with Mexico's Day of the Dead festival is thinking I'm either hallucinating or having some kind of voodoo-inspired nightmare. Fear not. I'm in Oaxaca where this annual celebration is just days away and skeletons are appearing in homes, shops, restaurants and public buildings. The Hotel Azucenas, where I'm staying, has a Day of the Dead altar just inside the entrance to its courtyard. And a couple of weeks ahead of my arrival, the hotel e-mailed me this message:

> *Dear Guests Visiting Oaxaca & Hotel Azucenas during the Day of the Dead, as you may know most homes and many businesses in Oaxaca (and Mexico) make beautiful altars of flowers, fruit and offerings for the dead during these days. You are invited to bring your own photos of family and friends who have died, if you would like to include them in our altar. And we (the living & the dead) look forward to seeing you in Oaxaca.*

At the time I received this note, I didn't know a whole lot about the traditions of *Dia de los Muertos*, but now here I am looking at my father on a Mexican altar for the *defuntos* (departed), along with a dozen or so pictures of the relatives of other hotel guests and a black-and-white image of two tabby cats. I very much like seeing him there, and I've already taken several photos of the altar to show Sam and the rest of the family. Fa would no doubt have thought me rather silly. But he would have smiled indulgently all the same.

The Hotel Azucenas's *ofrenda*, or altarpiece, is typical of the Day of the Dead shrines erected in homes, commercial establishments and public offices. This one's a riot of colour. It's covered with pink-and-purple plastic tablecloths in bold floral designs while above, also in pink and purple, are draped *papel picado*, or "perfo rated paper" – delicate paper cut-outs depicting dancing skeletons that remind me a little of the festive bone swags in Sedlec Ossuary

In a couple of tall vases on either side of the altar are bunch es of orange marigolds (known here as *flor de muerto*, and which since pre-Colombian times have symbolised death), combined with a few burgundy-red amaranths, a flower known, appropri ately enough, as Love Lies Bleeding. Leafy branches with oranges dangling from them create a glorious arch over the whole thing.

As well as photographs of the *defuntos*, the altar's tiered shelves display an assortment of skeleton effigies and sugar skulls (*calaveras*). Copal incense made from pine will guide the dead towards their home. There's food and drink, too – a glass of water placed in a prominent position (the dead are always thirsty), some tortillas, a few cupcakes and the loaf of bread with the saint's head embedded in it. On one shelf is a bottle of Noche Buena, a popular Mexican beer. A packet of Marlboro cigarettes, a dish of peanuts a bowl of plums and a few pomegranates are also dotted around.

It's important to leave a generous supply of food and other offerings on the altar, including the favourite treats of the deceased relatives. For this is time when the dead return to earth to visit their relatives, and they're hungry when they arrive.

Oaxaca is one of Mexico's most beautiful colonial towns. It sits in the southern part of the country at the convergence of the Sierra Madre Oriental and the Sierra Madre del Sur ranges. The province was a thank you gift to Hernan Cortez from the Spanish crown for his conquest of New Spain. In 1521, Cortez arrived to claim his prize and proceeded to build a dazzling showcase city with every thing a smart new metropolis should have – an elegant grid plan grand classical buildings and magnificent Catholic cathedrals.

The most spectacular, Santo Domingo, has a pair of stylish domes covered in black-and-blue checked tiles. Just inside its main entrance, a gilded ceiling depicts Saint Dominic's family tree.

On my first morning in Oaxaca, I wake to a flawless day. The air is crisp, the sky is clear blue and, walking down the hill from the hotel, the sun on my shoulders feels like a blessing after the grey clouds I left behind in New York. I'm heading towards the Mercado Abastos, an immense covered market on the edge of town just the other side of the railway tracks. That's where I'm hoping to find all the flowers, skeleton effigies and candy skulls sold at this time of year.

Plunging down the first entrance I see, I feel I've died and gone to heaven. There's something intoxicating about the profusion of goods on display at these kinds of markets. Cheap soaps, washing powder sachets and lipsticks are piled precariously on small tables. Thousands of shoes and leather sandals hang in ranks on plastic feet cut off at the ankles (a display method I've always found a little disturbing).

In the fresh produce section, plump cactus leaves and exotic vegetables I'm unable to name are piled high in a Thanksgiving-style salutation of abundance. Pyramids of fruit defy gravity (or are somehow glued together), while in the meat section, a row of headless plucked chickens lie on a table with their spindly legs sticking out at different angles like a line-up of poorly-disciplined Can-Can dancers.

Sounds drift in and out. Porters clear a path for their loads using high-pitched whistles. Manic mariachi tunes give way to the strains of a soppy love ballad that's part of the soundtrack coming from a DVD stall. Next to it, a competitor is screening a cheap horror movie. As I walk past, a woman howls in anguish as she rips off her own jaw, assisted by some rather unconvincing special effects and lots of fake blood.

Invading my nostrils is a pungent cocktail of odours – copal incense smoke, the heady scent of marigolds, the rich cocoa aroma of *mole* paste and, cutting through it all, the citric sharpness of oranges and limes. I long to buy everything but I know I'll never get it in the suitcase.

Then I stumble across what I'm looking for – great piles of

loaves like the one on the altar at the Hotel Azucenas. These are *pan de muertos* (bread for the dead). Table after table is loaded with them and embedded in the surface of each loaf are little heads of Jesus, the Virgin and various saints, all with colourful haloes in pink, red, yellow, blue, purple and even lime green. Across from the bread, one woman is selling heart-shaped buns with a dark red paste spread over them. I'm just guessing, but do these by chance represent bleeding hearts?

Moving deeper into the market, I find a stall selling strings of tinsel with tiny plastic skulls threaded through it. It's the start of the skeleton section. And what, you might think, could be weirder than going shopping for skulls and skeletons? Yet the merchandise feels festive rather than morbid. Everything is endowed with playful humour. There are plastic skeletons wearing sombreros, skeleton dolls (like the one on the hotel altar next to Fa's photograph), skeleton earrings with tiny dangly arms and legs, candy skulls in all sizes and miniature wooden caskets with little skeletons inside. In my favourite version, you pull a string at one end, causing the cadaver to sit bolt upright.

Meanwhile, small dioramas, or *nichos*, feature groups of skeletons installed behind glass in painted boxes, with brides and grooms in wedding outfits, families sitting around dinner tables and mariachi musicians ready to strike up a tune. Miniature skeletons – dozens of tiny plaster figures glued to wooden bases – are keeping busy. There's the skeleton dog groomer, the skeleton footballer, the skeleton singer dressed as Elvis, the skeleton at a computer, the artist skeleton painting at an easel, the skeleton dentist with her skeletal patient and (perhaps most paradoxically) the skeleton midwife assisting at the birth of a skeleton baby, which pokes out between the legs of its skeleton mother.

La Calavera Catrina turns up everywhere. She's the Lady of the Dead. Her image first appeared in the nineteenth-century works of José Guadalupe Posada, the Mexican printmaker, and today you find her on cheap plastic shopping bags, in *papel picado* cut-outs and in life-size effigies decorating lobbies and shop windows around town.

La Catrina is also available as a ceramic statuette. In this more elaborate and expensive form, she cuts a macabre figure – tall, willowy and flamboyantly attired in a long low-cut gown revealing her rib cage. With a broad-brimmed hat covering her hairless skull, she often appears cigarette in hand, a bejewelled clutch bag on her bony arm and a feather boa around her fleshless shoulders; a cadaverous Auntie Mame. In some ways, she's nothing but a burlesque bit of fun and fantasy. But, with her toothy grin and black, empty eye sockets, she's also menacing.

Mexicans were not the first to use scary skeletons to commemorate the dead. Nearly six hundred years ago, in the cemetery of the Parisian monastery of Les Saints Innocents, a mural was decorated with images rather like those stuck up in Mexican shop windows and on the shelves *ofrendas*.

The mural, completed in 1425, has since disappeared, but its images survive in a set of woodcuts made by printer Guy Marchant in 1485 showing dozens of dancing dead figures, each accompanying a living person. With grinning skulls, they prance around with courtly movements as they entice the living – kings, popes, clerks and labourers – to join them in a ghoulish caper towards the grave. The final image is of a dead king, whose flesh is being consumed by worms.

Images of the Danse Macabre, as it was known, became popular in Europe in the fourteenth and fifteenth centuries. As well as the dancing dead, other macabre themes started to creep into art, architecture and literature.

One tale, *The Three Living and The Three Dead,* told of the encounter of a duke, a prince and a count with three ecclesiastical corpses, who urge the aristocrats to repent their sins, for their status and riches will be of no use when they're dead. The story appears in paintings and prints of the time, with the corpses often depicted in a grisly state of decomposition, accompanied by variations on the ominous message: "What we are, you will be."

The use of personifications of death at this moment in history makes perfect sense – actual death was never far away. The Black Death is thought to have arrived in Europe in 1347, when a ship full of rats bearing diseased fleas dropped its anchor in the Sicilian port of Messina. Soon, a pandemic – the bubonic plague – was ripping across Europe at an astonishing pace. This, and a subsequent series of plagues, wiped out nearly two-thirds of Europe's population. It decimated whole towns.

And it was a brutal way to go. Perishing from the plague took only a few days, but it was an awful experience, accompanied by fever, agonising pain and black swellings the size of apples in the armpits and groin, from which oozed blood. These were followed by the appearance of blotches and boils. And the simultaneous presence of two varieties of the plague – one affecting the bloodstream and spread by contact with infected individuals, the other attacking the lungs and spread by respiratory infection – proved devastating. The death rate skyrocketed.

The only way to accommodate so many corpses was to dig mass graves. There was no time for funerals. The dead were buried without vigils, prayers or even last rites (eventually, to assuage people's fears of dying without remission of their sins, the church permitted laymen to administer extreme unction).

"The stench of their putrefying bodies carried the tidings," wrote fourteenth-century Florentine author Giovanni Boccaccio, "and what with their corpses and the corpses of others who died on every hand the whole place was a sepulchre." The mortality rate was such that, as Boccaccio put it, "a dead man was then of no more account than a dead goat".

For the citizens of medieval Europe, such a rapid spread of disease was horrifying. Medicine was in its infancy, and doctors knew almost nothing about the source of the contagion. Some ascribed it to far-off earthquakes, others to swarms of locusts. Ancient Greek and Roman medical literature contained no clues. In a vain attempt to find someone to blame, angry mobs massacred hundreds of Jews across Europe.

With people around them dropping like flies from an unexplainable disease, artists and poets looked for ways of turning death into something tangible. Grinning skulls and skeletal dancers turned mortality into a figure that was threatening but also rather comical. Grief and consolation are absent from the manuscripts, sculptures and paintings of the time. Art expressed either shock at the brevity of earthly life or the hope of salvation. We can only imagine the very human feelings that lay between.

The potency of the macabre retained its currency, appearing a century later in strange, disturbing tomb carvings. Instead of depicting knights in armour or bishops in ecclesiastical robes, some sculptors started to carve their patrons' marble effigies as skeletons, or as naked, decomposing corpses.

Cadaver tombs (or transi tombs, as they're also known) show the bodies of those they memorialise in various states of decay. One tomb, now in London's Victoria and Albert Museum, represents John Baret, a wealthy English clothier who died in 1467, as an emaciated corpse, with his rib cage and femurs exposed and his bones protruding through his sunken skin. In other tombs, worms penetrate the limbs and frogs eat into the flesh of their occupants.

In some instances, sculptors created "before and after" versions. In the Fitzalan Chapel at Arundel Castle, West Sussex, a rare "double-decker" tomb sits above the body of John, the seventh earl of Arundel, who died in 1453. On the top section is his effigy in a suit of armour; below is a withered cadaver, the ominous sign of things to come. (Curiously, the shrivelled marble corpse doesn't depict his actual cause of death – gangrene arising from a cannon-ball wound sustained in battle. Victorian archaeologists confirmed this after partially excavating the grave, finding a body with a leg missing.)

In another double-decker tomb in a Dutch church in Vianen, the lower section shows the unfortunate Reynout van Brederode, a noble who died in 1556, as a skeleton crawling with infestations of creatures resembling eels or worms. Beneath a grandiose classical wooden canopy, his body is in a grotesque state of decay. Inside the chest cavity his internal organs can be seen, while his legs are part flesh, part bone.

So here we find a different attitude to the fate of the body. Unlike the mummies of the Sicilians or Egyptians, these pieces of tomb art make no claims that the corpse will survive death – quite the opposite in fact. Corporeal decay is the whole point of these disturbing sculptures. And looking at these gruesome representations of putrefaction, you can't help wondering why anyone would want to be depicted like that. Some suggest that these graphic displays were meant to emphasise the miracle of the Second Coming. Never mind the state of your remains, they seemed to say, come the Resurrection, Christ could put you back together again.

Visions of corporeal corruption also served as warnings of what was to come. "He that will sadly behold me with his eye may see his own morrow and learn for to die," reads the inscription on John Beret's tomb. Most powerfully, perhaps, these marble figures speak of equality in death. Mortality, they say, cares not whether you're a king or a pauper. Death is the ultimate enforcer of democracy.

Perhaps, like so many of us, these medieval nobles were grappling with the meaning of death, and trying to prepare themselves for it by picturing it. Did that help? Who knows? Still, whatever effect these tombs were intended to have on viewers, they betray a curious obsession for human decay. Their rotting bodies and corpses riddled with worms, mice, snakes and other creatures make even the most disturbing of Oaxaca's skeletal ghouls look benign.

After it's buried, a human body starts to deteriorate immediately. Soon, the corpse becomes a festering ecosystem. No frogs are present at the corporeal feast (the medieval sculptors got that bit wrong), but the body provides nourishment for a host of other organisms. Sir Henry Thompson, the Victorian champion of cremation, puts it eloquently: "Already a thousand changes have commenced," he writes. "Forces innumerable have attacked the dead. The rapidity of the vulture, with its keen scent for animal decay, is nothing to that of Nature's ceaseless agents now at full work before us."

Thompson might put it poetically, but putrefaction is not something many of us want to contemplate. For the curious, however, here's roughly how it goes: bodily corruption is categorised in several stages – putrefaction, black putrefaction, butyric fermentation and dry decay. In the first part (self-digestion), the natural enzymes that inhabited the body while it was alive start attacking their host, breaking down the cells that keep us in one piece, generating a liquid that causes the skin to peel off and creates those unfortunate leaks that have precipitated so many funeral industry innovations.

Following in the footsteps of the human enzymes, invasive tomb raiders such as maggots, beetles and mites also start to devour the body. Meanwhile, fed by the new supply of bodily liquids, the corpse's bacterial colonies – what Mary Roach calls "the ground troops of putrefaction" – start to multiply. When we die, explains Roach in *Stiff*, these bacteria no longer feed on what we've just eaten. They feed on us, producing gas in the process. Since mechanisms the body normally uses to expel gas have stopped working, it builds up inside the body. This is what causes a corpse to bloat.

When most of the soft flesh has gone, it's time for beetles to take over from the maggots, attacking tougher stuff, such as skin and muscles. Meanwhile, the body continues to dry out and, if in contact with the earth, it becomes covered in mould. Hair, which takes longer to decompose since it's made of keratin, a protein, finally disappears – although in the right conditions hair can survive for centuries. Depending on where it's buried, it can be months before the organic part of the body has disappeared, leaving only the skeleton.

In the light of all this, skeletal remains seem – to my mind anyway – the least disturbing state for a dead body to be in. And while everyone from medieval artists and Halloween revellers to heavy metal bands with names like Exhumed, Impaled Nazarene and Obscene Eulogy might like to use skeletons to frighten their audiences, set next to decaying flesh, these bony frames don't look so scary. In fact, with her feather boa and flamboyant hat, Mexico's La Catrina makes being a skeleton look rather good fun.

No, it's the process of reaching her state – the bit between the last heartbeat and the dry bones – that worries me. Having seen the grotesque cadaver tombs of medieval Europe and read the descriptions of the process of human putrefaction, I'm not drawn to the idea of being left below ground, my flesh slowly disintegrating at the hands of bacteria, maggots and beetles. And while I've never feared of being interred alive, I now wish I hadn't read the terrifying descriptions in Edgar Allen Poe's *The Premature Burial*. I'm becoming convinced that burial is not for me.

Unpicking the cocktail of cultural, religious and artistic influences behind Mexico's Day of the Dead celebrations is no easy matter. The first connection is obvious. Falling on November 1 and 2, the festival is directly linked to All Souls' and All Saints' days, celebrated by Catholics around the world, including Mexico's former colonial rulers. In Spain on All Soul's day, families flock to cemeteries, as they do in Mexico, taking with them flowers and candles to put on the graves.

Yet the customs and skeletal iconography of Day of the Dead have roots in cultural phenomena that predate the arrival of the conquistadors and Spanish Catholicism. In the Museo Rufino Tamayo, one of Oaxaca's loveliest museums, you can see the power of the skeleton in the pre-Hispanic imagination. Amid the artefacts on display are ten simplified Aztec stone skulls hanging on a wall in two vertical rows and, in a glass case, a decorated human jawbone. Most startling is a ceramic figure seated on a throne. With an exposed rib cage, round staring eyes and an ornamental crown, this is a pre-Colombian skeleton king. He was created long before the Black Death swept across Europe, and at a time where no contact with that continent existed. Yet he wouldn't look out of place in one of Guy Marchant's fifteenth-century Danse Macabre woodcuts or amid today's skeletal trinkets in the Mercado Abastos.

Skulls and skeletons appear in pre-Colombian sculpture. Take Central Mexico's *tzompantli* (rows of carved stone skulls). You find them at Tula, the thirteenth-century capital of the Toltec empire, where there's also a wall depicting serpents consuming human skeletons. These have the same "lanky limbs" and "prominent joints" as the skeleton dolls found in Mexican markets today, notes anthropologist Stanley Brandes. Of course, none of the irreverent humour of the Day of the Dead skeletons appears in these carvings – perhaps unsurprisingly so, since many are at sites where human sacrifices would have taken place. But the images may have left their mark nonetheless.

Meanwhile, the Europe's Danse Macabre imagery made its way to the New World in the sixteenth century, when the conquistadors arrived, bringing with them their religious art.

In a museum at Toluca, in southwest Mexico, the decorations on a funerary catafalque (a raised platform on which high-ranking individuals lay in state) show animated skeletons, some dressed up and engaged in various activities – writing at a desk, firing a cannon, helping a nun to card wool, riding in a carriage, walking bent over a cane and wielding a scythe. There's no skeletal midwife assisting at the birth of a skeletal baby amid these decorative figures, but you feel she'd fit right in.

Both pre-Colombian and Spanish peoples held feasts for their dead. The Aztecs even created effigies from food. In one Aztec tradition, wooden images of people who drowned or died in ways that ruled out cremation were covered in dough and placed on altars. Meanwhile, in Europe, seventeenth-century Spanish Catholics baked special bread for the dead on All Souls' day, as well as small, sweet pastries known as *panellets*, or "little breads", which are still prepared in Catalonia.

Yet the pink candy skulls, skeleton dolls and Catrinas may owe their prominence in Mexican craft and culture to something darker, too – demographic catastrophe. For when the Spanish arrived on the continent, they brought with them their diseases – not only smallpox but also illnesses such as the flu that to locals, who had never encountered them, proved deadly. During the sixteenth and seventeenth centuries, in their own version of the Black Death, indigenous American people suffered a series of devastating epidemics, wiping out huge chunks of the local population.

Writes academic David Stannard: "That is why, as one historian aptly has said, far from the heroic and romantic heraldry that customarily is used to symbolise the European settlement of the Americas, the emblem most congruent with reality would be a pyramid of skulls." So equally important in fostering macabre imagery in early colonial Mexico was what Brandes calls the "ubiquitous presence of death".

And perhaps there's something more universal in the skull mania that breaks out in Mexico every November – our endless fascination for the human cranium. Skulls have physical and philosophical potency. As three-dimensional objects, they have a sculptural beauty. Each is unique. The three wiggly lines that appear where the cranium's different sections meet are like fingerprints – no two are the same. But it's their features to which we're so often drawn – gaping black eye sockets, empty recesses and grinning jaws that can't easily be disassociated from the face of a living human.

Former guardians of the brain and the organs of the senses, skulls also seem to represent the spiritual nucleus of the individuals who once occupied them – so much so that, at times, we can't help talking to them, as Hamlet does when he addresses the skull of Yorick, the king's jester. "Where be your gibes now," Hamlet demands, "your gambols, your songs, your flashes of merriment that were wont to set the table on a roar? Not one now to mock your own grinning?"

Modern artists often play on our powerful association with skulls. In Picasso's prints and paintings, they become abstract shapes, particularly in his cubist work. Yet the staring black eyes and toothy grins have the same striking impact as they would in a more realistic depiction.

More recently, of course, it was not only the 8,500 gems he used that brought Damien Hirst, the prominent British artist, global media attention when in 2007 he unveiled his spectacular diamond-encrusted skull, a work entitled *For the Love of God*. Unlike the candy craniums in Mexican markets, Hirst's creation (which eventually sold for £50 million) has genuine teeth and dazzles so brightly that it's hard to gaze upon. Still, the artwork sparkling with diamonds and the Mexican calavera sparkling with sugar crystals both take as their inspiration the same object – the remains of a human head.

One evening, I head down the hill from the Hotel Azucenas into town to see what's going on. Well, that's not quite accurate. I'm actually driven by the thought of a large margarita, and I remember from a previous visit that they make excellent ones at an open-air bar opposite the nineteenth-century French bandstand in the Zocalo, an elegant colonial square just south of Avenida Independencia. The bar's still there. And I'm not sure how much tequila the barman put in my drink, but for the rest of the evening I seem to be part of a Danse Macabre of my own.

Heading off in search of a restaurant, I run into a procession of students dressed in skeleton, devil and monster outfits cavorting wildly, whooping and screaming as they proceed down the cobbles accompanied by a small band. Meanwhile, in the Zocalo, just in front of the church on one side of the square, a stately open-air dance is taking place to the sound of a large brass band orchestra. Elegant old couples in their Sunday best shuffle around alongside mad-looking devils in bright red outfits and a host of skeletons, including one in a white bridal outfit and straw hat.

The dancers move with measured precision to the slow tangos and bossa novas of the band. Every so often, a man in a suit holding a microphone interjects with announcements and everyone stops to watch individual couples perform in front of the band. Finally, just before the last dance, prizes are awarded. Appropriately enough, one of the devils wins a microwave and the skeleton bride gets a set of saucepans.

Meanwhile, inside the cathedral, a choir and an orchestra are performing Mozart's *Requiem Mass*. The music has reached that dark and urgent moment when the choir sings at full volume. With the doors of the great building wide open, trumpets and cheering from the festivities in the plaza outside blast down the nave and rattle around the transepts, competing with Mozart for attention. Every so often, great bangs – which I'm hoping are fireworks –

bounce off the ancient stones. I almost expect to see a red devil hanging off one of the church's huge chandeliers. The mad musical cacophony continues throughout the night, with skeleton dancers romping through the streets to the music of an assortment of brass bands, student orchestras and drummers.

You might think dancing and death would make unlikely bed-fellows. But in some cultures, dancing is at the heart of the funeral itself. I first encountered this at an Ashanti funeral party in Kumasi, a city in southern central Ghana. In a big open enclosure tents and seating were arranged on all four sides with a shrine in the middle covered in white fabric and decorated with flowers commemorating the deceased.

Visitors arrived dressed in fabulous outfits in red, for members of the immediate family, and, for everyone else, a stylish matt black fabric printed with glossy black designs. For the women flamboyant dresses and large turbans were de rigeur, while the men looked magnificent in toga-style robes. They'd be the African equivalent of ancient Greek senators if it weren't for the occasional pair of Gucci sunglasses or Rolex watch.

At each new arrival, the drummers started beating frantically on their instruments and, to greet the most important visitors, a dancer would come forward to offer a welcome, prancing in front of them in a kind of ritualised bowing and scraping. As the party got going, the dancing and drumming intensified, with set pieces in which individual dancers would become wrapped up in strange sinuous movements, placing their feet slowly and deliberately on the ground as if marking out their territory (this low-impact dance creating maximum visual effect with minimal physical input is sensible, given West Africa's hot, humid climate). When inspired members of the assembled crowd would join them.

Best of all were a group of Muslim guests (one of the female members of the deceased's family had married into a Muslim tribe). The men were elegantly attired, carrying metal sticks and wearing long, heavily pleated smock-like shirts in colourful striped fabric. With white caps or more luxurious velvet floppy hats, they gave the appearance of a medieval band of minstrels. The smock shirts came into their own when the men started dancing. "They dance with their dresses," said the woman next to me, and she was absolutely right. As they twisted and turned, the lower half of the smocks fanned outwards, turning their wearers into spectacular human spinning tops.

In the 1930s, British anthropologist Godfrey Wilson came across funerary dancing when studying the death rites of the Nyakyusa people of East Africa. Wilson found the events "very jolly" compared to funerals back home, with the men obliged to dance on and off in the days leading up to the burial ceremony. There was lamenting, too. But as the female mourners' wailing trailed off, the men's dancing intensified, with more and more joining in, all wearing skirts and ankle bells. The idea, explained Wilson, was to frighten off evil spirits as the deceased headed off to the next life.

Some might dance *for* their dead. But Madagascans dance *with* them. Like Day of the Dead, Madagascar's *famadihana* or "bone turning" ceremony is a riotous occasion. But unlike the skeletal figures dancing through the streets of Oaxaca and other Mexican cities, the bones being paraded around in Madagascar are real.

Every five or seven years after the death of a relative, during the dry season in July and August, the Merina people of Madagascar take their dead out from their resting places and wrap the bones in silk to keep them warm. Touchingly, if a husband and wife have reached a certain stage of decay, their bones are combined, reuniting spouses separated at death. Families eat, drink and dance around with their ancestors hoisted up on to their shoulders, occasionally tossing them exuberantly up into the air before returning them to their tombs. It's a great big seven-year party for the dead.

Every evening when I return to the Hotel Azucenas, it's good to see the picture of my father on its colourful decorated altar, to say hello again to the figure standing in the wintry Dorset landscape. On November 2, hundreds of families will be doing the same thing beside their *difuntos'* graves. In Oaxaca, unlike other places in Mexico where all-night vigils are more common, this final part of the *Dia de los Muertos* takes place during the day. And for many Oaxacans the place to go is the Pantéon Général, the town's main cemetery.

The Pantéon Général sits at the edge of town, removed from the hum of the city's traffic. Here, the streets still cleave to Cortez' grid but grand stone plazas and ornate classical façades have given way to small shops and low-slung dwellings whose adobe walls are decked out in bright colours. Surrounded by tall trees, the cemetery has a huge four-sided cloister with buttercup yellow walls and a hundred arches. Inside, the graves are a hotchpotch of grand mausoleums of white marble, plain tombstones and simple rectangles of raised earth whose sole decoration is an iron cross.

When I arrive on the morning of November 2, the place is alive with activity. A street market has been set up outside the gates with dozens of stalls selling snacks, fruit, drinks, cheap plastic toys and plenty of flowers. Next to the market is a funfair with all kinds of rides for children. Meanwhile, people pour in through the cemetery gates clutching great armfuls of flowers or wheeling them along in plastic bins on rollers with water slopping about inside.

The cemetery looks glorious. Beneath a lucent sky, the white marble gravestones and tombs are decked out with bright orange marigolds and maroon amaranths. Inside the cloister, visitors crowd around the spectacular sand floor paintings that are another part of the Day of the Dead tradition. Hundreds of people are here ambling through the cloisters and or wandering down the avenues of the cemetery itself. Some haul around buckets of water filled from standpipes dotted around the place. Everywhere, people are hard at work scrubbing headstones with sponges or carefully picking out the letters of inscriptions with new gold paint. It's a spring cleaning for the dead.

A few mariachi bands stroll around looking for customers who might pay a few pesos to have their relative's favourite song played by the grave. To save money, one family has brought along a boom box. It sits on top of the grave cranking out dozens of tunes, all for the price of a cassette tape and a couple of batteries.

Meanwhile, at one of the wealthier tombs in the cemetery, a family has enlisted the services of a preacher who, with the help of two assistants and a mariachi band, is conducting a private mass.

Some just seem to be enjoying the fine weather and the presence of others. At one grave, an old man and his wife sit opposite each other on the benches on either side of their family tomb, silent, motionless and expressionless. Elsewhere, whole families are perched on graves, chatting and eating. Today, the living outnumber the dead and it's hard to see the tombstones for people and flowers.

I don't fit in here. I'm the only one without jet-black hair and a set of relatives under the turf. But no one seems to mind. People smile warmly or simply ignore me as I wander about. By the end of the afternoon, as the sun falls behind Oaxaca's surrounding hills, deep purples and warm ochres spread across the cemetery. People start slowly packing up their cooler bags, buckets and watering cans as they bid their relatives goodbye – that is, until next year.

On my last day in Oaxaca, a strange thing happens. I'm walking past the church of San Felipe Neri, not far from my hotel. The doors are open, so I mount the steps to go inside. The exterior of San Felipe Neri has a spectacular baroque façade in golden sandstone with ornate columns topped by florid ionic capitals, cherub heads with angel wings and a crowned figure above the entrance representing Filippo de Neri, a sixteenth-century Italian priest.

Since I first admired this glorious frontage, I've been anxious to have a look at the interior. This, it turns out, is rather unusual. Art Nouveau murals lead up to a gilded apse carved with figures of saints. At its centre – adding a dash of colour to dusty carvings – is a figure of the Virgin who, in a turquoise nylon robe, wouldn't look out of place among the Day of the Dead skeleton dolls.

But in the end, I don't spend much time looking at the décor. I'm more interested in what's going on in the church, which is full of worshippers. A service is underway. Priests stand at the altar, folding and refolding pieces of linen over a challis (Catholic rituals always look to me as if someone is doing a tiny laundry service) and an electric organ hammers out a solemn hymn.

As the music draws to a close, the congregation rises and

people start shaking hands and hugging each other.

Then I realise what kind of service this is. In front of the altar resting on a low table is a polished steel box with silver handles. This is a funeral. My heart misses a beat. I'm surprised at how shocking it is to see the real thing after the vaudeville theatricalities of Oaxaca's nightly revelries.

As the service ends, I quickly leave the church, not wanting to get in the way of the departing mourners. Moving to a respectful distance across the street, I watch the pallbearers bring the coffin out into the sunlight and down the steps to the sidewalk, where a large silver hearse is waiting. For a while, people mill around, talking quietly and shaking hands. One woman hugs another in a tight embrace as her friend sobs on her shoulder. The look on her face is one of utter desperation.

I step aside to let a group of small children pass. They're carrying balloons, wearing skeleton outfits and their faces are painted white with panda-black skeleton eyes. As those playing the dead cross paths with those mourning the dead, the collision could not be more jarring. The two seem to have nothing to do with each other. They are strangers speaking different languages, inhabiting different worlds.

A few months after my trip to Oaxaca, I visit to Dorset to help Sam clear out the house. As a family, we seem to have spent much of our time engaged in this activity. Like garden weeds, possessions always seem to multiply and every so often we cull what's no longer needed. It's something Sam and I have always enjoyed doing together, leaving us with a feeling that it's not just the house that's a little clearer – it's our heads, too.

This time, though, it's not as simple. Sam's new house next door is finished and in a month's time, Kate and Ian and the boys will be moving into Summerfields. They'll probably use any furniture Sam doesn't need, but we want to get everything else out before they arrive. It's time-consuming work, sifting through books and ornaments. We carefully pick over each item, and for anything we don't want, we try to think of some friend or relative to whom it might be useful or would bring pleasure.

One day, Sam and I get a break when my uncle and aunt come over for lunch. I'm extremely fond of Alastair, my father's brother, and his wife Monica. As children, Kate and I spent many summer holidays with the four cousins in their big farmhouse, riding horses and lingering over family meals around the kitchen table. Alastair was a warm, fatherly figure. I never felt too far from home when he was around.

But now, as he walks through the door, I realise I'm totally unprepared for the effect his presence has on me. He and Fa were always very alike in looks, though Alastair had a larger frame and rounder features. But with age he's come to resemble Fa even more closely. And I'd forgotten how much his voice – oh, how I love that voice – is exactly like Fa's, with its quiet confidence and soft tone. The voice the brothers shared was an educated one, well spoken, and full of generosity and warmth. For the first few moments after Alastair and Monica arrive, I can barely breathe, let alone follow the conversation. I'm too busy gazing at this man who's so like my father and, even more astonishingly, is talking with his voice.

A couple of years before Fa died, I recorded a phone conversation with him. I made the tape, as I told him at the time, because I wanted to capture some of his childhood recollections for a bit of family research I was conducting. When I found out his illness was terminal, I labelled the tape and put it safely away in a drawer. I haven't listened to this tape since he died. Perhaps it's because I fear hearing his voice will bring back the pain of losing him.

Now I'm hearing his voice again. Part of me wants to cry. Yet I'm also filled with immense happiness at seeing those familiar facial features and hearing that voice. I'm reminded of the comfort and security I so often felt when observing my father in animated discussion. The world was safe as long as he was in it. As I gaze at Alastair, I realise that we can revisit our *difuntos* without decorated altars or bone-turning ceremonies – but through the living people whose genes, relatives, friends and memories they share.

10

THE FINAL CHAPTER

Small Packages, Neatly Tied

In Evelyn Waugh's *The Loved One*, a "mortuary hostess" at the Whispering Glades funeral home tries to persuade Denis Barlow to buy a "Before Need Arrangement." The hostess assures him that there's nothing morbid or dangerous in giving some thought to this topic. On the contrary, she says, fear of death can cause "vital energy" to "lag prematurely" and "earning capacity" to diminish. She encourages him to: "Choose now, at leisure and in health, the form of final preparation you require, pay for while you are able to so do, shed all anxiety."

I'm not at all happy with the idea of leaving this world. I enjoy my presence in it far too much. So if those Terror Management theorists want a candidate who can speak for them at conferences as a living example of their hypothesis, they can sign me right up and I'll happily talk about the ways in which I'd like to live on whether by leaving my money to charity or my books on the book shelves. Certainly, the idea of creating some sort of legacy does seem to provide solace in the face of my undesirable but undeniable shelf life.

Of course, we don't always have to arrange our own legacy to live on. Often it happens by itself, even in something as simple as a phrase. My friend Gay Firth had one I'll always remember. We were neighbours in London, and whenever we met for dinner, I'd offer to accompany her home afterwards. She'd always insist she'd be perfectly fine on her own. "Darling," she would say emphatically, "I *promise* I won't mug anyone on the way." I stole this line and I now use it on my friends. Like the citizens of Sagada when they invoke their dead ancestors, I think of her every time I say it.

In her sixties, Gay was diagnosed with an extremely rare form of cancer. She spent her last months in London's Royal Marsden hospital. There, she spent the hours meticulously planning her memorial, from the hymns and readings to the flowers, guest list and reception. When her notebook was lost during the move to another hospital room, she was inconsolable. It coincided with a worsening of her condition. But for me, this event, more than anything else, marked the start of her final decline.

For Gay, thinking about the readings and music for her memorial provided a welcome distraction from the endless rounds of tests and drugs that ultimately proved futile. And even though she lost her notebook, after she died, the notes were found and a close friend who'd been in on much of the decision making put together service. In the end, Gay got the send-off she'd wanted.

Planning your own funeral is not such an eccentric thing to do. My father, in his own way, did it. And for someone who claimed death required no fuss, he certainly thought a lot about it. Many years before he died, he wrote a few short verses about dying – poetry and art again expressing the inexpressible. Death even became part of his filing system, in his carefully labelled "How To End It!" folder.

When General MacArthur planned his exit, he set down details such as which uniform he should wear when lying in state. Others, like Gay, have wanted to select their guests. John Osborne, the British playwright who died in 1994, left instructions that a note should be posted on the church door bearing a list of those who should *not* be admitted. More than a decade's work went into the optimistically code-named "Operation Hope Not", the plans for the funeral of Winston Churchill, and some say he had a hand in the arrangements.

Happily, setting it all down is getting easier. On a website called mywonderfullife.com, you can plan your own funeral and store all the details online. After setting up an account, you create an online "book" with virtual pages where you name up to six "angels" to carry out your wishes, and send them an e-mail request to accept or decline the responsibility. Then you can specify whether you want to be cremated, buried or perhaps have your body donated to medical science. You can write your own headstone and obituary, upload photos, leave letters for people to read after you've gone and suggest music and readings for the memorial.

Creating the site was the idea of Sue Kruskopf, a Minneapolis-based advertising executive, and her friend Nancy Bush, whose fifty-three-year-old husband John died of cancer. After going through the experience of arranging his funeral, Sue and Nancy wanted to take some of the guesswork out of the whole process.

It's a sensible idea. For while we're often reluctant to contemplate our own deaths, leaving a few instructions as my father did relieves friends and families of much of the angst and uncertainty surrounding our departures (not to mention potential rows over everything from the choice of music at the funeral to where to bury the remains).

But it also seems to me that for those of us suffering from "mortality salience", devising an appropriate send-off provides some small consolation for the fact that the one thing we'd most like to control – the end of life – we cannot. Waugh's hostess may be overstating it when she says funeral planning helps us "shed all anxiety", but perhaps picturing what will happen in the aftermath of death (our favourite music echoing down a church aisle; our ashes streaming out from a plane above Mount Everest), allows us to look ahead to a time when, although we're gone, our shadow lingers for a brief moment on earth.

I haven't thought much about music or reading. But I've now got clearer ideas about what I want to have happen to my remains. As stated earlier, I DO NOT want to be embalmed. Do not bury me either. Going back to nature is all very well, but I've acquired too many images of putrefying cadavers on this journey to contemplate interment as an option.

Of course, that means my lovely Ghanaian Empire State Building coffin won't be used for its intended purpose. In any case, it's far too beautiful an object simply to be left to rot underground. I'm thinking that, with a few shelves fitted inside, it would make a great cocktail cabinet, particularly in an Art Deco-style interior. Or perhaps a museum would like to have it.

Then there's cremation. Cremation is quick and efficient – it was my father's choice, after all. Some have even found it inspiring, as George Bernard Shaw did in the days when you could follow the coffin to the furnace. In a 1913 letter, the British playwright describes his reaction to his mother's cremation: "The violet coffin moved again and went in feet first. And behold! The feet burst miraculously into streaming ribbons of garnet coloured lovely flame, smokeless and eager, like Pentecostal tongues, and as the whole coffin passed in it sprang into flame all over; and my mother became that beautiful fire."

As I've found out, however, cremation with its smoke and carbon emissions is not the most environmentally friendly way to leave this world. Still, perhaps there's a third way in which I can dispose of my "organic matter". It's a method that combines being returned to nature by burial with having ashes to scatter. It's an alternative to earth and fire – water. And, from what I've learned, it appears to be remarkably gentle on the environment.

In alkaline hydrolysis (a process one company is calling "resomation", based on the Greek word resoma, which means rebirth), an alkaline solution is used to accelerate the natural decomposition of a body. In a dissolvable silk shroud, the corpse is inserted into a stainless steel pressure vessel, which weighs the corpse and adds the appropriate amount of alkali and water. Once the liquid is heated, breakdown of the "organic matter" gets going.

After about three hours, all that's left are the bone remains, which are put into a cremulator and turned into a fine white ash. The process uses far less energy than cremation and creates no harmful emissions. After treatment the liquid can be used as fertiliser, and hip replacements or pacemakers emerge in perfect condition so can be recycled.

It's early days, and who knows whether it will catch on or not but resomation seems to provide an appealing alternative to burial and cremation. The whole thing has a more natural, gentle feel than cremation. "Think of it as the last hot bath you'll ever take," one proponent of the process told me when I asked him about how it worked.

Of course, even if I'm resomated, my body will require some sort of container to transport it to the site of the pressure vessel. Here, I'll follow my father's example and go for a cardboard box or something equally simple – perhaps one of those flat-pack self-assembly versions from the EveryBody Coffins company. I've watched the video on the company's website and it really does look easy to snap together. It takes less than two minutes, and requires no nails, screws or tools – rather like a very basic Meccano kit. It costs about $150 and I like the idea that if my friends, or anyone else who happens to be around, want to decorate it, they can. I I'd known about these at the time, I'd have got one for Fa.

Like my father, I'm not really bothered about who (if anyone) shows up for the resomation although, unlike him, I won't proscribe the gathering of friends and relatives who want to have a party or hold a ceremony of some kind to mark my departure. But as with cremation, that's just the first step. Cremation and resomation are like double burials – the "rites of secondary treatment" documented by anthropologists. As Robert Hertz wrote, cremation is "usually neither a final act, nor sufficient in itself; it calls for a later and complementary rite".

This, of course, is the scattering. And this is where it gets interesting. Liberated from the constraints of a burial ground and freed from worries about the need to dispose quickly of a rapidly rotting corpse, you can pick somewhere meaningful as your final resting place and have yourself scattered at a time that suits everyone.

The other great advantage of being resomated is that, as with cremated remains, you can divide up the leftovers – in this case pure white ash. For me, this is particularly good news. I've been struggling to choose a single place for my remains from all the destinations I've visited, lived in and loved. But with a decent supply of calcium dust, I can create an itinerary. I can spread myself thinly.

Of course, my plan relies on willing volunteers. But this is the whole point. I'm thinking that the distribution of my remains could be the reason others – family, friends, acquaintances or strangers – get to see some of the places I've seen and have new experiences of their own along the way. And like Miss Vincent-Jones, who left a sum of money to her godson for a "fine dinner", I'm going to set aside some funds to pay for it.

Volunteers need only a small sample of my resomation dust. They may have their own ideas about how to transport the tiny corporeal parcels that were once part of me. But I have one suggestion – those clear acrylic Muji pots for holding pills and other small items. They suit my aesthetic – stylish but neat – and with lids that screw on tightly, they're eminently practical. I've travelled with them for years. They hold my earrings, earplugs and headache tablets. They might as well be used for my last journeys.

The question of how to organise all this and who does the scattering is more complicated. Travel is expensive, and while there will be no shortage of my ash, there might be limits to my cash. What's more, if there's a rush of applicants to participate in my scheme, which ones do I choose?

The solution may be to devise some sort of competition, judged by me, or by the executors of my will, if I'm no longer around. Like applicants for a fellowship or grant, would-be volunteers could write an essay or make a video stating why they want to go on such a journey and what they hope to get out of it. And, of course, those who want to fund their own trips would be more than welcome to a scoopful of my remains. Once I've figured out the details, I'll post it on my website – or perhaps leave the instructions on mywonderfullife.com.

I've chosen seven destinations to which people can take small portions of my ashes. And if there's any money left over, perhaps the last portion could be sent to Angels Flight, the Californian company that turns cremains into firework displays. Of all the death rites I've witnessed on my travels, the funeral pyre I watched on that warm night in Bali was the most thrilling. I've always loved fireworks and the service laid on by these innovative pyrotechnicians might be the closest way of creating something with the impact of a Balinese cremation.

Meanwhile, in no particular order, here are the places I've selected for a portion of my remains:

Number one: the Empire State Building, Manhattan, New York City, United States. The wire mesh fence on the Observation Deck is not too densely woven, so it should be easy enough to reach through and scatter a few grains of ashes. Please make sure choose a day when, as Fa put it, "prevailing winds are moderate", and that you scatter *with*, and not *against*, the direction of the breeze (I don't want to temporarily blind some unsuspecting tourist). And *do not* drop the Muji pill pot. From such a height, even something that small could give a pedestrian below a nasty bump, or at least a fright.

Number two: Vishwanath Gali, Varanasi, Uttar Pradesh, India. While Hindu cremations are going on beside the river, the place I really want to be is behind the waterfront, where a labyrinth of tiny lanes is stuffed with even tinier shops, cafés and temples. This is Vishwanath Gali, an ancient bazaar. Colour pops out of every corner – fuchsia pinks, mustard yellows and vibrant lime greens, each hue more brilliant than the next. Here you find glass bangles by the thousand, trays of the city's famous sweetmeats, rolls of richly brocaded silk and jars of nuts, candies, aniseed, chillies and spices. Being in the midst of all these goodies – as well as crowds of women in saris, the occasional cow and barefoot *sadhus* (holy men) in flamboyant robes of orange, gold and silver – is my idea of heaven, so please leave a small portion of me here. While you're in the bazaar, spare a thought for me as you drink a cup of *chai* served from a tiny clay cup, which you dash to the ground after use – dust to dust.

Number three: Echo Valley, Sagada, northern Luzon, Philippines. Whoever is drawn to natural beauty, tranquillity, fresh mountain air and the scent of pines should be the one to take a portion of my ashes up here. I'd like them thrown across Echo Valley to join the Igorot ancestors in their craggy limestone resting places. I don't need a pig slaughtered in my honour but perhaps I can have my name invoked occasionally at local ceremonies and ritual feasts (ask Siegrid about this). Stay a while if you can. I recommend the Saint Joseph Resthouse in the room called "Andrew". With a bed, a wooden stool and a wardrobe supplied with three metal clothes hangers, it's sparsely appointed. But with windows on two sides, it has a glorious view of the mountains and the town below. Try to be there over a weekend to catch the Saturday night buffet at the Log Cabin restaurant, cooked by Chef Akay (a Frenchman whose real name is Philippe).

Number four: Mercado Abastos, Oaxaca, Mexico. I get the same feeling here as I do in Vishwanath Gali. The smells are different (cilantro, quesadillas, *mole* sauce, sugar cane and fresh bread, as well as the ever-present, distinctively Mexican aroma of laundry detergent) but the sense of life and activity are equally intense. The place is immense – you can walk for hours and not come across the same stalls. So there'll be plenty of places to choose from when it comes to scattering some of my ashes. Look out for the sections for shoes, flowers, woven baskets and crazy miniature items (although perhaps avoid the food sections – I don't want to end up in someone's dinner), but the more people, noise and piles of goods the better. I'd like part of me left amid the throb and rhythm of the market, in with the mango skins, bits of string and cigarette butts – the detritus of human energy and motion.

Number five: Karimabad, Hunza Valley, northern Pakistan. I've been here several times over the years but my first trip was the most memorable. Arriving in darkness to a full hotel, I took up the manager's offer of a tent in the garden and, fully dressed, crawled into my sleeping bag, unaware of what surrounded me. Next morning, clambering outside into the dawn light, I felt like I'd died and gone to some sort of heaven. The garden on which my tent was pitched sat on a rocky escarpment overlooking one of the world's most dramatic landscapes – a valley where the great ranges of the Karakoram, Pamir, Hindu Kush and Himalayas fight it out in a grand confusion of jagged peaks and gaping ravines. The fiery colours of early autumn – deep russets, pale golds, the occasional flash of green – blazed brilliantly against lead grey slopes. The early morning sun worked its alchemy, transforming snowcaps into sparkling diamonds and the river in the valley floor into a snake of pure silver. I hope to get back there someday while I'm still living, but I'd also like a tiny piece of me left there after I'm dead.

Number Seven: Fa's Hill, North Poorton, West Dorset, England
It wasn't intentional, but the grassy slope on which we scattered my father's ashes has acquired his name, at least among friends and family. "I drove past Fa's Hill the other day," Sam will say. I'd like someone to leave a tiny portion of me there, partly to join my father but also so I can show the glorious countryside in which I was raised to someone who's never been there before. Drive around a little while you're in the area. Highlights include the spectacular coastline and pebble beaches, the magnificent Iron Age hill fort at Eggardon and one of my favourite churches, the Church of Saint Mary the Virgin, Powerstock, with its early Norman chancel arch and charming Victorian floral paintings on the nave walls.

I may add to this list as I continue my travels. And the places themselves may change with time. But as I go through these locations and consider what it is I love about them, I'm wondering if this was how Fa felt as he put together his instructions for us, inserting the picture of the church and explaining why that piece of beautiful Dorset landscape was the spot he'd chosen.

The emphasis of my scheme is slightly different from Fa's however. I'm certainly happy that tiny pieces of me will end up in some of my favourite places. But it's more than that. What really excites me is the idea that my ashes might be a reason for others to embark on adventures of their own. And who knows where they might lead? This thought allows me to look beyond my own mortality, which is important. When it comes to death, my rationalist philosophy leads only to extinction, and that's not something I'm willing to contemplate.

Of course, I won't be around to enjoy the trip or take in the view. But imagining others getting something out of my death – even if it's just the chance to drink *chai* from a clay cup in India or to gaze across the Hunza Valley – gives me a kind of seat at the table. I get to be a small part of my post-mortal future.

In this, I join the ranks of philanthropists, medical researchers, teachers, sports coaches, parents, and others who hope that they can provide a springboard for the creativity and productivity of those following them. It's the idea that, even though the power supply has been switched off, we may still be able to generate a few sparks of electricity. That's what I call living on.

ACKNOWLEDGEMENTS

Many friends, strangers and colleagues have advised, supported and encouraged me in writing this book, giving me generous portions of their patience, time and expertise, as well as their personal stories. I'd particularly like to thank Jennifer Senior, Cait Murphy, Melissa Milgrom, Charis Gresser, Jon Zeitlin, Bob Still, Babak Goodarzi, Janet DeNeefe, the Iran Heritage Foundation, my sister Kate and, of course, my mother, Sam.

Others have helped me on my travels, guided me around their countries and welcomed me into their communities. Many thanks to Maryam Mohamadi, Kawther el Obeid, Abena and Anthony Appiah, Nicola Chilton, Prhativi Dyah, Marsha Dubrow, Lucy Jackson, Siegrid Bangyay, Villia Jefremovas, Fernando Zobel de Ayala and Jessica Koth.

I also want to thank my publisher, Coptic Publishing, and my agent Elizabeth Sheinkman at Curtis Brown. And finally, I might never have completed this book without the calm, the quiet, and the company of the diverse creative individuals I found at Yaddo, the artists' colony in Saratoga Springs, New York State.

BIBLIOGRAPHY

GENERAL READING

–Ariès, Philippe, *The Hour of Our Death*, Weaver, Helen (translator), Second Vintag
Books Edition, New York, 2008
–Ashenburg, Katherine, *The Mourner's Dance: What We Do When People Die*, Nort
Point Press, New York, 2003
–Barnes, Julian, *Nothing to Be Frightened Of*, Vintage, New York, 2009
–Cullen, Lisa Takeuchi, *Remember Me: A Lively Tour of the New American Way a
Death*, HarperBusiness, New York, 2006
–King, Melanie, *The Dying Game: a Curious History of Death*, Oneworld, Oxford, 200
–Harris, Mark Donald, *Grave Matters*, Scribner, New York, 2007
–Lynch, Thomas, *The Undertaking: Life Studies from the Dismal Trade*, Pengui
Putnam, New York, 1997
–May, Todd, *Death*, Acumen, Stocksfield, UK, 2009
–McKenzie, Kenneth and Harra, Todd, *Mortuary Confidential: Undertakers Spill th
Dirt*, Citadel, New York, 2010
–Metcalf, Peter and Richard Huntington, *Celebrations of Death: The Anthropology o
Mortuary Ritual*, Cambridge University Press, New York, 1991
–Murray Parkes, Colin, Laungani, Pittu, and Young, Bill, *Death and Bereaveme
across Cultures*, Routledge, London, 1997
–Quigley, Christine, *The Corpse: A History*, McFarland, North Carolina, 1996
–Roach, Mary, *Stiff: The Curious Lives of Human Cadavers*, Norton, New York, 2004
–Nuland, Sherwin, *How We Die: Reflections on Life's Final Chapter*, Vintage, New
York, 1995
–Waugh, Evelyn, *The Loved One: An Anglo-American Tragedy*, Penguin Classics, Lor
don, 2000

1. THE LAMENT

–Alexiou, Margaret, Tradition and change in antiquity, in *The Ritual Lament in Gree
Tradition: Interdisciplinary Approaches*, Rowman & Littlefield, Lanham, MD, 2002
–Canetti, Elias, *Crowds and Power*, Viking Press, New York, 1962
–Danforth, Loring M., *The Death Rituals of Rural Greece*, photography by Alexand
Tsiaras, Princeton University Press, Princeton, NJ, 1982

–Darwin, Charles, *The Expression of the Emotions in Man and Animals*, 1872, D. Appleton, New York and London, 1916

–Feld, Steven, *Sound and Sentiment: Birds, Weeping, Poetics and Song in Kaluli Expression*, University of Pennsylvania Press, Philadelphia, 1990

–Gorer, Geoffrey, The Pornography of Death, in *Encounters: An Anthology from the First Ten Years of Encounter Magazine*, Basic Books, New York, 1963

–Holst-Warhaft, Gail, *Dangerous Voices: Women's Laments and Greek Literature*, Routledge, New York, 1992

–Jalland, Pat, *Death in the Victorian Family*, Oxford University Press, New York, 1996

–Kübler-Ross, Elisabeth, *On Death and Dying*, Scribner, New York, 1969, and Scribner Classics, New York, 1997

–Liao, Yiwu, *The Corpse Walker: Real-Life Stories, China from the Bottom Up*, Pantheon Books, New York, 2008

–Lutz, Tom, *Crying: The Natural and Cultural History of Tears*, W. W. Norton & Company, New York, 2001

–Lysaghtm Patricia, *Caoineadh Os Cionn Coirp: The Lament for the Dead in Ireland*, Folklore, Volume 108, Folklore Society, Gale Group, 1997

–Merridale, Catherine, *Night of Stone: Death and Memory in Russia*, Granta, 2000

–O'Connell, Eileen, The Lament for Arthur O'Leary, in *The Ireland Anthology*, Seán Dunne (editor), St. Martin's Griffin/Thomas Dunne Books, New York, 1957

–Ó Tuama, Seán, *Repossessions: Selected Essays on the Irish Literary Heritage*, Cork University Press, 1995

–Patton, Kimberley Christine and Stratton Hawley, John (editors), *Holy Tears: Weeping in the Religious Imagination*, Princeton University Press, Princeton, NJ, 2005

–Perry, Hosea L., Mourning and Funeral Customs of African Americans, in D. P. Irish, K.E. Lundquist, and V.J. Nelson (editors) *Ethnic Variations in Dying, Death and Grief: Diversity in Universality*, Taylor & Francis, Washington D.C., 1993

–Radcliffe-Brown, A.R., *The Andaman Islanders*, Free Press, Illinois, 1948

–Rottenberg, Jonathan, Bylsma, Lauren M., and Vingerhoets, Ad J.J.M., *Is Crying Beneficial?*, Current Directions in Psychological Science, Journal of the Association for Psychological Science, Volume 17, Number 6, December 2008

–Shirley, Evelyn Philip, Extracts from the Journal of Thomas Dineley, Esquire, giving some account of his visit to Ireland in the reign of Charles II, in *The Journal of the Kilkenny and South-East of Ireland*, Archaeological Society, Volume II, University Press, Dublin, 1859

2. BEAUTIFUL FIRE

–Connor, Linda H., The Action of the Body on Society: Washing a Corpse in Bali, *Journal of the Royal Anthropological Institute*, Volume: 1. Issue: 3, 1995

–Covarrubias, Miguel, *Island of Bali*, 1937, KPI Limited, London, 1986

–Davies, Douglas James and Mates, Lewis H., *Encyclopedia of Cremation*, Ashgate, Burlington, VT, 2005

–Eassie, William, *The Economy of Cremation, in Transactions of the Sanitary Institute of Great Britain*, Sanitary Institute of Great Britain, London, 1886-7

–Geertz, Hildred and Clifford, *Kinship in Bali*, University of Chicago Press, 1978

–Michner, Joerg, Crematorium to help heat homes in Swedish town, *Daily*

Telegraph, December 20, 2008
–*New York Times*, The Cremation of Mrs. Pitman, February 14, 1878
–Prothero, Stephen, *Purified by Fire: A History of Cremation in America*, University of California Press, Berkeley, 2001
–Thompson, Sir Henry, *Cremation: The Treatment of the Body after Death*, Cremation Society of England, London, 1884
–Wagner, Frits A., *Indonesia: The Art of an Island Group*, McGraw-Hill Book Company, New York, 1959

3. STARTLING STILLNESS

–Acton, Harold Mario Mitchell, *More Memoirs of an Aesthete*, Methuen, London, 1970
–Barnes, Carl Lewis, *The Art and Science of Embalming: Descriptive and Operative* Washington D.C., 1896
–Bradbury, Mary, *Representations of Death: A Social Psychological Perspective* Routledge, New York, 1999
–Carlson, Lisa, *Caring for the Dead: Your Final Act of Love*, Upper Access, Hinesburg VT, 1997
–Cockburn, Eve, Reyman, Theodore Allen, *Mummies, Disease & Ancient Cultures* Cambridge University Press, Cambridge, 1998
–Gilpin Faust, Drew, *This Republic of Suffering*, Knopf, New York, 2008
–Goolsby, Denise, Funeral homes undertake change, *The Desert Sun*, March 25, 2007
–Gore, Catherine Grace Frances, *The Royal Favourite*, (1854) Routledge, Warne & Routledge, London, 1862
–Jalland, Pat, *Death in the Victorian Family*, Oxford University Press, New York, 1996
–Kelly, David, The mummy returns: Utah partners hope to revive ancient funeral practice, *Los Angeles Times*, 14 July 2003
–Kemp, Elyria and Kopp, Steven W., The Death Care Industry: A Review of Regulatory and Consumer Issues, *Journal of Consumer Affairs*, Volume: 41, Issue 1, 2007
–Kübler-Ross, Elisabeth, *Questions and Answers on Death and Dying*, Scribner, New York, 1997
–Laderman, Gary, *Rest in Peace: A Cultural History of Death and the Funeral Home in Twentieth-Century America*, Oxford University Press, New York, 2003
–Langman, James, *Magical Mummies of the Atacama*, Americas, Volume 53, Issue 3 2001
–Mayer, Robert C., *Embalming: History, Theory, and Practice*, fourth edition, McGraw Hill Medical, New York, 2005
–Meskell, Lynn, *Object Worlds in Ancient Egypt: Material Biographies Past and Present* Berg, New York, 2004
–Mims, Cedric A., *When We Die: The Science, Culture, and Rituals of Death*, St. Martin's Griffin, New York, 2000
–Mitford, Jessica, *The American Way of Death*, Hutchinson & Co, London, 1963
–Mitford, Jessica, *The American Way of Death Revisited*, Vintage, New York, 2000
–Pringle, Heather, *The Mummy Congress: Science, Obsession, and the Everlasting Dead* Theia 2001
–*Psychiatry and Social Science Review*, Volume 4, 1970
–Quigley, Christine, *Modern Mummies: The Preservation of the Human Body in the*

Twentieth Century, McFarlane, North Carolina, 1998

–Steele, Donald W., *The Value of Viewing the Body*, The Dodge Company website

–Willis, Nathaniel Parker, *Pencillings by the Way: Written During Some Years of Residence and Travel in France, Italy, Greece, Asia Minor, Turkey and England*, Morris and Willis, New York, 1844

4. INSIDE THE BOX

–Bondeson, Jan, *Buried Alive: The Terrifying History of Our Most Primal Fear*, Norton, New York, 2002

–Burns, Vivian, Travel to Heaven: Fantasy Coffins, *African Arts*, Volume 7, No. 2, UCLA James S. Coleman African Studies Centre, 1974

–Colman, Penny, *Corpses, Coffins, and Crypts: A History of Burial*, Henry Holt and Co., New York, 1997

–Cooney, Eleanor, Funeral chic: Colourful coffins convey the deceased's interests, profession, *San Francisco Chronicle*, October 30, 2002

–Cressy, David, *Birth, Marriage, and Death: Ritual, Religion, and the Life-Cycle in Tudor and Stuart England*, Oxford University Press, Oxford, 1999

–Errington, Sarah, Burial Sights, *Geographical*, September 1, 2000

–Hughes, Robert, All-American Barbaric Yawp, *Time* magazine, May 6, 1996

–Kim, Hyung-Jin, South Koreans give their deaths a trial run, *Associated Press*, January 13, 2008

–Secretan, Thierry, *Going into Darkness: Fantastic Coffins from Africa*, Thames & Hudson, London, 1995

–Stewart, Henry, *The End of the Cemetery*, CUNY Graduate School of Journalism Research Centre, New York, 2008

–St. John, Warren, On the Final Journey, One Size Doesn't Fit All, *New York Times*, September 28, 2003

–Sumner Allen, Dan, The Mason Coffins: Metallic Burial Cases in the Central South, South Central Historical Archeology Conference, Jackson, MI, Middle Tennessee State University, 2002

5. PACKING FOR ETERNITY

–Aiken, Lewis R., *Dying, Death and Bereavement*, Lawrence Erlbaum Associates, Mahwah, NJ, 2001

–Becker, Ernest, *The Denial of Death*, Free Press Paperbacks, New York, 1973

–Berling, Judith A., Death and Afterlife in Chinese Religions, in *Death and Afterlife: Perspectives of World Religions*, Obayashi, Hiroshi, Praeger, 1992

–Flannelly, Kevin J., Ellison, Christopher G., Galek, Kathleen, and Koenig, Harold G., Beliefs about Life-after-Death, Psychiatric Symptomology and Cognitive Theories of Psychopathology, *Journal of Psychology and Theology*, Volume 36, 2008

–James, William, *The Varieties of Religious Experience: A Study in Human Nature*, Longmans, Green & Co, New York, 1902

–Jordan, David, *Gods, Ghosts and Ancestors*, University of California San Diego, 1999

–Lee Scott, Janet, *For Gods, Ghosts and Ancestors: The Chinese Tradition of Paper Offer-*

ings, Hong Kong University Press, Hong Kong, 2007

–Obayashi, Hiroshi, *Introduction, in Death and Afterlife: Perspectives of World Religions*, Obayashi, Hiroshi, Praeger, New York, 1992

–The *Onion*, World Death Rate Holding Steady At 100 Percent, January 22, 1997

–Portal, Jane, *The First Emperor: China's Terracotta Army*, British Museum, 2007

–Roach, Mary, *Spook: Science Tackles the Afterlife*, Norton, New York, 2005

–Scott, Sean A., "Earth Has No Sorrow That Heaven Cannot Cure": Northern Civilian Perspectives on Death and Eternity during the Civil War, *Journal of Social History*, Volume 41, 2008

–Solomon, Sheldon, Greenberg, Jeff, Schimel, Jeff, Arndt, Jamie, and Pyszczynski, Tom, *Human Awareness of Mortality and the Evolution of Culture in The Psychological Foundations of Culture*, Schaller, Mark, and Crandall, Christian S., Lawrence Erlbaum Associates, 2004

–Rapoport, Scott, Now You, Too, Can Call Out The Dead In N.J., *CBS News*, April 9, 2008

–Waters, Dan, *Chinese Funerals: A Case Study*, presented at the 34th International Congress on Asian and North African Studies, University of Hong Kong, 1993

6. RAISING PIGS

–Cohen, Adam, A New Kind of Memorial for the Internet Age, *New York Times*, July 25, 2009

–Comila, Felipe S., *The Disappearing Dap-ay: Coping with Change in Sagada, in The Road to Empowerment: Strengthening the Indigenous Peoples Rights Act*, Volume II Nurturing the Earth, Nurturing Life, the International Labour Organization, 2007

–*The Economist*, Bankruptcy and burials: The rising cost of Ghana's funerals, 26 May, 2007

–De Witte, Marleen, Money and Death: Funeral Business in Asante, Ghana, *Africa* Volume: 73, 2003

–Fison, Lorimer, *Tales from old Fiji*, Alexander Moring Ltd., The De la More Press, London, 1907

–Frazer, J.G., *The Belief in Immortality and the Worship of the Dead*, Volume 1, Macmillan, London, 1913

–Garces-Foley, Kathleen, and Holcomb, Justin S., *Contemporary American Funerals in Personalizing Tradition in Death and Religion in a Changing World*, Garces-Foley, Kathleen (editor), M.E. Sharpe, New York, 2006

–Greenberg, Blu, *How to Run a Traditional Jewish Household*, Fireside, New York, 1985

–Hunt, Melinda (author), and Sternfeld, Joel (photographer), *Hart Island*, Scalo Publishers, 1998

–Jalland, Pat, *Death in the Victorian Family*, Oxford University Press, New York, 1996

–Klinenberg, Eric, *Heat Wave: A Social Autopsy of Disaster in Chicago*, University of Chicago Press, Chicago, 2003

–Leland, John, It's My Funeral and I'll Serve Ice Cream if I Want To, *New York Times* July 20, 2006

–Lysaght, Patricia, Hospitality at Wakes and Funerals in Ireland from the Seventeenth to the Nineteenth Century: Some Evidence from the Written Record, *Folklore* Volume 114, Issue 3, December 2003

-O'Connell, Brian, Lifting the lid on Irish wakes, *Irish Times*, March 25, 2009

-Piluden-Omengan, Dinah Elma, *Death and Beyond: Death & Burial Rituals & Other Practices & Beliefs of the Igorots of Sagada, Mountain Province, Philippines*, Giraffe Books, Quezon City, 2004

-Post, Emily, *Etiquette in Society, in Business, in Politics, and at Home*, Funk & Wagnalls, New York, 1922

-Scott, William Henry, An Engineer's Dream: John Staunton and the Mission of St. Mary the Virgin, Sagada, in *Studies in Philippine Church History*, Anderson, Gerald H. (editor), Cornell University Press, Ithaca, NY, 1969

-Van der Geest, Sjaak, Between death and funeral: mortuaries and the exploitation of liminality in Kwahu, Ghana, Africa, *Journal of the International African Institute*, Volume 76, Issue 4, 2006

-Williamson, Robert W., *The Mafulu Mountain People of British New Guinea*, Macmillan and Co., London, 1912

7. FOREIGN FIELDS

-Bray, Alan, *The Friend*, University of Chicago Press, Chicago, 2003

-Brooke, Rupert, The Soldier, 1914 in *The Poetical Works of Rupert Brooke*, Keynes, Geoffrey (editor), Faber & Faber, London, 1946

-Buck, Sir Edward John, *Simla, Past and Present*, Thacker, Spink & Co, Calcutta, 1904

-*The Calcutta Review*, Volume XXXI, Thacker, Spink & Co, Calcutta, 1858

-Dunlap, David W., Dig Unearths Early Black Burial Ground, *New York Times*, October 9, 1991

-Chaker, Anne Marie, Shipping News: How Funeral Directors Earn Free Flights, *Wall Street Journal*, May 17, 2005

-*Daily Mail*, Woman wins legal battle to be buried with her lover, January 31, 2009

-Deloria, Vine J.r., *Custer Died for Your Sins: An Indian Manifesto (Civilization of the American Indian)*, Macmillan, New York, 1969

-Holmes and Co., *The Bengal Obituary*, or, *A Record to Perpetuate the Memory of Departed Worth*, W. Thacker & Co, London and Calcutta, 1851

-Horrox, Rosemary, *Fifteenth-Century Attitudes: Perceptions of Society in Late Medieval England*, Cambridge University Press, Cambridge, 1997

-Jacobs, Andrew, Jewish Newark's Urban Pioneers Rest Uneasily, *New York Times*, October 15, 2000

-Jordan, Rosan Augusta and de Caro, Frank (curators and editors), *British Voices from South-East Asia*, electronic exhibit reproducing an exhibition held in Hill Memorial Library at Louisiana State University, 1996

-Kipling, Rudyard, *The City of Dreadful Night*, Alex Grosset & Co, New York, 1899

-Longworth, Philip, *The Unending Vigil: The History of the Commonwealth War Graves Commission*, Leo Cooper, Barnsley, S. Yorkshire, 2003

-Elias, Lopez, Nameless Are Memorialized at Old African Burial Site, *New York Times*, October 2, 2007

-The Lewis Historical Publishing Co, *A History of the City of Newark: Embracing Practically Two and a Half Centuries*, Volume II, New York, Chicago, 1913

-Moodie, Susanna, *Roughing It In The Bush*, Richard Bentley, London, 1852

-Nelson, Judy, The Final Journey Home: Chinese Burial Practices in Spokane, *The*

Pacific Northwest Forum, Volume VI, Number 1, Winter-Spring, 1993
–*Reuters*, Eternity with Marilyn Monroe goes back on auction block, October 15 2009
–Slackman, Michael, In a New Age, Bahrain Struggles to Honor the Dead Whil Serving the Living, *New York Times*, September 18, 2009
–Smiley, Lauren, Exporting the Dead, *SF Weekly*, January 21, 2009
–Smith, Claire, and Wobst, Hans Martin, *Indigenous Archaeologies: Decolonizing The ory and Practice*, Routledge, New York, 2005
–Thomas, David Hurst, *Skull Wars: Kennewick Man, Archaeology, and the Battle fo Native American Identity*, Basic Books, New York, 2000
–Yalom, Marilyn, *The American Resting Place: 400 Years of History Through Our Cem eteries and Burial Grounds*, Houghton Mifflin Harcourt, New York, 2008
–Yung, Judy, Chang, Gordon H. and Lai, Him Mark (editors), *Chinese American Voic es: From the Gold Rush to the Present*, University of California Press, Berkeley, 2006

8. DEM BONES

–Andrews, William, *Old Church Lore*, The Hull Press, London, 1891
–*BBC News*, Saint's remains arrive for tour, September 15, 2009
–Bondeson, Jan, *Buried Alive: The Terrifying History of Our Most Primal Fear*, W.W Norton & Co., New York, 2002
–Danforth, Loring M., *The Death Rituals of Rural Greece*, photography by Alexande Tsiaras, Princeton University Press, Princeton, NJ, 1982
–Favazza, Armando R., *Bodies under Siege: Self-mutilation and Body Modification i Culture and Psychiatry*, The Johns Hopkins University Press, Baltimore, 1996
–Golden, Tim Salvador, Skeletons Confirm Reports of Massacre in 1981, *New Yor Times*, October 22, 1992
–Green, James W., *Beyond the Good Death: The Anthropology of Modern Dying*, Univer sity of Pennsylvania Press, Philadelphia, 2008
–Gregorian, Dareh, 9/11 Victim Identified, *New York Post*, April 2, 2009
–Higgins, Kathleen, *Death and the Skeleton, in Death and Philosophy*, Malpas, J. E. an Solomon Robert C. (editors), Routledge, London, 1999
–Hoyt, Mike, The Mozote Massacre: It Was the Reporters' Word against the Govern ment's, *Columbia Journalism Review*, Volume 31, January-February, 1993
–Kulich, Jan, *The Ossuary: Kutná Hora – Sedlec*, Gloriet Publishing House
–Lazure, Guy, Possessing the Sacred: Monarchy and Identity in Philip II's Relic Col lection at the Escorial, *Renaissance Quarterly*, Volume 60, Issue 1, 2007
–Muldoon, James, *Varieties of Religious Conversion in the Middle Ages*, Universit Press of Florida, Gainesville, FL, 1997
–Quigley, Christine, *Skulls and Skeletons: Human Bone Collections and Accumulation* McFarland & Company, Jefferson, NC, 2001
–Sherrow, Victoria, *Encyclopedia of Hair: A Cultural History*, Greenwood Press, West port, CT, 2006
–Sheumaker, Helen, *Love Entwined: The Curious History of Hairwork in America*, Uni versity of Pennsylvania Press, Philadelphia, 2007
–Smith, A.J. (contributor), *The Complete English Poems*, Penguin Books, London, 199
–Turner, Mark, *The Artful Mind: Cognitive Science and the Riddle of Huma*

Creativity, Oxford University Press, New York, 2006

–Wills, Gary, Venice: *The Lion City: The Religion of Empire*, Washington Square Press, New York, 2002

9. HELLO AGAIN

–Binski, Paul, *Medieval Death: Ritual and Representation*, Cornell University Press, Ithaca, NY, 1996

–Boccaccio, Giovanni (author) and Payne, John (translator), *The Decameron*, Volume 1, Kessinger Publishing, Whitefish, MT, 2003

–Brandes, Stanley, *Iconography in Mexico's Day of the Dead: Origins and Meaning*, Ethnohistory 45, 1998

–Brandes, Stanley, *Skulls to the Living, Bread to the Dead: The Day of the Dead in Mexico and Beyond*, Blackwell Publishing, Malden, MS., 2006

–Cantor, Norman F., *In the Wake of the Plague: The Black Death and the World It Made*, Harper Perennial, New York, 2002

–Carmichael, Elizabeth, and Sayer, Chloë, *The Skeleton at the Feast: The Day of the Dead in Mexico*, University of Texas Press, Austin, 1991

–Haley, Shawn D., and Fukuda, Curt, *Day of The Dead: When Two Worlds Meet in Oaxaca*, Berghahn Books, Oxford, 2004

–Huizinga, Johan, *The Waning of the Middle Ages*, Dover Publications, NY, 1998

–Norget, Kristin, *Days of Death, Days of Life: Ritual in the Popular Culture of Oaxaca*, Columbia University Press, New York, 2006

–Oosterwijk, Sophie, Food for worms – food for thought: The appearance and interpretation of the 'verminous' cadaver in Britain and Europe, *Church Monuments*, Volume XX, 2005

–Oosterwijk, Sophie, Of Dead Kings, Dukes and Constables: The Historical Context of the Danse Macabre in Late Medieval Paris, *Journal of the British Archaeological Association*, 2008

–Stannard, David E., *American Holocaust: The Conquest of the New World*, Oxford University Press, New York, 1992

–*The Times*, Hirst's diamond-encrusted skull goes to unknown investors for £50m, August 31, 2007

–Tuchman, Barbara Wertheim, *A Distant Mirror: The Calamitous 14th Century*, Ballantine Books, New York, 1987

10. THE FINAL CHAPTER

–Dent, Alan (editor), *Bernard Shaw and Mrs. Patrick Campbell: Their Correspondence*, Alfred A. Knopf, New York, 1952

–Mydans, Carl, By a General's Friend: Memento of 25 Years, *Life* magazine, April 17, 1964

–Myers, Alyse, I'm Honoring the Dead (and Look at These Great Seats), *New York Times*, July 5, 2009

More stories, pictures, resources and web links:
www.makinganexit.net, makinganexit.tumblr.com, @makinganexit

Lightning Source UK Ltd.
Milton Keynes UK
UKOW022359011111

181326UK00002B/3/P